ATHEISTS
CAN GET TO
"HEAVEN"

Cover Design: Orion Nebula photograph expanded for cover by author.
Original astro-photography by Edward J. Pavlu III
(Used with permission)

ISBN: 1-4196-9875-3
ISBN-13: 9781419698750

Visit www.booksurge.com to order additional copies.

ATHEISTS CAN GET TO "HEAVEN"

PERSPECTIVES FROM THE JOURNEY
Beyond
THE TUNNEL OF LIGHT

W. MICHAEL KING

TABLE OF CONTENTS

ATHEISTS CAN GET TO "HEAVEN"

Foreword ix
Preface...xiii

THE JOURNEY
Beyond THE TUNNEL OF LIGHT

Chapter One: Personal Introduction 1
Chapter Two: The Road Trip Begins 5
Chapter Three: Visions...13
Chapter Four: The Exorcist.. 21
Chapter Five: The Forces of Defiance..45
Chapter Six: Primed 51
Chapter Seven: The Emergence of Individuality......................................65
Chapter Eight: The Crater of Self-Deprecation 77
Chapter Nine: The Retreat: Discoveries 103
Chapter Ten: Reconstruction..121
Chapter Eleven: Commencement 139
Chapter Twelve: Transformation...149
Chapter Thirteen: The Test...163

Chapter Fourteen: Celestial Threat 181

Chapter Fifteen: Mentors.. 191

Chapter Sixteen: Humbled & Informed.................................... 215

Chapter Seventeen: Decision..237

Chapter Eighteen: The Return 249

PERSPECTIVES — FROM THE JOURNEY
Beyond THE TUNNEL OF LIGHT

Perspectives: Overview.. 271

Perspectives: Responsibility 275

Perspectives: Children of the Universe......................................289

Perspectives: Creation of Deities, Emissaries and Belief Systems.................295

Perspectives: Magic, Science and the Evolution of the Individual 313

Perspectives: Ethical Behavior & Tribes 321

Perspectives: Choices and Responsibility for the Species...........................327

Perspectives: Challenges and Strategy for a Personal Journey.....................331

AFTERWORD
Inspirations 345

APPENDIX
May the Force be With Us... 349

ACKNOWLEDGEMENTS
ACKNOWLEDGEMENTS 357

DEDICATIONS

*To my life-partner, Rosy,
for your love, perseverance, dedication,
encouragement and inspirations!*

*To our children:
For the inspiration and stimuli
you have brought to my life.*

To my mentors and protégés......

FOREWORD

I magine that at the moment of your birth, when your body first experienced the sensations of being out of your mother's womb and feeling air for the very first time, you were an open canvas, a fabric of being ready for imprinting with the colors and the human concepts of life. At that instant, were you actually a "blank canvas?" Were you open in spirit, pure in being, and free of any influences or proclivities? What *are* your natural tendencies?

In the wondrous assemblage of your being, your fabric already carried the indelible imprints of the heritage from your ancestral bloodlines. Your genetic construction imbued you with natural talents, abilities, and tendencies that in combination cause you to be a unique individual. When you were born, you were the most recent extension of your familial path that had preceded you through hundreds of generations.

Then what happened?

You developed and evolved through a progression of experiences, information, and teachings that when superimposed onto the fabric of your natural self, shaped you. Some of these influences and experiences wholly complemented the inherent nature of who and what you are. Other influences could have failed to complement your nature, setting up conflicts that might have impeded the efficiency of your path toward optimal self-advancement. In some individuals, the influences applied could have dramatically conflicted with their nature, possibly resulting in many diverse consequences to their personalities such as through turmoil, anger, withdrawal, or confusion.

When you were young, influences occurred and experiences gathered that might have been easy, or difficult, for you to cope with. Collectively, all of your influences and emotions embedded within you to form a "belief system"—which is your mental acceptance, your personal conviction, of values and truths that constitute a foundation upon which you reference your life. It can be an amazing and formidable challenge to probe into that reference foundation, see the vistas beyond its boundaries, discover your true nature, and develop a new reality that you can use to evolve yourself.

Memories of events may fade over time, but the inadvertently implanted emotional reflexes within you can remain influential to your personality and behaviour. Implanted effects can have many consequences for you. These may span the whole range of positive to negative, from intended and volitional reactions to circumstances and people, to emotionally reflexive where you act without the use of deliberate thought.

When you ask yourself the question, "Who am I?" first listen with your mind then open your emotional heart. You may experience deep and unexplained emotions, reminding you of some forgotten memory of long ago, or dreams of something that you cannot recall nor define.

Observations of individuals tend to indicate that it is not precisely what occurred to you that remains with you as your reference system in life: it is how you reacted and "believe" what happened that matters as you define yourself.

This book will expose you to situations and events I encountered during the *Journey*. These could be quite striking, surprising, or even present daunting challenges to you. When anything you read here sharply influences you, ask yourself: "How would I react or respond to this situation, event, or challenge if it were presented to me? Are there analogies to these events in my own life?"

Rationally gaze inside yourself and deliberately examine your processes. You may learn more about the mysteries of your mind by examining your responses to the descriptions presented to you during this *Journey!* Take advantage of this invitation to make an assessment through your own exploration into what might be a vast unknown: your inner self.

Consider as you read along through the descriptions offered to you during this *Journey* that any sharp emotional experiences you may have, might be simply reflex responses that strike out from your embedded *blind belief* system and that these responses - *can be altered*. You are encouraged to open your mind to possibilities that may transcend your current belief system. It takes courage to resist the defensive reaction to reflexively judge yourself harshly, and close your mind off to increased potential. Ultimately your mind-set may change and by the force of your will, personal breakthroughs may dramatically improve your essence of yourself: your self-esteem.

People tend to resist change, and frequently the basis of this resistance is fear: the fear to leave whatever is familiar. Where did the fear come from? When you look at yourself in a metaphorical mirror of reflection, what do you see? Can you view yourself objectively, absent emotion, or are there impulsive negative reactions that invade your self-esteem?

This book starts with the story of the **Journey** of one person who has experienced many events, both physical and metaphysical, facilitated in part by genetic legacies and by clinical death experiences. Along the way of the *Journey*, projected descriptions indicating the potential for ultimate human evolution will define the nature of "heaven" (which is continuance of your soul beyond the human body) as a result. The **Journey** relates many experiences, that when retrospectively considered yield **Perspectives**, and these may provide incentive for you to use in introspection and, perhaps, apply to your everyday life.

The consequence is that the attainment of full human evolution, a state of being religions would call "the eternal soul" is possible without depending on the control of emissaries or institutions that make the assertion they represent a deity, nor tribal structures that demand obedience to their precepts. Logically, this evolution could be any individual's ultimate responsibility to himself or herself. My personal experiences, gathered during clinical death and my *Journey* that took me far, far beyond the tunnel of light, emphasize these conclusions.

Given my discoveries and descriptions that I will reveal to you in this book, even some that might provocatively challenge your assumptions, any individual, including atheists, may indeed evolve into eternity and "go to heaven!"

PREFACE

I slouch back in my desk chair, idly gazing at the familiar desktop screen of my computer. Succumbing to uncertainty as the screen holds my gaze, not yet willing to make a commitment to do what I suspect I eventually must do, I steeple my fingers to my nose, my thumbs as a chin rest—and stare. *"This is different,"* I mutter under my breath, *"Has the time finally arrived?"*

It is the third week of November 2004, and I have just had an inspired vision that took me by surprise. Rosy, my wife, and I were shifting furniture around in our bedroom to complete our remodeling, when the flash of inspiration came. It looked like a bright flash centered in a rectangular, sky-blue field, as if I had glanced at the sun. Within the flash were the words: *Atheists can get to heaven!* As I caught the message, the bright flash and the blue field zoomed away from me. As it moved away, I saw it clearly: It was a book cover—my book cover. For a moment, it was elating.

Furniture in place, I had drifted into my office, setup a word-doc file, and keyed in the words from the vision that were, at first, powerful to me. I saved the file—slouched back—and revisited the dilemma that I had lived with for years: whether to openly write about what I had discovered, or stay a private person, exposing my experiences to only a limited number of protégés. Because of my life-long preference for staying completely out of the public eye, rarely publishing even in my technical field, I had already resisted disclosing my experiences and discoveries for ten years. Now a simple vision comes along, a clarions call to bring me to action and unveil my personal journey for anyone to see.

"Damn it!" I sighed, frustrated at my own unwillingness to break my pattern. I drifted away from the computer and tried to empty my mind of the persistent and provocative message of the vision. Atheists *can* evolve into eternity and thrive in what religions would call heaven - at least as easily as "believers"—was something I had directly experienced for myself during an extended "near-death experience." But I had gone farther than most, even breaking out of the *tunnel of light* and thriving in a great adventure. I learned that there is no singular deity as such; that we are, rather, children of the universe. I learned that the tapestry of the universe moves through us, envelops us, and connects us to sources of knowledge and ability that has been the source of inspiration for prophets, poets, mystics and seers for millennia. We can indeed evolve to the point where we consciously graduate from the physical body, prevail beyond its boundaries; and ultimately, that our evolution is entirely up to us—as individuals. We evolve by freeing the energy tied up in restrictive beliefs and low self-esteem, and learning to utilize the energy to thrive. Anyone who has the courage to peer beyond the limitations of self can find wondrous discoveries that reveal the magnificence of one's being.

In the past, I had been successful in avoiding the exposure that *issuing the book* would imply. Nevertheless, the message held in the inspired vision became intractable—I just could not make it go away. I knew that to meet my responsibilities to myself, I had to eventually write the story—issue myself out of hiding—and it seemed that the vision was announcing that I had procrastinated far too long. The message of the vision was clear, and so I made the commitment get through my issues of reluctance, and began writing this book.

W. Michael King
May 2008

ATHEISTS CAN GET TO "HEAVEN"

THE JOURNEY
Beyond
THE TUNNEL OF LIGHT

CHAPTER ONE

PERSONAL INTRODUCTION

S o that you may have an overview of who has written this book, I'd like to give you a brief introduction. I've experienced a rather diversified life in both the personal and professional realms. About age four, comparatively early in life, I was drawn toward music and particularly the piano. Music was a talent that I shared with my mother, who would duet with me. Learning and playing the instrument seemed very natural. Because of my expressive ability at the keyboard, I entered (by my parents' and piano teacher's urgings) into competitions at the young age of six.

I must admit that socially I was a very timid child, and it required tremendous effort for me to be "in performance" at anything, especially the piano. In order to perform, I had to learn how to mentally block out the fact that I was intimidated to be in front of a large audience. For the most part, I was quite scared before my performance started.

Fortunately, as soon as I started to play, I would lose myself in the music, and the audience would disappear from my conscious mind. The instrument would become an extension of my fingers, my expression, and my *feeling* of the music!

I also had a great deal of curiosity about how things worked. Early television's science show, *Mr. Wizard,* with Don Herbert, stimulated my curiosity, which my parents supported. Later, science fiction shows such as *Space Patrol* added to my inspirations about what *might be possible.*

Photography also became an early interest, motivated initially by my technical curiosity. My photo work was widely used in school publications, and I was encouraged when a major newspaper (to which I was apprenticed) published my photographs while I was still in high school.

My musical passion eventually converged with my technical interests in electronics, and I became involved in the professional recording industry. I found it easy to learn proficiency using microphones and mixing consoles and be a recording engineer, and I later produced records. This all happened before the age of 21, thanks to the nurturing help of my first mentor, whom I met when I was about 14 years old. These interests and activities overlapped my other technical curiosities and my involvement with high-performance cars.

Opportunities then opened for me in the design of electronics systems, opportunities driven by the impetus of the Cold War of the 1960s and JFK's commitment to the space program. Responding to those opportunities, I soon became involved in the design and development of various government-funded space, aerospace, weapons, and communications projects. Many of these systems and projects were highly classified. Decades later some of these projects would be seen by the public in television coverage of operation *Desert Storm* in the Persian Gulf region, or hinted about in some novels.

The diversion of government funding from technology research into the Vietnam conflict prodded my engineering career increasingly toward commercial projects, including computers, medical electronics, and a multiplicity of communication networks. During this period, corporate managers increasingly sought my help to train their staffs in my particular area of technical expertise, which is electronic systems design (with a focus on electromagnetic fields and waves). While the training goal of management was to increase their staff's proficiency in this field, I realized that it was only marginally effective to teach technology *per se*. Individuals, I learned, could memorize the facts and principles of technology yet still be ineffective when called upon to work through issues, due mainly as it turned out, to self-confidence issues in their personalities that impeded their technical competence.

Self-confidence issues often attend self-esteem issues, and these can impede self-trust, and thereby, objectivity. Since objectivity is a fundamental attribute required for experiments in science and technology, any marginalization of self-trust would threaten effectiveness, and potentially, the validity of results. Consequently, to expand their self-trust I became a mentor to many of these individuals. Following the trend in technology at that time, I became an independent consultant. This transition dramatically increased my connections with clients and with many individuals who became protégés in several countries.

My career as a design consultant for electronic systems engineering (with specialties in electrostatic field boundary displacements and the propagation or capture of electromagnetic fields and waves) fortunately required extensive travel. While *fortunate* might not always have been my word for this traveling, given the time-zone stresses and inconveniences to family life, it did at least provide some highly valued compensation in the form of *travel points!*

Over the period of more than 45 years, I logged approximately ten million frequent-flyer miles through the demands of my career. As might be expected, the benefit was that I could take vacations essentially anywhere, anytime, with my wife and partner Rosy, and sometimes with the entire family (our children).

From the beginning of our relationship in 1980, Rosy and I have particularly enjoyed traveling to ancient sites of classical history, lolling on the beaches of South Pacific islands soaking up the sun's rays, navigating the roads through the Alps, or tromping through tropical rain forests—to give but a few examples.

Despite all of our travel adventures, including several road trips touring most of Europe, something was missing: a road trip within the United States! That missing experience brings us to the real beginning of this story.

CHAPTER TWO

THE ROAD TRIP BEGINS

Rosy and I decided to close the gap in our experience—of not having toured our own country. We planned an extensive four-week driving trip through the Western states, choosing as our focus the national parks in Arizona, Utah, New Mexico, and Wyoming. We scheduled our trip for the month of June 1994—before the start of summer vacations, while the weather would be pleasant and mild.

Little did we know when we started the trip that unexpected events would occur to take us far beyond the plans we had in mind. Those events changed our trip into an adventure, and the adventure changed my life. Profound experiences would yield dramatic and dynamic changes in our outlook of life and reality.

If you like to drive on the open road, road trips can be a lot of fun! There are no airline schedules to follow! There is little in the way of structure that would cramp spontaneous impulses to explore remote or unique areas. With our 4-wheel-drive, heavy-duty vehicle, we started on our general travel plan, though we would often modify it along the way.

We first visited the Painted Desert and Grand Canyon regions in Arizona, which are well known and frequently visited national parks. Rosy, the truth be told, has always had a severe and unrelenting case of *wanderlust,* amplified by her passionate curiosity about many things. (I am convinced that this tendency is probably the result of an embedded attribute in her DNA.)

When Rosy looked at the Arizona map and noticed the National Monument of Canyon de Chelly and Canyon del Muerto – *Poof!* – We had an instant change of plans! Rosy's "curiosity gene" can easily overcome something as insignificant as established travel plans, and I learned long ago *not* to try to thwart that curiosity!

While many of the national parks are well known and frequently visited, Canyon de Chelly National Monument (which includes Canyon del Muerto) seems to be less known, and therefore less visited. These canyons are located in northeastern Arizona, near the New Mexico border.

From the air, or on the topology of a map, these two canyons appear to take the general form of a "Y" turned 90 degrees, with the short center leg pointing in a westerly direction. Canyon del Muerto is on the north side of the "Y." The name *Chelly,* I learned, is probably a corruption the Spanish conquistadors sounded out from the Navajo word *tsegi,* meaning *rock canyon.*

We learned that the two canyons are sharp rifts in an otherwise generally flat surface called the Defiance Plateau (sometimes called the Defiance Uplift), which covers several hundred square miles. It was surprising to see the canyons as we approached from a distance: they simply appear as a break in the surface that emerges with little visual warning, similar to the magnificent view that emerges when approaching the Grand Canyon. It rumored that the first conquistador from Spain to see the Grand Canyon exclaimed, "Madre de Dios!" – as he fell to his knees in reverence – and these two canyons have a similar effect.

The Canyons Chelly and Muerto form impressively deep rifts in a flat landscape with scattered brush, small trees, boulders, and rocks. The visual impression is that the canyons are narrow in width as compared to the depth. The walls rise about 1,000 feet above the canyon floor with little slope to the rise. *Precipitous* accurately describes the effect. The floors of the canyons appear rather quiescent, generally flat and peaceful. In each canyon there is a creek running through the length, which makes them both suitable for agricultural use by a small population.

Despite the impressive grandeur of the vista, even as seen through the windows of our moving vehicle, I suddenly started to have a feeling – almost a premonition – that was growing in contrast with the serenity of what we were seeing. At first, it was too vague to identify. Yet, it was a nagging feeling, deep within me, that something was different about Canyon del Muerto!

I mused that perhaps the serenity of the view was in some way, very deceiving. Something was not in harmony with other factors of history lodged here: *I could feel it.*

Call it a feeling, or a premonition, of something powerful that I could not quite grasp, let alone identify or define. At this un-expected moment, as we were about to get out of the car at a scenic overlook, the feeling was intensifying to the point of be-coming an *immersion* experience – as if some unrelenting feel-ing were entering all of my being.

Most of the time in my history, whenever I have a feeling about something, there is at least some hint as to what forces might be involved in causing the sensations to surface. My inabil-ity to grasp even a nuance of what I was experiencing within me at that moment provoked a combination of curiosity and a mild form of anxiety. I only knew *something* was happening to me. Despite the feeling, we walked to the view atop the canyon wall, bracing ourselves against the pressures of a hot wind sweeping across the Defiance Plateau.

On the overlook at the rim of Canyon del Muerto, the first impression is the sheer depth of the canyon, looking across what was once a uniform plateau, now broken by the rift. The depth is fascinating because of the contrast between the red walls and the light sand of the floor. The brightness of the floor in the reflection of the sun seemed to cause the floor to want to raise itself to the surface of the plateau, pulling your visual attention, beckoning you into the rift.

We could see the sandy floor, punctuated with green plants and small trees, generally following the path of a gentle stream framed like a photograph by the red canyon walls, the soft flow of the stream reflecting the blue color of the sky. Every element of shelter, water, and arable soil is available to support a small culture, looking as if it were willing to provide a comfortable and embracing home.

The motions of the clouds interspersed in the blue sky became reflections super-imposed on the stream. This made the movement of the clouds a highlight to the water's surface – as if the moving clouds were part of the flow of the stream itself. Truly, it is a lovely and compelling sight, and it all combined to build an image of tranquility and nature's beauty.

The contrast between the red sandstone walls and the tan, sandy, meandering floor and stream, is striking. Within this setting, the canyon's panorama reveals many ruins – fascinating vistas of several prehistoric cliff dwellings. The natives had built these dwellings from about the fourth to the fourteenth centuries, according to historians.

The dwellings are located variously on the floors of the canyons, in caves, and notably hewn in the sides of the canyon walls as well. One of the predominant structures is a dwelling in the wall called the White House Pueblo. The name comes from the lighter-tan, nearly white, alabaster color of the sandstone forming the wall in that location. It is easy to appreciate the "Pueblo" since the natural color gives the structure a beautiful contrast to the red sandstone backdrop. The contrast causes the pueblo to visually pop forward from the wall, like a bas-relief.

The Pueblo, occupied from about 1060 to 1275 A.D., looked impressive for its time. A preserved mummy found in a nearby cave, dated to about 1250 A.D. Reports are that the Navajo, at least by that tribal name, are comparative newcomers to the area, having started to settle in these canyons at the beginning of the 18th century.

On this particular hot summer's day, the wind velocity increased, tearing undeterred across the surface of the Defiance Plateau. I could imagine the shapes of the pressures, and feel the swirling of the wind currents. They whipped about noisily, propelled in eddy currents into and around the rifts in the plateau. The wind, being true to the name of the plateau, seemed to give the impression of defying any mere human to withstand its hot and dehydrating energy.

The wind sheared off an infinitesimal fraction of its energy by impacting our bodies – unrelentingly – as it pressed against us, played with us, taunted us to surrender to its forces.

The wind seemed to grow hotter, heated by compression as it came swirling down into the canyon from the rim. There was a subtle lamenting sound, like a soft human moan. I felt that all of the effects experienced in this moment seemed to converge into a conspiracy of nature: the canyon beckoning to pull one in; the image of the floor rising to capture our attention; and its partner in power, the wind, cajoling us into the canyon, continually testing our mettle against its impressive force.

Something is indeed very powerful about this place. Still, none of this explained my feelings, my perceptions, now approaching an overpowering form of something undefined yet, intensely – impressive.

We braced ourselves against the forces of the hot, dry, strong, and gusty wind while it energized and toyed with our bodies and nudged ourselves against the guardrail at the very edge of the rim. I was fighting the unrelenting pressures not to fly into the canyon, feeling the tearing forces as my clothes fluttered violently in complaint, submitted as playthings of nature. I pushed against, and held tightly to our bastion of security, the protective railing along the edge of the rim. Having sensations at the edge of fear, I felt I could succumb to the dance of the forces, the pressures of the wind leading me in the dance.

The images of the canyon continued to assemble and reassemble in my mind. The increasingly intense inner feelings, though still undefined, were starting to overwhelm me. They carried a high sort of familiarity, a déjà vu, like that of an old experience long held but submerged in memory, trying to fight its way to the surface of my mind.

"What is this feeling – the distant memory stirring in me?" I quietly asked myself as the feeling tenaciously persisted.

"Something is trying to fight its way to my surface like a pervasive dream lodged in the distant past, oscillating to approach the surface, then defeated, only to retreat back into the shadows."

Standing at the rim to look down into the canyon's depth, a faint recollection began to come back. A piece of my history was beginning to emerge, and it seemed incredible. I had not experienced this level of perception and raw emotion in many years.

Suddenly, the feeling intensified with the force of a catapult, rushing into a whirlwind of energy: power, piercing pain, turmoil, anguish, and then, as if I were ensconced in the eye of a hurricane – a solace – as if it were the peace of death.

The continuing moan of the wind emphasized these sensations, these naked emotions, as if in combination they were trying to envelop me in re-experiencing something. As my thoughts trailed into the canyons, my vision blurred as I dropped my resistance and allowed my consciousness to probe into the depth of my being.

Then in a brilliant flash, it all exploded out of a deeply locked up vault, a place of confinement where it had been for a very long time! The memory flooded out into a full exposure that I could no further conceal, no longer deny.

Under my breath, I gasped in exhaling to the wind as I stammered… *"…Oh…. my…dear…"*

Now shaken in an instant, tears welling in my eyes as my emotions reenergized, saturating me in a regression to events of a previous time long in dormancy: my early youth.

Observation

During life, people are frequently affected by vague or direct recollections. Events that were significant to us, through prior experiences, become embedded as buried emotions that surface unexpectedly. When emotional reactions pop up that are not understood, you can benefit from asking questions of yourself, such as "Where is the feeling coming from?" to gain insight into your past that causes current reactions. Are there missing pieces for you?

Do you understand the cause of your emotional responses?

CHAPTER THREE

VISIONS

As a quiet child on summer vacation, I would often stroll around in my back yard, enjoying the warmth of the sun. My mind would wander, thinking about things I wanted to do, projects to work on, or just dreamily staring into the sky studying the cloud formations. One lazy afternoon, as I gazed into a blue and cloudless sky, I saw a glint, like a flash or reflection, off something bright and metallic. That glint turned my attention to a specific direction in the sky. Then, I suddenly saw it: An airplane, starting to fall in mid-air, was twisting about!

I knew something about airplanes, because for a time my father had worked for Douglas Aircraft, nearby.

The twin-engine, propeller plane, about the size of a DC-3, was in trouble! I could vividly see the break-up of the portside wing as it fell away from the fuselage! The wing itself and some metal fragments flickering about the sky were highlighted by glistening reflections of the sun off of the aluminum as it twisted in the air, and then the spiraling plunge of the fuselage. I tracked the movements, first of the fragments of the wing that had separated, and then of the fall of the fuselage itself.

My immediate reflex was to excitedly run inside the house to tell my mother what I had seen, shouting *Mom, Mom!* - as I ran, looking for her. My mother quickly responded to my pleas as I took her hand and pulled her outside to the place where I had been standing.

When I pointed to the position where I had seen the debris and the aircraft falling, my mouth fell agape in shocking surprise and confusion: there was nothing in the sky to be seen; nothing at all. *There was not a wisp of anything in view, only the sight of the blue sky.* There was not even a hint of drifting debris suggesting an airplane failure, smoke, or anything else!

My mother, being a gentle and nurturing person, quietly assured me that I might have seen a reflection. Maybe I had seen a cloud formation, or even a heat mirage, she offered, in an attempt to quell my excitement. Though I felt a bit of embarrassment because I had dragged her outside to see my vision, followed by a letdown, her gentle words did have a soothing effect. As my emotions settled down, I spent the rest of that day reflecting on what I had seen, trying to understand my emotions. It had seemed so real, yet it was not there for my mother to see.

What had happened? Did I actually see anything?

My embarrassment caused me consternation and confusion, partially because of my timidity and tentative self-image at that time of my life. I worried I would be thought of as someone who told tall tales and made up imaginary stories, as so many children do, though I never had that tendency. Somehow, it seemed important: I wanted people to take me seriously. It would take only a few hours that same day to resolve the mystery of what I had experienced.

Imagine my mother's surprise, and my relief, when the evening newspaper reported an airplane crash! The story described the break-up of the wing and the fall of the fuselage in the same detail that I had reported to her. This vision was not my imagination at work. *It was real.*

The crash had occurred in a distant location, too far away from our residence for me to see it, yet I had had a clear view of the incident. I clearly recall mother's excited expression when she called out to my father, *"Michael saw this!"* as she ran across the room waving the fluttering newspaper to show the article to my father.

My parents discussed my report and the implications of the event between themselves for quite a while that evening. They were excited about what I had seen, and the newspaper's detailed confirmation. Though I didn't realize it at the time, I can say now that this was a defining "signal" (if not an omen) to alert me to other events that I would eventually be compelled to experience. I had yet to understand that a new reality would follow me, alter me, and be with me, forever.

Apart from my excitement over seeing the event, the vision of the airplane falling was not in any way personal or emotional to me. It was simply a vision like a video clip in today's television news report. (Television was not yet widely available at that time in the late 1940s.)

My detachment changed dramatically a couple of years after the airplane vision when I had another, more dramatic, even phenomenal experience which took place in our living room on a warm summer afternoon.

On that day, my parents' good friends came by our home to say good-bye before departing on an around-the-world shipboard cruise. The couple was elderly, older than my parents were. I knew that they were well-heeled Europeans, enjoying life in high luxury. According to my parents, they had fortuitously escaped with their fortune to the United States in the mid-thirties, before World War II invaded their homeland.

The couple didn't have children of their own, and they always embraced me with affection as if they were my aunt and uncle. They were frequent visitors to our home, and as patrons of the arts, they enjoyed attending mother's parties that centered on classical music and opera, and listening to mother and me play the piano.

I responded with fond feelings toward them both. She displayed the high bearing of her social status (she was a baroness): tall and proud – like Marlene Dietrich, with a sultry voice to match. He usually appeared a bit disheveled on the other hand, with frizzy gray hair rather like photographs of Albert Einstein. He was a practicing surgeon in the United States. The baroness and her husband arrived that summer afternoon to bid us farewell and to enjoy a social tea with my parents. I was playing at the dining room table when the baroness began to explain their extensive cruise plans to my parents. Their voyage would take them across the Atlantic on a luxury ocean liner for their first trip back to their homeland since the war. As I listened eagerly, not wanting to miss any of the details, an incredible *energetic wave* swept over and through me.

Suddenly a dreadful emotion immersed me, enveloped me! It brought me immediately to a state of panic. Some kind of dreadful force seemed to be welling up within me. Spontaneously overwhelmed and hysterically out of control, I ran across the room toward the baroness! I dropped, sliding across the floor, and grabbed her legs near her ankles. I reached up and tugged at her skirt as if I were trying to hold her down to the floor. My guess is that it looked as if I were having some kind of "fit," screaming as I did so.

Then, in a burst of tears, I cried and screamed at them as my voice cracked through my emotion: *"Don't go! Stay here!"*

She was stunned, and stared at me in silence with a startled expression. My parents were probably stunned, though to be honest I didn't even notice them at the time. My wholly directed intensity was toward the baroness. I vaguely heard an echo of my mother exclaiming *"Michael!"* but no more than that.

Responding to the baroness's urging, I released my grip of her legs. Then I seemed to be able to see myself from a height – as if my position was near the ceiling above. I have a clear memory of seeing myself writhing around on the floor, even to the detail of the clothes I was wearing. It is a powerfully indelible memory that will still bring tears to my eyes. My father seemed stunned, like a deer in the headlights, motionless. The baroness's husband was exclaiming something in their native language, beyond my comprehension.

It was the most powerful premonition I had had to that point of my life. Yet, the premonition itself was undefined. *I simply had to stop them from going on their cruise.* That was my only mission. Overcome, wholly saturated in emotion as never before, I could not be consoled or dissuaded.

I did not relent.

Amid all my screaming and crying, my father seemed stunned and motionless, because it was my mother's and the baroness's hands that reached out to comfort me. My parents' attempts to console me were futile, and my ranting continued. The baroness, however, knelt down to face me and tried to *hear* and understand what I was saying. It was obvious that she was trying to make some sense about my message and what was happening to me. This was a difficult task because of my hysteria. I was begging them, shouting, desperately pleading, as I writhed around on the floor: *"Please…. Please… Don't get on the ship! Don't go!"*

Suddenly she seemed to understand my distress. She suddenly seemed to grasp the message within my screaming! The baroness gently stroked my face with her velvet glove. She *heard my message* and she softly said in a deeply intoned and consoling voice: yes, they would change their plans!

It was as if a crack immediately broke open in my emotion.

She then said, in her European accent, as she looked up from her kneeling position toward my parents, anything should be heeded that was powerful enough to cause such a severe reaction in me. The baroness was still kneeling as she urged me off the floor to my knees. When I stood, wobbling, she bent toward me and hugged me, soothing me, as I was still gasping, sobbing, and trembling.

As soon as she had said *yes, they would change their plans;* a suffocating and terrifying burden lifted from me. Then with deep, short, and rapid breaths, I stood. I had a sensation of fatigue, near exhaustion, which quickly set in now, with my mission accomplished. I continued to sob – and tremble – for a while as the emotion wound down within me.

I walked instinctively, almost staggering on my wobbly legs, slowly out into the sun. My father tried to follow me yet mother held him back saying, "*He needs to be alone.*" I vaguely heard the adults continue their conversation in hushed whispers, though my feelings were still rattling through me.

I had learned to seek solace in the sun when there was any feeling of turmoil within me. For as long as I can remember, the sun itself seemed to be *a friend,* as its radiance of energy enveloped me. The radiance somehow helped me balance my emotions as I comforted myself in its warmth – isolated in its embrace.

The couple fulfilled their promise to me and rearranged their schedule. Reported in the news several weeks later, the story appeared: there had been a ship-to-ship collision at sea; the original cruise ship that our friends were going to travel on had sunk.

I remember seeing my mother's mouth drop open as she gasped while reading the newspaper story to my father. She immediately telephoned the baroness with much excitement, yet I remember only her excitement and not her words. As this was unfolding, I felt that I needed to hide somewhere, elevating my mother's concerns for me, her only child.

She felt she had to *do something.*

Observation

Children tend to have natural, unbridled, emotions, perceptions, and reactions during the first phase of their lives. Those perceptions and, perhaps, visions can be very powerful.

Powerful experiences can set up impressions that remain embedded in their beings throughout life. It is NOT what actually happened that matters later in life. What really matters are the emotions and "remembered events" that become embedded, that a person believes in to be "real" that influence reactions, that can drive self-image later in life.

I can only observe and suggest that the reactions of adults, parents or authority figures that surround the child can significantly affect what emotions are embedded that can reflexively surface later in each life.

If the "adult" reaction attempts to thwart or negate the feelings, the child could become suppressed and may learn to disassociate himself or herself from feelings, even in the broadest sense.

Suppressing feelings can sublimate reactions, yet still leave them close enough to the surface that they can eventually be evaluated. **Crushing** feelings into submersion can leave little to work with later, to evaluate for evolving self-knowledge.

I've found it valuable to ask myself questions as an adult when feelings pop to the surface that have no immediate, or superficially apparent, reason for the feelings.

So, asking oneself "where did THAT come from?" can be a beginning to understanding the basis of one's reactions. If the answer is not readily known, reflect back into earlier times and try to find parallel events that might provide triggers to unravel tangles in the mind.

There is **always** a cause for reflexive, impulsive emotions.

Do you understand the factors that occurred and still influence your being?

CHAPTER FOUR

THE EXORCIST

In our normal flow of life, my mother and I frequently shared physiological and emotional experiences. It seemed that we were mutually *connected*, no matter how physically far apart we were, and our connection automatically activated when something abnormal happened to either of us. If I suffered an injury, she would feel the same pain, or if she felt strong emotion, I would sense the feeling. When I'd ask her about this she'd pooh-pooh it, saying that such perceptions were just part of the normal bond between a mother and child. The overpowering emotion I had displayed with her friends, however, including my writhing about on the floor, seemed to frighten her. (It would be some time before I discovered the true basis of her concerns.)

My mother, a devoted Catholic, had contacts within the office of the Archdiocese through her volunteer work with the church. She had heard rumors that there was a bona fide (church-recognized) exorcist residing somewhere within the Archdiocese, and she presented her concerns through the chancery office, asking them to locate him.

Imagine my surprise, one day, when mother explained that she wanted me to meet *a special priest*. This priest, reputed to have *special abilities,* lived in the Archbishop's residence, a mansion, she said. To my questions about what that meant, her response was, *"Abilities that can help you."*

Whenever mother had concerns about me, particularly over things where she didn't have direct control, she would tend to use the word *special.* As her only child, born to her after eight years of marriage, late in her years (for her generation) when she was 37, I was undoubtedly special to her, though I usually found this confusing. In my own reality, in no way did I *feel* special. I did know this: I did not like to be forced to meet strangers, just as I did not like being compelled to perform for others at the piano!

I continued to ask why it was important for me to meet the priest. She did her best to assure me that it was, actually, to help me. She eventually escalated her urging to overcome my reluctance and protests: "You *must* see him!" I protested to Mother: *"Why must* I see him?" This time her response was, "Because he is an *exorcist."* I asked, *"What is an exorcist?"*

In a reassuring voice, she answered, "An exorcist can remove the trouble and turmoil from you that caused so much crying and emotion about the baroness. When trouble is removed, there is more room for God's grace in you!"

Therefore, it happened that I had been committed to meet someone for some purpose that I did not fully understand. I did clearly realize, though, that her insistence for me to meet this particular priest was because of my emotional outburst regarding our family friends and their shipboard cruise.

So now the trauma that I wanted to forget was continuing! I was to meet a special priest despite my vigorous protests! Her words did not assuage my anxiety or turmoil about meeting him. I continued to whine, to insist, "Why?" but no answer could completely satisfy me. In my mind, she was still forcing me to do something I didn't want to do! Although overwhelmed as I was by the specific event with the baroness, there had been many other events of less intensity. Those other events I never talked about – to anyone. Most of the precognitive perceptions that enveloped me during my childhood didn't seem important enough to mention to my parents or anyone else. Therefore, yes, even though the event with her friends was both tumultuous and exhausting, it was unique only in its intensity.

The archbishop's mansion was located in a gate-guarded area – unusual in my youthful experience and probably unique for Southern California itself in the late 1940s. Throughout our drive of about an hour, my anxiety was growing, but I remained quiet in the car. By the time we arrived at the mansion, however, my anxiety had taken over. I seemed to withdraw from what was happening, or going to happen, to me.

Everything seemed blurred.

I barely remember my mother driving up to the gate, saying something to the guard, and then driving by the guard post. The gate opened to admit our passage onto the property.

My first clear recollection picks up after we entered the mansion. I'm not even clear what the mansion looked like on the exterior, or even where we parked our car. Until we entered the mansion, all images seem somehow diffused or obscure to me, like I was in a daze. I was moving under the guidance of my mother as if I were sleepwalking.

Once in the mansion, everything seemed very plush. Though I had many ideas about what a normal home might look like, I had no idea or exposure as to what *a mansion* would or should look like. There were musty scents, probably from the thick draperies. There were also warm wood tones everywhere, and it all seemed replete with elegance. I found it hard to be comfortable in this unfamiliar environment, especially given my distraught feelings and the circumstances of why we were visiting the mansion.

Whoever greeted us at the main entry, a woman I believe, escorted us to an area down a long hallway. Toward the end of the hallway, a priest seemed to be waiting for us. Our escort presented my mother to this priest. The priest, a younger person compared to my parents, had a dark wood desk in an entry niche or anteroom. I can clearly recall that he stood as we approached his desk, and we were warmly and enthusiastically greeted.

There was a closed door behind his desk, toward my left. There were plush draperies framing this doorway, and the door itself was of a heavily paneled dark wood with a distinctive grain. After greeting us, he promptly turned and opened the door. The dark wood creaked as he walked through and into the main chamber, closing the door behind him. My attention drifted away, looking at the wood floor and the carpet runner with a burgundy floral pattern set against an ivory background.

After a few minutes, the creaking sound of the door interrupted my study of the carpet. Another priest appeared from the chamber, escorted by the one who had greeted us. The new priest, an older and balding man, turned toward my direction and briefly looked at me. I tried my best to avert his gaze. I wanted to hide. Immediately, even before I saw all the details of his physical image, I felt something incredible – like a powerful heat wave that both flooded me and wrapped itself around my body.

I snapped my eyes to focus on the image of the new priest, and then I experienced a sort of tingling, like a mild and continuous electric shock! The tingling sensation rippled through me, seemingly carried by the heat wave. I had been experimenting at home in my garage with building radios to feed my technical curiosities, and I knew what mild electric shocks felt like! My anxiety now had the fuel of a new source of energy! *Now* I felt discomfort and it rapidly became a sense of intimidation!

I quickly concluded that this new priest had to be *the special priest* because of the sensations! Our introduction to the special priest was nurturing and gracious, first to Mother and then to me, but I shied away when he started to approach me. I was relieved when he turned away and stopped his approach, and though his name of *Father (something)* clearly implied a Spanish heritage during the introduction, only the title of *Father* clearly got through to me. I was mentally in some state between a blur and being fully lucid, trapped in a powerful combination of the *electrified sensations* and *heat* that was nearly overwhelming.

My mother, after her introduction to the new priest, started a quiet conversation with him. Thankfully, this produced a respite from the events confronting me, and relief from the physical sensations. At least they weren't dragging me in to immediately engage with the special priest. I turned away from looking at him, distracting myself, darting my eyes between the carpet runner and my feet! I took a few deep breaths and tried to calm down.

Then cautiously, sheepishly, I elevated my head. I allowed myself to tentatively glance toward him. That took major courage! What I saw surprised me. In my religious upbringing, I had seen many artists' drawings of saints. The pictures usually had halos of gold and other colors of aura surrounding the saints' heads. When I looked at this special priest, I saw an aura surrounding his body. It seemed to be all around him, and it was slowly filling the distance between us.

"Was this priest a saint?" I wondered, which only increased my tension. I seemed to be feeling his aura. It radiated from him and *it seemed to reach out and touch me! It was expanding, and it was enveloping me!*

His aura, when I noticed and focused on it, seemed to resemble the heat-thermal waves that my parents had explained to me during drives across the hot Mojave Desert. Then, as I attempted to focus on these waves, I glimpsed many swirls of colors that outlined his body, and those colors were enveloping me as well. The aura seemed to be the cause of my sensations of heat and electricity.

I was already accustomed to seeing vortices of colors, particularly in the presence of my mother. We would sometimes see them together and talk about what we were both seeing. Seeing vortices, however, is very different from being touched by them and having them cause sensations in my body. It was a very powerful experience to deal with.

Here in these few moments was just the beginning of this incredible day in my life, a day that would leave indelible impressions within me.

The special priest gently clasped both of mother's hands in his as their greeting neared its end. Then he turned to look at me. He moved away from Mother as she stood outside the main chamber. The priest turned to reenter the chamber. As he moved away, the sensation of his aura field collapsed toward him, and away from me. I started to shiver.

The priest who had first greeted us pressed his hand behind my right shoulder. He gestured in a way that seemed intended to gently nudge me to follow the exorcist into the other room. I got the message. I followed reluctantly, scuffing my feet along the way.

My mother, not invited to enter the chamber with the exorcist and myself, remained in the hallway. When I realized that she would not be following me, I glanced back at her, feeling terrified! The consternation was awful, caught in the rift between what I was being directed to do, and reaching out to cling to the safety of Mother!

Yet, I was unable to muster enough strength or conviction to run back and hold on to her. I was used to obeying priests from my training in parochial school. I was doing what I had been programmed to do, essentially moving like an automaton.

The priest who had nudged me into the chamber now pointed me in the direction of a chair, but I could only stand there. He then closed the door of the chamber behind me, and I found myself alone – with only the exorcist, who was already sitting down.

My apprehension surged and my heart rate with it. Suddenly, I felt very cold, actually shivering with feelings that I tried to ignore, but could not. Each beat of my heart seemed to be pounding in my ears. Each heartbeat caused a surge of shivering throughout my body.

The exorcist was sitting on a plush sofa across the elegant room from where I was standing. Obeying his gesture, I sat down in an overstuffed chair opposite him. My recollection is that we were about six feet apart. At first, I just quietly sat there:

I really didn't have anything to say. Actually, I didn't know *what* to say.

We were there together, orchestrated to be so for some purpose, with some vague objective to help me – somehow. I wasn't really certain what the help was supposed to be about, what it was supposed to do for me!

My mind was racing!

"Help me? Why? How?"

"What am I doing here with this priest?"

"What is the electricity and heat I felt when I saw him?"

I took some consolation because I was there under the direction of my mother. At least, I believed that I could trust her judgment, and she was (after all) *just outside* the door in case I needed to bolt away and run for help. Heavens, how I wished she could cuddle me at that instant, but she had been excluded from my direct encounter with this special priest.

The priest started to talk to me in soothing tones. He asked about my feelings, and he reassured me that *I was in God's grace.* I was feeling dazed, I was just starting to settle down and accept whatever was going to happen, when something changed. I just barely nodded my head to acknowledge his words when, like the motion of a warm breeze, I felt his presence start slowly to expand again across the distance that separated us. Rather than feeling like tingling electricity riding on heat, the sensation this time felt warm and friendly, even embracing, as he seemed to somehow reach toward me through his aura. The uncertainty for me was that something was occurring, but I didn't know what. I only knew that it was powerful, out of my direct ability to influence or control, and it was becoming very, very, intense.

My anxiety surged again, which swept away the *warm and friendly feeling.* I did not realize it at the time, but I now know that I was impulsively attempting to hide, to block the sensations. I must have been successful because it suddenly seemed that the temperature dropped in the room. The *cold feeling* caused more anxiety, and my body began to tremble.

Somehow, I found the courage to gaze into his deep brown eyes. Perhaps I was seeking help, something to alleviate my discomfort. That seemed to calm me down. I could easily see the priest's aura and I focused on that. The more I connected with his aura, the warmer I became. His aura came to me in what seemed to be an expanded sense of his spiritual being, and that warmth became comforting for me. We somehow were connected, similar to what I was used to experiencing with Mother.

The exorcist started *talking* to me. I have to admit, though, that I am not certain: Were the words actually spoken, or simply understood? The communication was, however, quite focused but still gentle. My impression was that our conversation didn't occur as a flow of individual words, yet I precisely embraced and clearly understood the communication.

His message was very simple and very reassuring: *Be at peace, Michael. You are safe.* His words carried a very familiar Spanish accent.

The exorcist-priest was a Spaniard like my mother. In our home, we sometimes had visiting relatives and family friends from Spain, so I was used to hearing Spanish names and accents, and accustomed to a mix of Spanish and English. In the reality of my situation, it all felt so very familiar, as if we'd known each other for a long time.

A glow of warmth replaced the wave or surge of cold that had rushed through me moments ago. All of my fear yielded to acceptance, and my acceptance became a cuddly, nurtured, feeling of love. Though there was no physical contact between us, the power of our connection was compelling. Whatever tendency I might have had to try to avoid or even run from this encounter had now dissipated.

Apart from the exorcist's abilities, whatever they might be, I began to have a tentative feeling that his energy and personality characteristics were similar to my own – a very comforting perception! For the first time in my life, I was directly experiencing another who seemed to be similar to Mother and me.

The exorcist asked me to tell him about my vision of the airplane crash. This was easy, even exciting for me, because that experience was not riddled with heavy emotion. Then, after we had begun a flow of communication, he asked me to tell him what happened with my mother's friends about the cruise ship when I had become *very upset*.

Tentatively, yet dutifully, I responded. That was the event, after all, that upset my mother! That event was what caused me to be here with this priest!

I took a deep breath, swallowed hard and choked a bit, as I tried to tell my story, which carried echoes of the dreaded emotions. My voice broke and stammered and the exorcist used the peace of his gaze and aura to help reassure me.

He attentively listened to my account of how the dreaded premonitions had taken me over that day. I did not really understand the reasons for my actions, only that they happened. Begrudgingly, I tried to describe how I had been totally overtaken with raw feeling, that I was feeling guilty over how my actions had affected my mother, and how much I regretted being out of control. Finally, I admitted my concern, echoing something I had overheard from my mother talking to the chancery office: that evil spirits had possessed me. My composure temporarily broke, and in the whining voice of a timid and frightened child, I asked, *"am I evil?"*

He smiled and listened patiently to my emotional story, increasing his reassurance and nodding his head frequently as though he already knew what I had experienced. Had mother told him? When did she tell him, and in what detail?

The recollection of those powerful and disturbing events caused my emotions to stir again! My residual emotional problem, my anxiety, was that my perceptions of the priest and his aura were profoundly powerful. *Powerful* was close to what I had experienced just before the overwhelmingly intense precognitions with my mother's friends saturated me! I did not want to become overtaken completely out of control, again!

Then, it dawned on me. He already probably knew what I had experienced because if he had similar abilities to my mother and me, he could already feel it. As my story unfolded, actually before my version was fully completed, he attempted to assure me that I was perfectly normal. He said that extra-sensory awareness was perfectly normal *for me*, and the *devil had not invaded my soul, so I was not evil! That must have been it! The word "devil" caught my attention!*

My mother was concerned about *what had invaded her son.* Not long after the tremendous turmoil with her friends and their cruise, I overheard her talking on the telephone to someone, probably in the chancery office. She was saying something about her son possibly being *possessed!* In the religious context of my upbringing, *possessed always meant possessed by something demonic!*

The exorcist explained that I should not be afraid of unique feelings, these perceptional abilities, but I should embrace them. He said that God had given me *a gift of special knowledge* and that it was *God's will that I carry this cross of burden.*

His presentation caused me to feel that it was *God's order* directed specifically to me. I became convinced and compelled to carry *this cross of burden,* and that all of this was pre-ordained: *the way of God's will.* Then came the admonishment that would influence me, haunt me, for decades. The priest's advice, which seemed like a command to me, was: *"Do not let others know what you can see, feel, perceive, or experience."*

According to the exorcist, God directed His will to me privately and God compelled me to carry *His cross of knowledge* that came from Him. Then he added it should remain a private matter between God and me - because others would not understand.

Interpreting the exorcist's instruction came down to this: *He ordered me to hide my abilities and hide the reality of myself from society.*

In a reverent gesture of reverent acknowledgment, trained as I had been not to question any direction from a priest, I cast my eyes downward. I was slowly nodding my head to accept his admonition. I was neither questioning nor understanding the implications involved with my acceptance of – and compliance with – his instruction.

He stood and walked slowly toward me. I automatically knelt before him, being obedient to my training. He made movements that to others, had they seen these motions, would have looked like a traditional blessing from a priest. He was *signing the cross* in front of me but not uttering a single word, and his motions seemed to direct his aura more intensely to me.

He placed his hands upon my shoulders, and I will *not ever, forget the sensation*. It was as if a powerful wave of sparkling electricity was flowing through all of my body and within my being. My body trembled with the surge!

When the priest removed his hands from my shoulders, he took my hands in a gentle grasp to help me stand from my kneeling position. I arose before him, a quivering child.

I had difficulty walking at that moment. The residual presence of the energy surge from his hands was still tingling or resonating throughout my being. So in quiet compliance, I just stood as still as I could, wobbling as I attempted to balance myself. He kept his hand on my right shoulder as we walked the short distance to the door. The creaking as it opened seemed to underscore my feelings. We walked out to the anteroom, where Mother was waiting, seated on a couch. She stood up and smiled, but I did not run to her. The exorcist still had his hand on my shoulder, and he nudged me to stand against the desk.

Quietly, I stayed in the place where the exorcist had left me as he walked the few steps over to meet my mother. I remember getting the message, somehow, that I was to stay in that position, as the exorcist approached her with his soft voice. I supported myself against the desk because I was still feeling wobbly.

His aura now appeared different somehow, more localized about his body, while partially directed toward my mother. He placed his hand on her shoulder, and that gesture seemed to nudge her to turn away from me. He softened his voice to a whispered level to say whatever it was that he needed to say, though I could still hear some of what he said to her. I could also feel the peace and satisfaction beaming from my mother, so warm and loving that it glowed. As he started speaking to her, I felt a sense of grace and beauty that today I would call *nurture*. I could see changes in my mother's aura, which shifted from a brilliance of many hues, like ribbons in motion, to become deep blue. Her facial expressions changed as well, from a mild frown when he started to approach her, to a beaming smile as their conversation progressed.

His presentation to my mother about me was, at least by my memory, rather brief. From my mother's reaction, there is no question that his words were soft and reassuring.

His message seemed to be quite to the point. *He assured her that evil spirits had not taken over me!* He continued that I was just learning how to express myself *in God's service.* He blessed her, signing the cross before her, and said something to the effect that I was a continuation of her own being and ability. I was *fine* - not to worry, in other words.

I didn't *feel* fine. I felt exhausted. I didn't hear all the details he related about our conversation together, though I admit I was too tired to care.

My focus became a yearning: I wanted Mother to hold me. I was not really paying much attention to the exorcist. Actually, I had been energetically detached from him, so Mother's reaction was my whole focus.

It had been an exhausting day for me. I felt drained of energy. I was not inclined to try to probe into their quiet conversation. I clearly recall, though, the image of the two of them together. They looked very much like a partnership of close friends, maybe kindred souls – as if they had known each other forever.

I glimpsed the reflection of tears contrasting with her dark brown eyes as she thanked the exorcist for his service to us. Mother motioned toward me to come to her, and it took all of my restraint not to run at full pace to her arms. Instead, I just shuffled across the room. She reached toward me and gently put her arm around me and asked me how I was feeling. I didn't directly answer, but I looked up at her and feigned a smile. We slowly walked out of the mansion and got into our car, in silence.

When we had driven beyond the guarded gate, Mother's questions broke the eerie silence. She wanted to know the details about what had happened with the priest, but I really did not know how to answer. After all, my emotional display with her friends had stirred things up enough! My usual response would be to withdraw when confronted by challenges that I could barely deal with – especially if any fuss were involved! Withdrawal seemed to be my reflex. It was safe.

Therefore, at first, I just shrugged my shoulders with my face cast downward, trying to avoid her glances as she drove the car. *"Nothing happened,"* I cautiously answered in a quivering voice. I struggled with my voice as it wobbled, unable to feign a normal voice. However, it is essentially impossible to deceive an empath, particularly when she is your mother! Since the connection between us was mutual, I could feel her dissatisfaction with my response. I could even feel her quandary about how to help me break out of my shell.

She continued in a low tone of voice to urge out more information. *"Michael,"* she said, *"You were with the priest for a long time, and I could feel your emotions."*

It did not seem like a long time to me. Time stood still for me in that chamber. *"Miguelito, por favor. Te amo,"* she would say, reverting to Spanish to sometimes set a mood with me. Somehow when she used the Spanish version of *little Michael*, my emotions would melt. This was no exception. Withdrawal would not work. I had to find a way to deal with her insistence.

This caused a conflict for me: a priest, a special priest, had told me *not to tell anyone*. From my background in Catholicism, priests had specific authority. They had authority, more so than nuns did. *Priests were to be revered! Priests had to be obeyed!* Nevertheless, I could feel her ramping up her intensity to get me to open up to her verbally.

Typical of our relationship, *she intuitively found the key*. Mother asked the *one question* that could dislodge my silence! Instead of asking what happened in that room only a few feet away from her, she asked me, *"What did you feel in the presence of the priest?"*

Before I had time to think and react, she immediately piled on something even more specific. She asked, *"What did you feel when he placed his hands upon your shoulders?"* I jumped to a conclusion: *She must already know*!

"How could she know?" I thought.

Those few words implied she had specific knowledge, and that caused the welling emotions to flood out of me.

That last question did it!

If she already knew the essentials, then I *could not be guilty of violating the instruction* from the exorcist. I told her: *Everything*.

I told her about the colors of the vortex, the aura, the sensations of electrical energy shimmering through my body! I described the convergence of our communication. I told her about his aura as it approached and enveloped me, and I told her of her aura when she was with him. I tried to describe my feelings and perceptions the best I could.

Finally, I excitedly described the sparkling surge of electrification that trembled like a wave through my being when his hands rested on my shoulders.

Mother glanced in my direction, and did not say very much. She turned her attention back to driving the car and it seemed that all was standing still as she absorbed what I had said. Then she glanced back at me, nodded, and smiled. With great mastery of understatement, she said, *"And that was all?"* I felt stunned by the immediate acceptance. Relieved, I smiled and simply nodded *yes* to her.

From her easy acceptance and what seemed to be her satisfaction with my report, I had the feeling that she completely understood what had happened.

Much later, while still driving what seemed to be a long way home that afternoon, Mother seemed to want to get something out – a revelation perhaps. Her voice dropped to a very soft tone and I could hear her murmuring something – as if she were rehearsing what to say. Then, with a noticeable pulsing hesitation between her words, finally she said:

"Michael…. my family name…." she halted before she could continue, *"and… your name… … We are descendents of …"*

The pause was palpable as her voice broke and she swallowed, and then paused again. She again took a deep breath and briefly glanced toward me.

I felt that she was hesitating, wondering whether to reveal something important. It must have been very difficult for her. The fact is that whatever she was struggling to get out to me was so submerged, her uncertainty so deep, that it was influencing her piloting of the car, which was now wandering a bit within the lane. Quickly adjusting to control the car distracted her from her message to me, and the rapid sideways movement caused me to slide and lean against her side (cars didn't have seat belts then). Settling back into the drive, regaining her composure, I could feel that she was ready, maybe reluctant, to continue; yet, she was saying nothing. I was becoming impatient.

I awaited her next words with high anticipation. Eventually, after what seemed an interminable time, she continued, "We are descendents of a *conquistador….*"

As she said *conquistador* there was a crescendo of emphasis, an uplift of dignity. I heard the pride in her voice! Her face tilted upward in a way that underscored her tone, like the haughty pose of a Flamenco dancer. Then she paused again, and said….

"… Álvar Núñez Cabeza de Vaca," as she took in a deep breath, having finally gotten that much out.

There was another pause. Again, it seemed interminable, probably because of my youthful impatience. I had long known that my heritage is Spanish. My grandmother (who was living with us) was from Seville and my grandfather from Granada. Mother was a *Sevillana*, a point of pride for her.

Mother's lengthy pause only served to increase my eager, youthful anticipation. Somehow, through our empathic connection, I had a feeling about what was coming. Clearly, Mother *knew something* that she had been withholding. She had been waiting for the moment – I suppose waiting for a propitious moment – to tell her son. It seemed directly related to my recent experiences, and the feeling from her was intensely embracing.

The moment had come. I think of this even today *as a decisive moment, the disclosure of truth*! With all that had occurred during this profound day with the exorcist, it just had to come out – could no longer be withheld. She had received some form of verification that she needed through the encounter with the exorcist. There were glistening tears in her eyes as she continued,

"He was ……… much more than a conquistador."

My anticipation had now become anxiety as she said…

"He had 'special' power—Special abilities from God."

Then there was another pause as if she were contemplating how much more to specifically reveal to me.

"Those abilities flow through our veins. This is our inheritance…"

Her voice was starting to trail off, and was almost in a hush when she muttered to complete her thought: "… *of our blood."*

The expression, *"Oh – my – Lord – God,"* emotionally expressed through a stammer – captures the essence of my feeling at the time, even without fully comprehending what this all really meant to me.

I began to tear in my synergistic connection with her, and then withdrew as I attempted to suppress a sob. My inclination to cry was intense, yet I did not realize why, so I said absolutely nothing. My mind went numb. I was attempting to grasp the implications of her revelation to me. In that withdrawal, asking questions did not seem necessary.

With an intonation that seemed to say that her verbal ordeal was about over, she breathed easier. She brought her attention back to driving the car as she said: *"You will learn more, in time."*

I acknowledged her words with a polite but tentative smile as I gazed at her. I gently touched her shoulder with my head, and then I turned quietly away.

That seemed to end this phase of our conversation. It was common to know between us when a conversation had ended. The remainder of our drive home was quiet and even serene. Perhaps a gap closed, a gap long held open between us. Throughout my childhood, I had heard tales about conquistadors and even our ancestry. I had overheard conversations between Mother and my cousins when they would occasionally visit. Sometimes I would eavesdrop and hear my name mentioned in these conversations, which, I would guess, melded with this new information and made it seem more normal. By the time we had arrived home, I had mentally filed Mother's revelation away into the background of my mind.

Decades would pass before I would be motivated to research and study details about my ancestor: Álvar Núñez Cabeza de Vaca. His ancestry, like my own, was from Seville and Granada. He was treasurer of the New World expeditions for Charles I, King of Spain (1516–1556). Known in Spain as *Carlos Primero*, he would later be simultaneously Charles V of the Holy Roman Empire (1530–1556) and Lord of the Indies.

According to my ancestor's published account, his ship struck a reef. Shipwrecked in the New World, he was captured along with a very few of his shipmates by a tribe of natives, probably in what is now Florida. Most of his shipmates that survived the wreck, did not survive the tribe's attack, including the priest accompanying them. The natives were a tribe he called the *Iguase*.

According to his book, *La Relación (The Report)*, later called *Naufragios (Shipwreck)*, his captors singled him out and separated him from the other captured shipmates. An Iguase shaman (shamans were generally called *sorcerers* – diableros, devil men - by the Spaniards) took control of his captivity, and forced him, for a prolonged period, to be his apprentice to learn magic and the healing arts. After some years, they permitted him to eventually leave his captors, and he left a changed man. He had become proficient in the healing arts – "magic" in the way tribal (and even civilized) society believed in that era.

On his trek of about nine years through what is now Texas and Mexico, he was usually alone, separated from other conquistadors who were sparsely occupying the region. At one point, he encountered former shipmates, also released by the Iguase. These survivors of both the shipwreck and their captivity witnessed him performing miracles with, or on, natives, often healing those brought to him by tribal leaders. Witnesses described these "miracles" as similar to those attributed to Christ, including an instance where he apparently brought a native princess, presumed dead, back to life. Seeing his abilities caused a problem, because these men had survived the shipwreck and captivity and had known him on the ship for his position with the Crown. Obviously, they could also see that he had changed, and proof came when they witnessed his abilities. Word got out and started to spread. Rumors of his miracles, his abilities in sorcery, were spreading all the way back to Spain. These reports aroused considerable controversy, even though he attributed all of the miracles to "our Lord" working through him.

When a society learns of something they do not understand, particularly of things related to foundational biblical stories and beliefs, they react, and the reaction can be tumultuous even devastating. The Spanish inquisition still controlled the populace through fear and persecution, yet in my ancestor's fortunate case the reaction was less harsh than what it may have been in different times or under different circumstances. I have little doubt that the society of the time treated him preferentially, as he did not go around egotistically claiming to have powers even though his countrymen witnessed him performing miracles. It probably also helped his situation that he was of noble blood and a treasurer for the king.

For a time, though, they placed him under house arrest. The arrest seemed to be both for his abilities and for his active (but very politically incorrect) attempts to defend the natives from the plundering conquistadors.

Society will either fear or venerate individuals with abilities to heal or raise the dead (meaning the presumed dead). The normal question for religious faith-based societies: Is the ability from heaven or from hell? In any case, there was at least justification for anticipating severe reactions in the "Christian" society of that time (he called it the "Christian land of Spain").

Assembling these reports that shamans (*sorcerers*) were involved in refining Cabeza de Vaca's abilities probably explains at least some of my mother's apprehension about our lineage and our own abilities. Sorcerers were often said to have gained their power from "the devil." Any hint that *the devil* was involved in my visions or premonitions would have provoked great fear within my mother, and probably concerns about her own abilities.

I feel that Mother really needed the consolation through confirmation that evil spirits did not possess her son, and the exorcist had provided that comfort for her. If intense cognitive premonitions – not understood or embraced by society *even today* – were common for her, I can only guess what challenges she might have faced in her life from the time of her birth in 1904.

Mother and I had a long history of talking about *our musical abilities that God had given us*. Those abilities, passed down from mother to son, focused in our musical expression at the piano. With that background, the idea of a *blood inheritance of abilities* was normal in our discussions. This helped me to the extent that I had some understanding of inherited traits, even at that age. She used to say with a smile, *"Like mother, like son."* Whatever it was that had passed down to me, I inherited, and I could really do nothing about it because it was *God's will*.

That evening, my father wanted to know what had happened during our visit to the Archbishop's mansion. Though I was trying not to be obvious, I listened with a feeling of high anticipation as Mother told him.

How she related the events of that day grabbed my attention because of its understatement, which made it easy for my father to accept. She reported that she had taken me to meet a special priest who knew about people like me, like us. She said that the priest also knew about our family. That made some sense to me, since the priest was originally from Spain. The priest had assured her that I was normal, *not possessed*, and that everything was fine.

My father of Scottish descent was born and raised in rural East Texas. A graduate of the Naval Academy at Annapolis and retired officer of the Marine Corps, I first met him after the close of the war in the Pacific. He had spent the first four or five years of my life at war, not ever seeing his son. Because of the way that war had separated us, we tended to be generally aloof with each other. He was a kind and supportive man, when he could decipher how to be supportive.

He was skilled enough in dealing with both my mother and myself to know when a conversation would go nowhere beyond a certain point. My father did not possess the strong religious convictions of my mother, although he would regularly attend Sunday Mass with us. With mother's added comment that the priest had given me *God's special blessing*, their conversation turned to another subject, something mundane. This was a typical reaction from my father when things he did not understand, would occur between my mother and me.

Later in life, when my father would mention something about my mother to me, and sometimes about me, he would say something vague about our shared abilities or talents. He implied that he knew we were somehow different or unique, sometimes using that undefined and nebulous word, *special*. In his musings, he would tend to comment on mother's I.Q., somewhere over 200. He would also proclaim that mother should "write her book," which in the context of our family discussions usually meant a book on philosophy, our ancestry, and perceptional abilities. With emotion, I can say to you that in many ways this is also *her book,* the book she could not bring herself to write.

My father would occasionally mutter with uncertainty that per-haps our link together was through our musical ability. We were both "obviously" adept at piano, particularly in expression and composition. He thought, "That must be it," in one of his tenta-tive and abstract conclusions.

We both, mother and myself, downplayed it all. My own solu-tion to the turmoil that these events had caused was quite sim-ple: *I professed to have no abilities, whatever, at anything.*

I even allowed my school grades to drop to *prove my point!* I tenaciously held on to that posture for a very, very long time. Why was this attitude so compelling to me?

Abilities at anything seemed to cause a fuss, and from all that I could discern, the fuss often tended to point at me.

As the surge and resonances of these events with the exorcist began to settle within me, a conflict arose that, in retrospect, contributed to my decision to hide my abilities. I realized that the admonition that I had easily accepted on the implied authority of the exorcist-priest was actually quite confusing for me to cope with: that I should embrace and accept my abilities as coming from God, *while concealing those very parts of myself* from others in society.

The conflict implied by that puzzle would have to wait for a very long time to be resolved. In the meantime, my reaction was to obey the admonition to hide myself from others, unless, of course, something came along that compelled me to move myself out of this safe hiding place to *follow the will of God.* Eventually, I translated this to mean *God wants me to hide and si-lently carry this cross*, to deny myself entirely by withdrawing and internalizing my true nature.

Retrospectively, I accept that exorcist-priest turned out to be a highly perceptive empath. He had simply found safety and sanctuary within the cloisters of the church. By giving tribute to God for providing these gifts to us, including my mother, he was doing his best to help me.

Observation

In the early development of each person, there are abilities and attributes that may be evident or hidden. These are often embedded within the inherited legacy from our bloodline that we now call "DNA." Musical ability, graphical abilities for architecture (to see perspectives in three dimensions), and either inductive or analytical reasoning skills are understood (according to the research data base developed by the Johnson O'Connor Research Foundation over more than 60 years) to be a few examples of "intrinsic aptitudes."

The characteristics of each person can be significantly influenced by "learned factors" that, as adults, tend to automatically influence the way people think and feel about many things. If a religious teaching that "music is forbidden" is embedded into a person with natural musical aptitudes, a conflict will be set up against the true nature of that person. The individual will be compelled to try to adapt his or her emotions about music in order to comply with the dictums of their environment.

In effect, humans will develop a defense mechanism, to the extent of even hiding or denying their nature, limiting them to only hear, feel, and observe what is comfortable for them. When something comes along that conflicts with the "rules" of their belief system, they will do their best to modify what they hear, feel, and observe in order to fit the dictum that they have been taught to "believe" as their reality – even it the result is unnatural to themselves as individuals.

Much courage is often required to probe into one's belief system to find the true foundation of self and bring it into reality.

I've found it valuable to use introspection and ask why something is believed and how the concept was incorporated into memory and life. Learn whether a belief is "efficient" as a use of your energy or not efficient when it produces conflict, emotional pain, or turmoil.

Every person has natural attributes, aptitudes.

Have you probed yourself to learn what your attributes may be?

If you have, have you learned how to develop your attributes?

CHAPTER FIVE

THE FORCES OF DEFIANCE

As a stream of reflections from my past resurfaced, here on the Defiance Plateau, perceptions again confronted and challenged me more than five decades after the profound events that I had experienced with the exorcist. Now here in Arizona I started to return to my authentic self! Once again, as early in my youth, I gave myself permission to be *wide open* to perception!

I find it magnificent that this happened through my interaction with nature: standing against the forces of the hot and powerful wind on the edge of a rift precipice in the Defiance Plateau. Somehow, I realized that I could no longer hold back what I had been suppressing, even though I had to *compel myself* to be vulnerable to my feelings. Standing on the rift precipice, I barely attempted to defiantly suppress my clairvoyance as the name of the plateau might suggest, but my attempt was blown away. The wind-force of change was now flowing through my being, and I could no longer be defiant. I had to invoke a process of self-renewal to embrace, regain, and to re-attain my natural state of being.

Now, on this plateau, reinforced with a commitment to self-enhancement, with a more open mind and confidence in self, I was once again willing to explore. What had previously seemed so threatening to my social order that I had to conceal it now had started to open. Once again I was allowing myself simply *"to be."* *I was empowered again!* I *could prevail* with these incredibly overwhelming precognitions! Marvelously, wondrously, I started to accept that my ability no longer seemed like *a cross for me to bear.*

Little did I realize at this moment, that I would receive wondrous rewards for my efforts to renew my being that I had worked so very hard to re-attain. Those rewards would become incredibly powerful, and magnificent, experiences.

My perceptions *surged* as I was balancing myself in a mutual contract with nature. I captured my balance between the compelling pull of forces from the canyon, and the contrivance of the wind. I successfully resisted the beckoned call of the canyon: it seemed to be cajoling me to let go of the guardrail and to enter in flight from above. The energy, the warm bright day and the sound of painfully suppressed pliant moan from the canyon, had triggered once again the memories of those perceptions from so many years ago.

Once again, a saturating and overwhelming feeling of power immersed me. My familiarity with the power of these empathic events demanded prudence in my actions, combined with a feeling of humility. This would not be an exception to my prudence, because it would have been folly *not to respect the forces* playing with me.

Very, very, cautiously, we were picking our footfalls slowly. We were guiding ourselves by gripping the handrail provided by the Park Service, defying the forces of the defiant wind. In sidestepping movements, we approached a plaque that was mounted on the railing. That plaque displayed information about the occurrences at this overlook into the Canyon Muerto. Immediately I saw a flash from history. I felt the muzzle blasts of heat and death that were *not* the impulsion of the wind.

We were standing on the spot where the conquistadors of 1805 had mercilessly fired their weapons into the tribe of Navajo who made their home in the canyon. In a classic act of disassociation and deception, they justified their tyranny by saying that they were just *teaching the natives* a lesson.

The natives, trapped in a cave and the canyon, had no other place to hide. At least 115 Navajo, including many women and children, perished in a needless slaughter. The Navajos say that these areas, the Canyons, are sacred. The powerful experience of my clairvoyant immersion is evidence: their statement is true.

Now, with the information provided by a simple plaque, I understood the formation and cause of what I was experiencing. My perceptions had openly exposed me to the feeling, the dreaded emotion, and the vengeful power of turmoil. I felt the hate and violence that had brought so many to their deaths. I experienced their tumultuous terror, followed by the quietude of death. The upwelling of my emotion was overwhelming as though I was experiencing the slaughter as it all was happening again. Yielding to trembles that shuttered through my body, my tears flowed.

For me, in vast understatement, it was a powerful experience. Again, I re-experienced being shaken as I had been so many decades ago. Paradoxically, the attributes that I had tried so fervently in youth to submerge, were now *raging* to the surface! They were coming with a vengeance and power that I could no longer deny, nor constrain.

Though I had not yet discovered the potential significance of these feelings, as they would be relevant to my future, I knew that attempting to even try to submerge them again would be untenable. Internalizing these intensities could even be potentially damaging for me as the unnatural state that submergence always has been.

Given my feelings and the exhaustion of my body from struggling with the forces within me and from nature, we returned to our Suburban. Rosy took over the driving responsibilities as we departed the area. Yet, my perceptions did not diminish as we distanced ourselves from the area of the massacre. While we were discussing my experiences at the rim, my awareness of my surroundings shifted, and I fell silent. Something was happening, and slowly I saw that something developing around me. It had an appearance like an approaching dark and charcoal - gray fog.

Then, in a natural flow of gentle movement, my consciousness shifted. I was moving into an alternate reality to occupy a sort of duality: with myself in the vehicle and *"somewhere else"* that was undefined. The force of the perception that I had been experiencing, that started on the rim, seemed to push me into this alternate reality. The *"somewhere else"* of my reality appeared to be a region. The region saturated me within the dark and charcoal gray fog, felt warm, even familiar. I was in the equivalent of a peaceful trance. I could both see and perceive through the mists of the gray fog, faint and shadowy silhouettes that seemed to be observing, studying me.

There was no obvious communication exchange during this sojourn, except for one lingering impressed thought: this is for a purpose; this is to prepare you for something. Whatever this was, it was so vague I simply could not bring it to the surface.

Suddenly, my reality shifted and I was back in the vehicle. I looked over to see Rosy dutifully driving. It surprised me that I was actually in our vehicle. Experiencing some level of confusion as I asked Rosy: "Whoa. That was overwhelming. Where did I go?" She responded to me by saying, *"What do you mean? Trust me. You never left the Suburban!"*

I was not so certain.

There was a residual feeling that continued with me during the days that followed. Something was going to happen. I could feel it. It was coming. I could only accept it, as I had found in so many other empathic impressions I'd encountered throughout my life.

Importantly, I was wholly opening myself, once again, to a state of full awareness – the cognizance in my natural and unfettered being, to simply "be."

Thus, following the implications of these experiences I worked to accept and compel myself to drop the pretenses, to drop the guises of protections and *allow myself to feel.* Whatever was happening had a renewed strength. My sense of purpose required monitoring, in vigilance to be myself, to regain those parts of myself that I had hidden and suppressed for decades.

I began to feel free, fully aware that with those feelings, there would be more experiences, more perception, and more responsibilities. I have found that responsibilities always attend abilities. I wondered if I could meet this regained state of being with alacrity, lose fear, and not revert to the familiar state of denying myself.

Observation

It is not necessary to be "empathic" per se, in order to explore. Every person carries the potential to use the tools of observation, perception, intuition and feeling in the broadest sense to inspect and explore anything and everything, including oneself.

To explore and learn through the freedom of an open mind, one must have objectivity and that comes first by letting go of psychological barriers that hold you back. When barriers are recognized, then accepted and dealt with, the next step is opening up your mind, giving yourself the permission to be free and explore.

CHAPTER SIX

PRIMED

Despite the intensity of my experience on the Defiance Plateau, Rosy's curiosity gene activated again and she urged that we continue onward with our trek. We were pushing ourselves to eventually get to Monument Valley of the Navajos. That had been our original destination before we diverted to the Canyon Chelly National Monument! She suggested a short cut to save time. We wended our way onto the back-roads of the Navajo Reservation. Essentially lost and wandering, we rambled into remote regions of unmarked "roads."

It takes a leap of vocabulary to call these paths *"roads."* They were little more than clay-mud paths, cleared through dense forests of northern Arizona near the Utah border. As our truck listed over gently, sliding sideways into a deep clay rut, the left front wheel buried itself in the red sticky clay. We got out of our listing vehicle to assess the situation. Immediately on opening the doors, we sensed the remoteness of our location. The musty scents of the earthy wet clay intermingled with the wafting methane-borne odors from the darkening forest. It was becoming late afternoon, quiet, without a single sound of mechanical civilization noticeable. Our setting struck me like a scene from the old television series, *Twilight Zone*, where a city couple became lost in unknown lands with unexpected consequences.

Rosy engaged the 4-wheel drive transfer case with the traditional "ka-thunk." Happily, the construction of our vehicle made it easy to deal with our quandary. Its drive, traction and power easily surmounted our predicament and we continued forward. Our truck gently slid gracefully, heeling over to one side and then the other scraping the frame along the clay, as we plied our way through the forest.

We struggled to navigate over bridges that were only marginally supportive of our large, and heavy, vehicle. I use the term *"marginally"* here with quite a bit of generosity. *"Begrudgingly"* might be a better term. Rosy navigated the large vehicle onto the apron of what seemed to be a particularly frail and narrow bridge. As we were *far away* from any known assistance, I had images of plunging into the ravine below. Groaning in strains under the weight of our vehicle, the complaints from the bridge seemed to underscore my feeling! (Undeterred, Rosy just smiled as she pressed on!)

We arrived in Monument Valley in the late afternoon, and studied the routes in the area. Our exploration there took us into the evening, and the landscape became beautiful with the change of light. We knew that in the evening and morning periods of the "golden light," as photographers like to say, optical magic happens! The sun angle and hues of light play spectacularly into the depths and shadows of the *"monuments,"* which are backdropped by the red soil. The wind dances in orchestrations with dust motions flowing in the swirls, and toys with the shadows in nature's choreographed beauty.

Monument Valley, which had been the backdrop for many Western movies during the reign of the actor John Wayne, is magnificent, particularly in the golden light. I found only peace in the beauty of this region of the Navajo. *"The feeling"* that enveloped me at Canyon Muerto was continuing to travel with me. I imagined the feeling as an unseen cocoon of energy immersing me, an oxymoron connecting to simultaneous power and peace.

I had learned through the trials of my life that it is useless to have anxiety, or to agonize, about what might happen in the future. My life was becoming less stressful by applying a philosophy that we really exist only in the current moment that I call *"the now."*

I could only be patient while waiting to learn what the next moment of *"the now"* would bring to me.

Monument Valley was a delightful experience! The vistas are vast, and we enjoyed composing many spectacular photographs to add to our collection. Our trek continued as we exited Monument Valley through Arizona towards our next destinations: the national parks of Zion; then onward to Bryce Canyon, Utah. Our plan was to wend our way through Utah and into Wyoming to visit Yellowstone National Park. In between, we would have a stopover in Salt Lake City, Utah.

My sense of awareness had been pried open by the forces at the Defiance Plateau, and that openness was now continuous. I knew at some level that something was going wrong, but I was hesitant to probe deep down because I knew how overwhelming my premonitions could be.

Our tours of Zion and Bryce Canyons were marvelous experiences in the magnificent beauty of nature's vistas. In Zion, the sheer canyon walls pinch the river flowing along the canyon floor, bringing memories of Canyon Muerto immediately to the surface of my mind. We truly enjoyed the river's dancing-light reflections on the precipitous red rock cliffs. We were also fascinated with the processes of geology we learned that formed both of the canyons.

Zion provided a multitude of hiking trails to enjoy and explore the grandeur of the canyon. The river, forced through tight bottlenecks between the cliffs, set up potentially dangerous surges in the river's height. There were warnings posted: severe flash floods could happen at any moment, threatening people in or near the bottlenecks.

Truth be told, when it comes to hiking, horses, or mule riding, Rosy is far more adventurous than I am! After all, she has competed in equestrian events at the expert level for many years! (To be fair, though, we have both driven "formula" open-wheel cars around major race tracks "at speed.")

At one point, while struggling along a steep trail in Zion, I found myself muttering about the physical effort required. Facetiously, I voiced my suspicion that Rosy had probably increased my life insurance policy for her benefit, given the conditions of the hike! I complained louder as I lost my footing and grabbed a shrub to halt my slide down a steep incline!

For a moment I imagined myself hanging off a cliff, desperately clinging to the branch of a shrub surrendering its grip in the earth; torturously slipping as I became panicky – just like in the drama of the movies! I wondered if that was what my premonitions were signaling, but no, I found my footing and our hike continued!

In Bryce, Rosy wanted to tour the canyon by mule train. Grudgingly, not being a fan of mules I relented and accepted my fate: the challenges of mules! Actually, the mules didn't foist up my fears: the sheer drop-offs of the trails frightened me! Those mules tended to test my mild acrophobia by placing their hooves exactly upon the outer edges of the trail precipices. The view when looking down the side of the animal revealed only freefall – it seemed like hundreds of feet below to the canyon floor. I found it unnerving to be at the mercy of the mules' judgment, *assuming that mules actually have any judgment.* I could only hope that "suicide by cliff" was not in the mules' normal mindset!

Come to think about it, "suicide by cliff" was less probable than the mules' instinct to play the game of *"dump the tourist into the precipice!"* I've wondered as we clopped along if mules could be that conniving, or if they'd just "dump" the passenger to work less. It was easy to understand why the cowboys that were guiding our mule train were riding horses, *not mules!*

Despite the anxiety, thrust out from the recesses of my fear the mule ride, while challenging, was actually quite uneventful. I must admit, though, that I spent a terrific amount of effort trying to induce my tyrannical mule to clop along against the canyon wall, and not along the cliff's edge. It was a futile effort that only tired my body! Maybe mules are not the tyrants of the canyons after all! Perhaps the tyrant that exhausted me was only *my own fear* that combined with my inability to "trust" mules with my life!

To this point in our travel, I had survived the tribulations of the hike up the cliffs at Zion and the formidable Bryce mule ride (though my confidence had surely been tested). Bolstered and relieved, I was grateful that the "tours" of these two canyons were over. Actually as a city slicker, I rejoiced triumphantly in my accomplishments – my "survival" skills – and comforted by our next stop: the civilization of Salt Lake City!

I thought my feeling of dread would now be at a lower level of intensity, but I confess that the intensity stayed the same. I simply did not want to admit the magnitude of feeling and the anticipation that something profoundly ominous was going to occur. It was an unrelenting feeling that pulled up memories of similar premonitions from my past – premonitions of dread!

In the midst of this, there was a new feeling that felt increasingly physiological, even visceral. This new sensation was that of an insignificant or low-grade fever, and it was permeating my body. Although I was having some discomfort from this mild fever, it didn't seem to significantly impede my physical activity. Rosy and I both rejected it as a factor of any real concern. We thought that maybe I might be just fighting off the start of a common cold or maybe a mild intestinal "bug."

We nonchalantly toured the Great Salt Lake, visited islands that were accessible across causeways, heard the remarkable acoustics in the Tabernacle, and meandered about Temple Square. During this time, my intuitions tended to intensify in varying degrees – as if there were waves surging in ebb and flow upon me, compounded by the sweltering dank heat around the lake, or the chill of air conditioning in the tour van.

My immersions involved two sensations: the feeling of dread and the physiological feelings that were permeating my body. In effect, the superimposition of the two feelings seemed to merge, as if they were one. The combined result was an ominous involvement of my sense about my future that, even as profound at that might sound, I accepted as being inevitable.

One captivating experience happened in the city, indelibly etched itself in my memory. We were touring next to a large medical facility, located not too far from the Temple Square. On the roof of the medical facility was poised a helicopter-ambulance.

My focus became drawn and actually fixated, to the helicopter.

As I gazed at the machine, looking upward at the rotors, there was an instantaneous surge of intensity - like an amplification of what happened near Canyon Muerto. Without any emotion, with only a simple acceptance, I thought to myself: "The helicopter. Something about the helicopter connects to this puzzle of my premonitions. Would I tour in a helicopter? Would there be a report of a helicopter crashing in one of the canyons? Would a helicopter transport me in a medical emergency? Would this helicopter crash?" These thoughts hung suspended in amazement as I continued to stare up at the helicopter. "Is there a connection between the helicopter and the hospital that would involve me?"

My curiosity continued to explore the possible scenarios with increased intrigue. I had no doubt at all: something of powerful significance would occur – and soon.

Feelings and premonitions were now merging into the new reality of a physical event, perhaps based on my low-grade fever that seemed to carry no other symptoms. My feelings that connected *helicopter* and *medical* seemed to build up as a surge in my anticipations.

I wondered how the events and feelings of the past days would move forward in combination. In "the place" of the dark gray fog that I experienced after leaving Canyon Muerto, I now recalled some instilled reverberation that I heard as a whispered echo: *"Ready?"*

Now, tentatively I questioned: *"Ready?"*

If so, *"For what?"*

Even in asking those questions, the echo within my premonitions tended to confirm, *"Yes, this is preparation."* Given the dramatic nature of my past precognitive experiences, I suspected that I would recognize immediately the answer to the question, *"For what?"* as it started to occur, precisely *when* it started to occur.

After completing our tours of Salt Lake City, we continued our trip by driving into the Wasatch Mountain Range across Utah. As we drove along, I started to feel queasy with digestive upset. The upset manifested as spasms of my intestinal tract. We tentatively attributed the upset to (possibly) "something" in the meal the night before (pasta & scallops). Sometimes scallops, we thought, might cause a reaction. The intestinal upset did not seem threatening, just an inconvenience at worst.

There was now a combination of feelings: highly daunting premonition, low-grade fever, and intestinal upset. Added to those feelings, there was the premonition about the *helicopter* on the roof of the medical center. The layers of possibilities seemed to be building up. Prudent and cautious people might have found signs, even omens, in this combination! Nope! Not true in my case! To be fair, nothing really seemed uniquely threatening to me. We threw prudence to the wind as we continued our adventure, departing Utah for Wyoming.

We entered Wyoming at the southwest corner. The high country of Wyoming is open range territory. Cattle are generally free to roam: even across highways! The landscape and topologies of the high country are vast, green, and seemingly endless. About mid-way between our state line entry point into Wyoming and Jackson Hole on the rural highway, we noticed a moving and huge dark mass ahead of us. The massive shape was in motion, approaching our vehicle! "What…in…the…" was my exclamation, answered just a moment later.

An entire herd of cattle was charging down the highway, head-on to our position, without even a single cowhand in sight! We abruptly stopped in amazement! Thankfully, the herd navigated around us and obligingly did not challenge (or collide with) our bright red Suburban. Large vehicles are indeed useful! We often complain about "traffic congestion" in the cities, but the open range country offers its own traffic surprises!

Our drive brought us through Jackson, Wyoming, and into the Grand Teton National Park. Although we hadn't scheduled this park on our drive, the Teton Mountains are an amazing and inviting site! Some of the mountainous ridgelines jut out of the Earth at ruggedly sharp angles. These angles are visually descriptive representations of the violent seismic forces that thrust them out of the Earth's mantle so many millennia ago. They appeared to us as a massive series of jagged peaks, stacked like vertical shark's teeth side-to-side, purple-blue in the background and capped with small snow bonnets!

The visitor's center of the park headquarters included an active seismometer, recording the continuum of small movements in the geology. We learned that the areas in and around these mountains are seismically active with a history of significant earthquakes. That information matched the image implied by the extreme and violent energy required for the upward thrust displayed by the angles and formations of the peaks.

Parking our vehicle, we photographed the vistas at Jenny Lake. The view was lovely, with the lake in the foreground and the Tetons providing the backdrop. There was a beautiful contrast between the purple blue majesty of the ragged peaks and the white highlights of their snowcaps. The lake's smooth surface, punctuated by reflected images on the water of puffy clouds lolling in the sky, was serene.

Suddenly, while enjoying the panorama, I suffered intensely sharp intestinal cramps! I nearly doubled over with the stabbing pain! Clearly, the condition that had been only annoying to that point had suddenly become more severe. To the extent that I was able, I quickly parked the Suburban without much respect for the marked parking spaces. Suspecting that diarrhea was occurring, we found the support facilities in the lodge at Jenny Lake.

By the time I entered the lodge to hurriedly find the rest rooms, my hands compressing my abdominal area, I felt panicked to get to the toilet "in time." There are moments in everyone's life that embed indelible memories, and for me this was one of them. The problem was not diarrhea at all. What filled the toilet bowl was blood: A torrent of blood gushed out!

I decided in the flash of a moment to exhibit an incredible self-deception – to be in denial of what was happening to my body. My tendency to hide, as commanded by the exorcist, often meant hiding from myself, no matter how intense my premonitions. I fell into my own trap – self-deception. I reflexively tried to convince myself the blood loss had to be minor. Thus, I was invoking my reflex to downplay all events, even those that could be highly significant. Besides, I did not want to worry Rosy.

The rapid blood loss seemed to reduce my pain, which played nicely into my downplaying reality. Relieved by the (temporary) reduction of spasms and sharp cramps, I returned to Rosy, who was patiently awaiting my return to our vehicle. I calmly reported to her:

"I don't want to worry you, but I think I have a small problem. I have had some significant bleeding internally. It might be only a hemorrhoid, though it came out in a torrent, like diarrhea. I'm probably fine because I feel better now. We have a wonderful opportunity to capture some great photographs, and I want to continue our sightseeing around the lake."

Rosy replied with serious concern, evidenced by the tone of her voice: "Michael, this might be a serious problem!" She wisely continued, "We should abort sightseeing Grand Teton Park and *quickly* press on to Yellowstone." She said *"quickly"* with a very sharp emphasis!

By then, it was about 2pm.

When one, who is ensconced in self-deceit, also makes a reflex decision to be in self-imposed denial, what would be the logical course of action to take in such a condition? I assured Rosy that I was okay to continue, and I decided to drive our vehicle to Yellowstone National Park, of course!

After all, we had never been to that park, *and we had reservations at a hotel* in Grant's Village within the park! Those reservations were difficult to arrange at this peak time of the visitor's season! I only had one point of focus: *Protect the hotel reservations! Continue our trip!* What other *orders of action* would you expect such a mind locked in self-deceit to request of his wife and partner – given the situation? After all, the impact of the experience at the Jenny Lake Lodge was (pardon the pun) stamina "draining!" Would you expect *protect the hotel reservations* to be the driving force of concern at that moment?

Increasing fatigue set in as I drove the short distance onto the highway. Finally, I subtly (very sheepishly) said to Rosy, in my first tentative signal of acknowledging reality: "I think you are right. We should make no further stops for any sightseeing." I paused, and then continued… "Let's just get to our hotel, so that I can lie down and rest and let this problem pass."

Rather than allowing the path of reason to prevail, I fell back into my own pattern of only believing what I wished to believe. Somewhere, someone must have written that self-deception can become so powerful that it circulates around in a self-imposed loop! In that loop, it rapidly becomes absurd stupidity - accepted as rational thought. If no one previously wrote that, I offer it to you now.

While I was still in the driver's seat, Rosy quietly, *very-surreptitiously*, studied a map. She had not argued with me when I insisted on driving. Actually, she didn't say a word.

Apart from the mechanical rumbles of our truck, all was silent. Rosy eventually said, "There is a hospital in Grant's Village. The hospital is actually quite near the hotel!"

"Great!" - I replied. I continued to feel compelled to get to the hotel in time so we would not lose those reservations! We could confirm our reservations by checking into the hotel, and then proceed to the hospital for what I tried to convince her was convinced was a needless checkup! What a relief!

Rosy said that she could get to the hotel and maintain our room reservation even in the unlikely event I needed some type of treatment. "We could then continue our trip touring Yellowstone," she explained, without interruption. "*Wonderful!*" - I thought. It is fascinating how something as simple as that could set my mind at ease!

As I continued driving, spiking, surging, spasms and cramps returned with much greater ferocity. A reality check began to set in! My distress compelled me to reevaluate my priorities! My body was in trouble: serious trouble. Suddenly, I felt threatened!

After half an hour of driving, I became progressively weaker to the point of feeling very shaky, even faint. I recognized that my physical stability wasn't sufficient to continue to drive, let alone sightsee. I pulled our Suburban over to the shoulder of the road, and softly asked Rosy to drive. I gripped the door as tightly as I could, to avoid falling off the running board as I exited the truck. I had to steady myself against the hood as I walked around the front of the vehicle. As I stepped up to the right-side running board to become the passenger, my pain surged. I was then writhing in pain, which made it impossible to avoid deceiving Rosy about my situation.

Rosy started driving, now *on a mission*. The internal stabbing sensation was becoming excruciating. I gripped my abdomen and doubled over, suppressing my tendency to be vocal about the feelings. Rosy had decided that we were going directly to the hospital, and she was now in the pilot's seat! Rosy in normal circumstances is often a "quick" driver. When "on a mission," as I have found her to be when she is jumping her horses, she becomes intensely focused. Now, acknowledging her responsibility to get me to the hospital *she was intensely focused,* and inclined to drive quickly.

Within the park, though, the roadways are narrow, bracketed by trees, and slowed by sightseers stopping on the shoulders as they watched for wildlife. The impediments to speed, even at the 45 MPH limit, must have been emotionally frustrating to my loving Rosy. Our hotel, and the hospital, was 50 miles into the interior of the park, and these became long, even torturous, miles. We probably averaged only 25 to 35 MPH, inhibited by slow vans pulling trailers, and other slow downs as tourists stopped to view wildlife. I imagined how emotional this experience would be for me, had the circumstances been reversed, where Rosy had become physically stricken and threatened, and I was driving.

During the drive to Grant's Village, I distracted myself by looking up to see the plumes of steam from the superheated subterranean water as it escaped from the surrendering snow that was struggling in vain to survive the summer. I could detect whiffs of the odiferous sulfur escaping from the steaming geysers and the pools boiling on the surface. It looked like a scene from a "sci-fi" alien planet movie, or of the primordial Earth, seething with steamy, sulfur-laden pools mingling with both the steam and the snow. Unlike our visits to the other parks, it was much colder here in this more northern latitude. The scenic distractions soon gave way to a new sensation. I was becoming cold: very cold.

The drive to the hospital required about two hours from the incident at Jenny Lake. Time seemed to stand still for me, warped by my sense of urgency and pain.

By then, it was 4pm.

Rosy easily found the hospital and drove into the parking lot of the small facility. The stabbing pain had not subsided. I had become very weak, and needed her help even to get out of the Suburban and gain my stability. Even so, I slipped off the running board and stumbled to the ground below. Rosy gently guided me as I wobbled up the walkway and through the doors of the hospital. I noted that the reception desk was, thankfully, very close to the door.

With Rosy's support, I approached the counter. A responsive female receptionist immediately approached me. I clearly remember saying to her: *"I'm bleeding and I think,"* at that point, my legs turned to rubber and I started to collapse. I fell across the counter, and instinctively grabbed it for support. I did not know exactly why, but the receptionist suddenly turned away from me and shouted something urgent to people behind her. Though I was beginning to lose consciousness, I sensed that almost immediately a wheelchair and staff appeared. Although I was semi-conscious at that moment, I still held my grip of the receptionist's counter. Rosy had to bring me to awareness by commanding: *"Let go – Michael!"* as she pried my hands from the counter.

They guided me, placed me, into the wheelchair. In my state of semi-consciousness, I hazily remember someone pushing me in the chair at jogging speed and rapidly turning a hallway corner into the Emergency Room. Approaching an examination table, I heard a voice ask, "Can you stand up?" I actually did not know.

I vaguely remember the touch of hands embracing or guiding me as I attempted to stand up at the side of the table. As I partially arose from the wheelchair in a dubious position somewhere between sitting and standing, I remember saying in a low tone of voice to no one in particular, *"I've lost... I'm going to..."*

Before I could utter the hushed word *"die"*, I was gone.

I passed out into unconsciousness, flooded in a pool of my own blood. Then, with the peace and gentility that acceptance provides and with no anxiety or fear despite the firm knowledge that my body that I myself, was dying: All faded to black.

Then, everything involving all of my being, my entire environment, all of my heightened perception started to alter, and alter profoundly. After what I can only assume must have been a short period of transition in the non-being empty state of blackness, everything of my consciousness, "my being," became again energized as if I had no medical issue whatsoever!

My cognitive awareness was intensely re-activated. A sequence of events started to unfold, as experiences...all of my consciousness spontaneously illuminated, fully initiated again.

I was in a heightened state of awareness: curious, intrigued, and willing to engage in the inevitable.

My life, all of my sense of being, was about to change: forever.

Observation

People are incredibly capable of using self-deceit to twist things around. They impulsively distort events into what they want to believe. I've found that much of all deceitfulness may start with various levels of self-deceit.

People can believe in their deceit to the point where they disassociate themselves from reality. When this happens, deceit itself becomes a personal belief "reference" and hence disassociation. The broader the scope that disassociation might embrace, the more difficult the task of regaining the tools of objectivity will be.

In the example described in this chapter, I simply did not want to accept my situation even though I had a huge stockpile of perception and information available to me. Self-deceit became an unspoken mantra, a way of life, and a truculent block to the use of reason. You might find it valuable to ask yourself: Are your realities veiled in self-deceit, masking your authentic nature?

CHAPTER SEVEN

THE EMERGENCE OF INDIVIDUALITY

I t has been said that for any given day, "Today is the first day of the rest of your life." That statement is true, but with one important exception: the day you die.

What would that statement become if, as soon as someone said it, you actually died? Alternatively, it could be, "Today, you will be changed forever!" The next question is strikingly obvious: Changed to what?

To an atheist, the change might be *the end of your consciousness*: the termination of your being. To a person deeply involved in religion, the change might be: *to be an angel with God in heaven.*

At the close of the previous chapter, I was entering the ultimate threshold of transition: my body was dying. Certainly, my impending death would qualify as powerful verification of my premonitions that seemed to start on the Defiance Plateau at Canyon Muerto. When I look back into my history, I realize that the premonitions I experienced over the years were mosaic pieces that, when assembled, always formed a pattern. The pattern seemed to be series of stepping-stones, one for each new experience, leading up to this moment of profound significance.

The result was that I was in full acceptance of my condition, and during this eventual failure of my physical being, I experienced no fear of my death. I was ready to die, even though I didn't truly know what that meant.

Somehow, I felt that it was okay because at some deep level, I knew I had been prepared. I had surmised that the series of preparations would have been pointless, wasted efforts – if my death was going to mean "complete termination" - the end of my being.

In my life before this time, I had struggled with much emotional turmoil and conflict. Conflict trapped me between the prohibitions of a very strict religious dogma about how to live and act, versus my feelings and perceptions about how life really worked. Religion seemed to permeate every aspect of my life. Church teachings and demands touched and infiltrated every dimension of living, from home life to education. I felt suffocated by seemingly endless, and unnatural, rules about how to think, feel, and act. The range of influence seemed vast: demands about attending church; being compelled to take sacraments to be in God's grace; the need to seek forgiveness for simple transgressions such as eating meat on Friday; to the more profound and unnatural such as the prohibitions about just having sexual feelings and thoughts, let alone acts. I had believed that my failure to please God was ubiquitous, that I had failed.

All combined, these seemed like dictums that flailed against my understanding of nature – at least my own nature if not all of nature itself.

Even the admonition of the exorcist played an increasing role in my turmoil as time moved on. My feeling was that if ability came to a person as a *gift from God,* then surely God must have *intended the gift* to be developed, not hidden, not smothered. The God I had come to know through the ubiquitous demands of the church was a flame-throwing punitive God, not a loving or nurturing God. God's weapon for control was a swift sword of guilt. My belief in His wrath, using that sword increasingly, vengefully, slashed away at my self-esteem.

I came to feel that I could never satisfy God's conditions to be in His grace. It seemed like an impossible dream. The risk of me driving myself into eternal damnation was frightening beyond description, and defiance of church dogma carried that risk. I had no alternative concept about how to think, feel, act, or for that matter, live.

Increasingly as I developed toward adulthood, I despaired. Fully controlled by guilt, I did my best to comply with the demands in every way I could. Yet, no matter how hard I tried to suppress my natural human tendencies, I began to experience sexual feelings. According to the teachings that I took literally, one had to extinguish sexual feelings to gain God's grace.

My continual attempts to banish these feelings only met in failure. I could not do it, no matter how hard I tried. I took my failure and internalized this with a simple conclusion: I, all of me in life, was not worthy - for anything. I was wholly inadequate: worthless.

Rather than defy the precepts of the church and risk the wrath of *eternal damnation* from God, I withdrew into depression, and that became a way of life. I had concluded that God must have intended this way of life for me as punishment for my continual failures.

Teenagers often view the world in an angry and depressed state, convinced that only they know how to cure all that ails this earth. My depression and confusion, however, seemed to surge deeper into my soul than just normal teenage rebellion. It consumed the joy of my existence. It was a horrible feeling to be carrying around at my age of 15 years.

I had thoughts that my multitudinous sins were so insurmountable that only an impending death with the sacrament of extreme unction, the last rites, would give me forgiveness and save me from eternal hell.

Before I lost the battle of despair, hope for me sprang forth from a dramatic series of events that challenged and inspired me to surmount these daunting challenges. Collectively, these events prepared me to be at peace as I now confronted my progression into the throes of death once again.

In 1957, at the age of 15 ½ years, I was driving the motorcycle that my parents had bought for me. I had originally wanted a Ford coupe, but the thrill of the motorcycle's acceleration had captured me. One morning while out riding, an automobile struck me broadside as I rode into a major intersection across a four-lane thoroughfare. I have no memory of the event itself because of brain trauma. I have no memories of anything leading up to the crash during the hours before.

You might be inclined to ask if, given my history of precognitive impressions, I had some premonition of this event. *Yes, I did,* a few days before the crash.

The perception was an extreme feeling of dread, of an intensity that seemed to engulf me like a fever. Yet, the premonition did not provide any detail of what, where, and how the events would unfold. I had withdrawn from discussing such warnings, even from my mother. Actually, the ominous feeling simply seem to meld into the depression I was experiencing at the time.

The impact of the automobile caused my head to snap to the side. The impact was sufficiently intense to cause the force of my head's whiplash to actually dent the hood.

At my request, my father drove me to see the automobile that stuck me, a 1949 Mercury, in a police impound yard. He pointed out the indentation in the hood - that matched the profile of my head. This incident occurred decades before any "helmet laws" existed, and I had not been wearing a helmet or any other protection. Reports by witnesses indicated that after the initial impact, my body was thrust airborne about 75 feet. When I landed, the reports continued, my body came to rest with another impact to the back of my skull: on the curbstone.

Imagine what it might be like for a teenager, already turbulent with the vortices of change in his body, stirring with passion, conflicts, and confusion, compelled to challenge the precepts and beliefs that had guided him. Then saturated in the backdrop of these forces, to awaken with no memory of what might have happened: To awaken in a hospital room surrounded by white-coated strangers, in wide-open wonder… and partially paralyzed.

Somehow, I had come to consciousness. My eyes were wide open, but I could not blink my eyelids. I could partially move my right arm, but something was not right. It felt very heavy. It took a while for me to realize that my right hand was in a plaster cast. My first sensation was confusion, not fear or pain.

The experience was something like a vivid nightmare: What was I doing here? Where am I? WHO am I? Why can't I move?

The sight of a blond woman, a nurse, gently talking to me, happily distracted me. She was approaching my face and saying that she was going to put eye drops in my eyes to clean them. Her hand reached out to touch my face. She said she needed to position me so the drops would flow into my eyes. I could see her hand come to my left cheek, and my faced turned toward her. Then it occurred to me: *I could not feel her hand on my skin.*

Panic set in! Panic turned to terror when I could not scream….

A gray-haired doctor, with a light strapped to his forehead, approached and peered into my eyes with a scope of some kind. He turned and muttered something to others standing along-side him. I lapsed into unconsciousness.

There were brief periods of consciousness, and periods of un-consciousness. I had no concept of time. During one brief flash, I thought: *Mom! Where is Mom?* Then I faded back to sleep.

During a brief interlude of consciousness, I saw my parents standing at the foot of my bed. I tried to talk to them. I could think my words, but my mouth didn't seem to produce any sound that I could hear. My mother seemed to be crying, and my father was expressionless. I do not recall having any emotions during these interludes of awareness. They seemed to be too brief for me to *feel anything.*

During my stay in the hospital ICU and for a period thereafter, I experienced oscillating waves of reality. These waves seemed to shift between what others would later report to be either delirium, then comatose states, and then temporary flashes of what seemed to them to be normal lucidity or awareness. While others were seeing my delirium or coma, as they later reported to me, I was privately experiencing an alternate and lucid reality.

At some point in the progression of events, probably immediately after the initial collision and during the airborne "flight" before I was halted by the impact against a curb, something thrilling happened: my consciousness projected into a huge region of white light.

As far as I can recall, the region or realm of light did not seem to have specific boundaries. Essentially, a vast field of whitish and translucent fog surrounded me in all directions. I had no idea what had really happened to me. I had no clue about what had occurred with or to my body, since I had wholly disconnected from my physical form in all ways that I could perceive.

As I tentatively explored the field of light that had enveloped me, I saw images of others inhabiting this light realm with me. The details of those images are no longer specific for me, though they seemed like silhouettes against the light.

In this alternate reality, I had continuing interactions with others who were sharing the realm of light with me. The undefined images were sentient, warm, embracing even though they did not assume human form. I felt peace and comfort in their presence: an embracing companionship enveloped me that felt nurturing. They would later give me support during the healing process of my body, and though I could sporadically feel intense physical anguish, I did not experience fear.

I do easily and firmly recall that I captured an implanted concept or idea within me while in this transitional state of existence. At this teenage point in my life, trained and wholly rooted in a focused religious upbringing, my development was not in any way sufficient for this experience in the realm of light and the subsequent changes. My understanding of religion, my religious training, could not, did not, provide explanation for my experience.

I would eventually come to understand the implanted idea as philosophical, as if a seed of inspiration had been set within me. The inspiration was simple: *I am an individual. I am able to control my destiny.* That simple message was emotionally stirring to me! It resonated as a beautiful melodic harmony that somehow felt as unfettered truth! Being able to control my own destiny implied a phenomenal sense of personal empowerment, even freedom, and that seeded both inspiration and motivation. Controlling my own destiny meant I would take full responsibility for myself, and the thought came to mind that personal abilities might be actualized by acceptance of responsibilities. Previously when I demonstrated abilities, I had accepted admonishments from outside forces to suppress myself. Suppression was the antithesis of my new inspiration. On a deep level, I felt that if I could overcome the embedded programming that was binding me, I gleaned a sense that I could thrive. I was motivated to try, and the open question was how to accomplish this goal to empower myself.

As time went by, the interludes of normal reality gradually became longer. My neurology seemed to be improving, and with that came flashes of conversation, and intense, increasing pain. During one period of lucidity, a doctor was explaining to my parents that there was no damage to my spinal cord. He continued by saying that blunt force compression to my basal skull area during the impact against the curbstone probably caused my paralysis. My mother leaned over to me and spoke softly through her tears. She was trying to assure me that God would heal me and my paralysis would not be permanent.

Eventually I learned that I had received what I had earlier wished for: the Sacrament of Extreme Unction. For a time I was pleased because I believed what the church said: the sacrament cleansed my soul of sin.

During the interludes of what seemed to be normal awareness, lucidity, I learned that a paralyzed body is a very small prison for an active mind, particularly a teenage mind. It was terrifying for me to be that confined! Sometimes, I would feel anger simultaneously with the terror, yet my body did not respond.

Occasionally as my paralysis lessened over time, there were flashes of excruciating pain from my pelvis. It became natural for me to shift my awareness into the white fog of embrace and nurture, where I found peace and comfort.

My structural injuries from this impact included multiple skull fractures, temporary coma (from the perspective of an observer outside of myself), paralysis, broken bones in one hand, and a broken pelvis. During my paralysis, physical therapists would apply electro-stimulation to my muscles to minimize the atrophy. The idea was that when my neurological systems began to function again, the mechanics of the body would be able to respond. About two months of therapy were required and my body slowly repaired itself.

All told, this experience formed a very influential piece in the mosaic panorama that pushed me along in life. One consequence, perhaps from the neurological effects or perhaps from my experience of the new dimension of life, was that my personality was forever changed.

Because of my inherent ability with music, my parents had my aptitudes evaluated by a foundation that specializes in measuring natural abilities, personality characteristics, and career-related attributes. A laboratory gathered these measurements before I entered into my teen years. The methodologies of the tests identity and evaluate intrinsic aptitudes in ways that are detached, separated, from learned experiences, and I.Q.

The database of this foundation, accumulated across decades, provides evidence that inherent aptitudes and personality traits are set into place very early in life, and are neither lost nor gained through life's experiences. Part of the testing determined if a personality was subjective or objective. Before the occurrence of the motorcycle crash, it was determined that I had a subjective personality in the 98th percentile rating. Subjective personalities are highly individual. They perform and work mainly for themselves as individuals, which would be ideal for a serious student of the concert piano.

After the crash and the extensive brain trauma, my parents noticed my personality had changed. They decided that the same foundation would retest me to determine if changes occurred. The new test results indicated that my personality had shifted to the 50th percentile, on the border between the two characteristics: subjective and objective. The foundation staff reported that they had *never* seen such a personality shift as this in their entire history. Objective personalities are gregarious and outgoing. Now, I was neither objective nor subjective in any clear way. This change signaled that I could easily shift between these two characteristics, based on volitional decisions or emotional response.

My new sense of myself was quite tentative. It had added to the confusion already existing in my life, sometimes emotionally tangled, and I didn't know how to adapt to my new personality. Rather than being set as a highly subjective personality, comfortable within myself, easily able to withdraw and work independently, I would now experience unexpected oscillations that reflexively caused me to be objective, even occasionally gregarious, seeking the companionship and friendship of others. "Gregarious" was foreign to my self-expression and nature before the crash.

I eventually learned that I was able to express myself anywhere in the range from subjective to objective, naturally, depending upon what my self-determined purpose or mindset might be. Though I emotionally fumbled my way through the brambles of my new and awkward life, this new ability brought a benefit to the way that I presented myself. Eventually, after a prolonged period of adjustment, my altered personality allowed me to engage in society with better diversity.

In ways besides the skeletal or physiological damage, the motorcycle crash was a shattering experience. The crash itself had been only a few years after my encounter with the exorcist. The stability of my religious system of belief started to unravel. I struggled to separate myself from years of devotional religion and a deity and reach for the concept given to me, embedded within me, while all of my being was enveloped in the realm of light. I found my religious beliefs brought conflicts and confusion to what I now comprehended to be my authentic nature.

As implausible as it might seem to you, the events surrounding the motorcycle crash and *my first near death* appear now as if they were necessary to expand my philosophy. During that clinical death, a seed of philosophy had been sown in me. This seed started to grow into a philosophical tree for an ascending approach to my life: a provocative, inspiring, understanding that I was, and am, an individual and unique being, with the ability to develop the skills needed to determine the course of my life and existence. I sensed that myself – I alone could, only determine my very existence, my development and continuance. Though many tough years of turmoil would be required to dislodge my dependency upon my early "religious belief system", my individuality would eventually become a mantra that I would staunchly maintain.

These new concepts and ideas brought discord to the givens of my belief system, including the conflicts over the exorcist's admonitions. Diving deeply inside my mind, though, I discerned: the cause of my turmoil was not what the exorcist said to me; the turmoil arose from how I responded to his admonitions – I just didn't know of an alternate approach.

My response when in turmoil was to withdraw into myself, even into depression. I was hiding from myself, in denial of my conflicts. Depression seemed like a safe place to be, so I often wallowed in that state, hiding and reveling in my presumed inadequacies.

To extricate myself from this pattern of concealment in depression, an astonishing yet plausible series of events occurred. First, there was the altered and amplified "state of being" that resulted from my death after the motorcycle crash. The new sense of "self-awareness as an individual" that had been implanted in me during the crash and recovery, initially added to my turmoil, conflicts, and confusion, since being a self-sufficient individual contradicted my religious dependencies.

Emerging from the safety of the self-rejection called depression presented the most daunting challenge of my life. To emerge, I would have to confront all the tenets of my early programming. When one emerges from anything, there will be confrontations and challenges as one encounters the new environment. If the emergence is from the prison of self-loathing as in my situation, the challenges are especially formidable.

Second, emergence from the state of death in the ER at Yellowstone eventually brought me into a new light of being, though many interim events were required to bring me to that state of readiness.

In fact, I had to emerge from a very deep crater of low self-esteem.

CHAPTER EIGHT

THE CRATER OF SELF-DEPRECATION

Emotional craters can be years, even decades, in the making. They start with initial seeds sown from emotional fragments, inadvertently embedded and accumulated during our early years. The fragments may be things that just happened to us that we did not understand, or our emotional reactions to those events. Later, energized by turmoil or conflict, they gather as shrapnel, twisting and swirling around with the force of knives gathered in the vortex of a tornado, slashing away the true nature of a person. The vortex of the tornado plunges into the esteem of a person, grinding deeper and deeper until self-respect is lost, and objectivity about self disappears into an abyss of darkness. The longer this continues, the deeper the abyss becomes.

These knives, the unresolved fragments of experience, can be emotionally traumatic events or they can be beliefs innocently accepted but tragically incompatible with whom we really are. The knives are often instilled: subtly by inadvertent circumstances, by manipulations through guilt and conditioning, or they can be violently impressed by physical trauma such as child abuse.

In my early life, the circumstance that significantly influenced me was World War II. My parents met when my father was serving in the Marine Corps, and married overseas in 1932. Mother's family was scattered in Spain and the Philippines, and all of her family became immersed in war. While overseas, they conceived their only child in early 1941. In late 1941, when my father was reassigned to serve on the Battleship Oklahoma stationed at Pearl Harbor, something caused him to send his expectant wife to the mainland, not to Pearl Harbor, and soon after her arrival in San Diego, I was born. The Japanese attack of Pearl occurred just three weeks after my birth.

My mother, a European, had no support infrastructure in San Diego, and my father intuitively suspected that it could be a military target because of the large presence of the defense contractors with Naval and Marine Corps bases in the area. As a result, we relocated to my grandfather's timber farm that was located in Sabine County Texas, near the East- Texas border with Louisiana.

Though my grandparents were kind and nurturing, we lived in rural isolation. I spent the first four years of my life socially isolated, absent the companionship of other children. I met my father for the first time at war's end – a profound experience for both of us since we were strangers to each other. A few months after meeting my father, my parents decided to relocate to California. I was terrified and overwhelmed at the prospect of moving into a new environment away from the farm.

At age 5, my parents placed me into parochial school. Separated from my mother for the first time, I was frightened to levels approaching hysteria when my mother started to leave me with a teacher and other children in the classroom. With the help and understanding of patient teachers (Sisters of the Holy Name) I eventually calmed down and settled into the routine of school, yet I remained isolated from other children. I did not know how to fit in no matter how much I tried. Eventually, as socially inept, I simply withdrew and tried my best to become invisible to others.

For reasons I have never understood, despite my attempts to be invisible I seemed to draw attention to myself – from the bullies of the school. Even when there were no physical threats, the frequent insults, name-calling and taunting that seemed intended to get me into a fight, took a toll on my self-esteem. Rather than lashing out in anger, I lashed myself into depression. At home in the evenings, I would steal myself away and overindulge on ice cream. I became overweight. Because of a fire that happened when I was age two, my head has permanent scarring, giving me a bald-cap even as a child. With my baldness and weight increase I was now both "baldy" and "fatty."

At lunch period one day in the fourth grade, a group of bullies surrounded me in a tight circle. They started shouting insults, violently pushing me back and forth like a ball across their circle. Eventually I lost my balance and fell on the asphalt ground. My head hit hard, and I suffered a concussion, briefly loosing consciousness. The bullies ran and found a teacher, loudly proclaiming that the fat kid had fallen and hit his head. Fearing retribution, I allowed the lie: I just had fallen and hit my head. The school authorities summoned my mother to take me home and even there at home, I maintained the lie. My parents must have suspected that something more was involved because from that day forward they drove me to the school and took me home even for lunch every day, arranging meeting places out of the sight of the students. This routine increased my isolation, while providing sanctuary, and I welcomed it.

I rarely entered the schoolyard without fear of assault, either by force or by verbal denunciations or threats. I would carefully time my entry to coincide with the bell summoning us back to class as precisely as I could.

My parents seemed notice my isolation. Their solution was that I should attend a summer-camp held by the Jesuits on the campus of Loyola University. I will never forget my first day at camp – not ever. Coach Parker and his assistants gathered us up and said "We're going to play soft-ball today. Please line up and we'll assign you to teams. The teams are the "shirts" and the "skins."

I had seen "baseball cards" that other kids traded, but had never seen a baseball game and had no idea about how the game itself was played. As our line moved forward, they took off or left on the shirts of the children. I was shaking in nervousness. My worst trepidation happened: I was to be a "skin." I had never been publicly shirtless before. Taking off my shirt would reveal my fatness, and they would ridicule me!

My memory is a blur about what was going on until someone brought me up to what the staff called "home plate" and they handed me a bat. One of Coach Parker's assistants took my hands to show me how to hold the bat, and he said "The ball will be pitched to you. Try and hit it by swinging the bat this way at the ball." He moved my arms with bat back and forth to give me an idea what to do.

Standing at the plate, I positioned myself for my first attempt at anything baseball. On the first pitch, my bat connected with the ball and it seemed to be traveling very far, over the heads of the other players. I just stood there watching the ball fly away. Coach Parker, his assistants, and all of the other team members started shouting at me *"Run! Run!"* I had no idea where I was supposed to run toward, so dropped the bat and I ran as fast as I could: far away.

I ran until I found a hiding place. Trembling in embarrassment and fear, I concealed myself in a crate under a staircase against a building. Some hours later, Coach Parker and his assistants found me. My parents were with him. Coach Parker said to my parents "Your son is not ready for this experience, and we can't keep him here at day camp." I was so terrified, I didn't, couldn't speak, even on the way home. That was my first and last experience at playing baseball or softball, and my only day at camp.

My only place for solace at school was in the music room at the piano. I would denounce myself for being inadequate, and I would shrug off any praise for my musical performance believing that I did not deserve the praise. In the shadows of my mind, I was an imposter, and that was an unfailing opinion that lingered throughout my school years. My experiences in school validated the admonishment of the exorcist that I had interpreted to mean one thing: hide myself from myself and from others. Even though it did not work well, hiding was the only thing I knew to do.

My conflicts moved me into increasingly deeper depression. Depression had become a way of life, a belief that this is how I was supposed to live with God's cross for me to bear. I learned how to feign myself so that adults would not realize my travail. My self-appreciation was flickering, slowly extinguishing. It had insufficient power to overcome my negative self-image, and that set the knives in motion. I had been trying and continuously failing to live up to a self-image that was not my nature, and to measure up to beliefs designed to control through guilt and prohibitions. I had imprisoned my true nature within myself.

My conflict came to a focal point through an event in the sixth grade, an episode I remember as a time of intense travail and embarrassment. One of our six parish priests would periodically "dignify" our catechism class in parochial school with a lecture. The Sister who normally taught our class emphasized that this was a *special privilege* for us on this day. The priest entered the room, and closed the heavy oak door behind him with a thud. The thud was a signal for us to immediately stand at attention to welcome him. He entered our classroom with airs, what seemed a fanfare, since visits to our humble classes by priests were rare.

Our teacher, Sister Mary Bernadette, brought a voice to the fanfare: "Children, we are privileged to have Father McCarthy with us today! He will give us blessing," she said as she dutifully bowed in the direction of the priest. He returned her bow, and then walked to the center of the room as he brought his hands together as if we were going to pray. Standing at the center of the room, he gestured the sign of the cross as he blessed our class. We bowed in silence, as we heard the blessing with his deep baritone voice extolling loudly in Latin. We automatically looked up when the blessing was over, as he extended the palms of his hands outward. With the down-stroke of his arms, Father McCarthy motioned us to sit down at our desks.

The classroom became completely silent. He briefly looked down and cleared his throat. *"Children!"* he roared in a voice that echoed down the high-ceiling hallways of the school, *"God is omnipotent! God knows ALL!"* His words seemed to carry a power that felt intimidating, made more so by his booming deep voice.

The lecture continued to impress upon us how humbled we were in His presence and that by serving Him according to His dictates; we would be with Him in heaven eternally by using our free will! Alternatively, failing to be of proper service would cause God to reject us, send us to hell because of our inadequacies. *"We must serve God!"* he proclaimed with a roar, or *"God would send us to the flames of hell for all eternity!"* It seemed thunderous and threatening. This was a punitive flame-throwing God.

At the end of the lecture Father McCarthy called on the class, "Do you have any questions, children?" His eyes panned around the room, and he had a stern frown on his face that seemed to dare anyone to ask a question.

As a very shy and uncertain child, I was quite intimidated. Despite that, I was sufficiently confused about the lecture and wanted to overcome my fear by asking a question. I hesitated, and then sheepishly raised my hand, quivering as I did so, simply to ask a question.

Father McCarthy pointed to me with his outstretched arm. He asked my name, and in a quivering voice, I said, "Michael," as I stood, as protocol demanded. I hesitated again, wanted to sit down, feeling like this was a mistake. He broke the silence when he said "Yes, Michael. What is your question?"

I swallowed hard, and asked respectfully: "Father, God is all knowing and we are to live by His commandments."

"Yes, my son," was the immediate reply.

"Father, if God is all knowing then He already knows if we will go to heaven or to hell."

"Yes, my son, but we can use our free will to be in God's Grace and go to heaven."

"Father, how can that be because He already knows what will happen to us, so there would be no purpose to what we might do?"

Father's frown turned to a stare and it felt like his eyes were throwing daggers at me. Then, with a bellowing voice, he said: *"Sit down! You have no faith or understanding about God's love!"*

My mouth was trembling, terrified at his response that seemed to come from God Himself. Trembling took over my body as I promptly sat down and slumped into my seat, hoping that he would not punish me for asking those questions. Father McCarthy snapped around and glared at Sister, seated at her desk, as if he was going to accuse her of teaching heresy. She said nothing, but seemed to blush in embarrassment.

Then, my worst fear came to pass: he turned back to the class and was walking toward me, abruptly jabbing his finger in my direction. He barked a command, *"Stand up!"* My trembling increased and I started to tear. I stood. Father asked me, in a shouting voice, *"Define understanding!"* It sounded more like, felt like, an accusation than a question. Haltingly, I replied, "Understanding happens…. when I clearly…." I hesitated, coughed, swallowed hard to get a pause groping for my answer…. "Know - something," I finally blurted out.

"What do you know compared to God's infinite knowledge?" he roared. I could feel something like a heat wave of fever from his face that came close to mine.

He ranted: *"How do you dare question God's gift of free will?"* I trembled as if I were facing God's rant, with no possibility of escape, and the prospect of hell itself facing me. He frowned, and sharply turned away, then turned his stare back to me.

"Sit down!" he commanded, waving his hand at me in contempt. *"You've proven you have no understanding!"* He turned toward Sister Mary Bernadette, and grumbled "Thank you" in a

curt voice. He then swept out of the room with the same flourish that had swept him in. This time the door slammed behind him.

My ordeal was over. I had failed again. I had humiliated myself.

Sister stood at her desk and announced, "Recess class. Please stand." We all needed a break.

This event, indelibly etched into my memory, left unresolved questions that troubled me for years. My confusion still centered on the lingering question: either God knew everything, including whether I would go to heaven or hell, or He did not know everything. It could not be both ways. If He did know everything, what would the purpose of my service to Him really be, since the outcome would have been predetermined? Then there was a flash of curiosity: *Why would an omnipotent being need service from puny and impotent humans?*

Never again did I ask a question about God, or religion, in a class. The humiliation that day resulted in more withdrawal. I was too embarrassed to tell my parents what had happened. I was afraid to admit my ignorance about God. I nearly failed to pass the grade that year because of frequent illness born of my depression. The gaps in my understanding continued to grow, and the swirling knives of turmoil became more active as I grew up.

I wended my way through high school, continuing to be burdened by occasional assaults by bullies that would sometimes seem life threatening, once being kidnapped and thrown into the Pacific Ocean while not knowing how to swim. There was also the burden of corporal punishment by the hands of the faculty that could be severe. A teacher would slap a student across the face for answering a question in class erroneously, or repetitively across the back of the neck turning the neck bright red, for an inarticulate presentation. My school days were fraught with fear of the students or the faculty.

I maneuvered my way into becoming the photographer for the school newspaper, wrote an occasional feature article, and contributed as a photographer for the yearbook. Working on those enterprises became my escape to the extent that I managed in four years of high school to attend but one gym class, averting ridicule over my body or my ineptness. Leveraging my philosophy out of the exorcist's lesson, I accepted that my emotional pain was a cross that God had given me to bear for my inadequacies.

Unfamiliar feelings and confusing feelings increasingly arose in my body through my teens, and these were sexual in nature. I consistently failed to banish these feelings, and since I could not control them, I became threatened by eternal damnation, even convinced that was my fate. It seemed unnatural to me, even at a young age, to have to confess sins that were just thoughts of desire, in order to circumvent eternal damnation – when the sin was just human nature. Surely, I thought if God created humans then human nature must serve the purposes of God.

Embedded beliefs tend to confine one to a very limited set of options. If the options provided in beliefs are insufficient to resolve the issues, trying to use them will cause further conflict. Perhaps that is their intent, to imprison our "sinful natures," supposedly for our own good.

My sense of inadequacy and worthlessness continued without resolution. One impressed principal of beliefs that exacerbated the depth of my crater during my young age was the absolute prohibition against sexual activity, even sexual thoughts, unless the people involved were married. If I had a vague sexual thought, I had sinned according to my beliefs. I was continuing to fail. Even marriage itself was said to be "true to God" only if performed through a ceremony sanctioned by the "one true" church. Any sexual activity outside of church-sanctioned marriage was assertively pronounced to lead one into eternal damnation – unless confessed and "absolved."

Having no other means, no objective rationale, to resolve my conflicts regarding my failure to eliminate impure thoughts, I made a major decision: conform to the rules to avoid eternal damnation, and marry at the age of 18 years. We who were faithful to the beliefs had been ingrained with the proposition that when we are married, love and sex are beautiful. That, of course, assumes that the two people, once married, are compatible. In my situation this, unfortunately, did not prove to be true.

At our age of 18 and both virgins, compatibility could not be determined without experience and we could not have experience before marriage without committing a sin against God. Worse, the many years of sex-negative-programming firmly implanted in both our belief systems, could not be easily undone. Consummation of our marriage didn't happen on our wedding night and days later when we succeeded, the experience was not joyful but awkward and unfulfilling. Because of the prohibitions against birth control, my wife became pregnant very soon after our marriage.

We took all prudent measures to be certain that the health of mother and child would be cared for, using the best standards of the time. The pregnancy progressed normally and I did my best to support my wife in all ways. The anxious moment finally arrived for the birth of our first child, about nine months and one week after our marriage.

During labor, there were cycles of mild contractions that alternated with periods where labor just stopped. The start and stop process of labor extended our anxiety for over thirty hours. I was allowed to visit my wife in the ward, on an off during this time. When hard labor started, the nurses directed me out to the waiting room because of the policy of not allowing expectant fathers to attend the delivery of their children at this time of history (even in the best of hospitals). Anxiously, I waited…and waited.

Finally, I saw the obstetrician walking down the hallway, and as he approached me he said, *"You have a daughter."* Something was wrong. I could feel it. Perhaps it was his tone of voice. There was no uplift or joy, just a very dry report of the birth. I nervously asked, "Is everything okay?"

His eyes cast downward as he said, *"We're not certain. We are calling in an expert to check our opinion. We think your daughter is a Mongoloid."*

"A what?" I frantically exclaimed. "Is my wife alright? When can I see her and my daughter?"

"You may see your wife in about an hour when we take her to her room," he offered, *"And you'll see your daughter through the window of the maternity ward about the same time."*

"Does my wife know about our daughter?" I urgently needed to know from my concern about her feelings. *"We haven't told her what we think about your child. We need to have another opinion.",* came the reply.

"What shall I say to her?" I asked in the uncertainty of confusion and turmoil.

"I suggest you say nothing until we know more." I was stunned, completely locked in confusion and uncertainty about what to do.

After what seemed to be a very long hour, a nurse appeared and pointed me toward my wife's room. I jogged down the hallway, and slid around the corner into her room. As soon as she saw me, she said, *"Michael! Why haven't they brought my child to me? I haven't seen her! Where IS she?"*

It was true. She did not know. Trying to obey what I thought was the approach the doctor wanted to use, I concealed my emotion and said, "They must be getting her ready to bring to you. I'm certain she'll come along soon."

We waited quietly together as we held each other, and waited some more. Eventually, a nurse brought in our daughter. The first thing that caught our attention was that she had a full head of dark hair - and oriental features.

Our beautiful daughter was a Down's syndrome child. As a teenage couple, God had given us a very heavy cross to bear.

Confused and in tumultuous emotion, I desperately tried to learn about the condition of our child, and what the future might look like. The day after her birth, our pediatrician gave us the best advice he could. There were two options, in his opinion: place the infant immediately into the institutional care of a State-run facility and go on with life without contact with the child; or, perhaps a mercy killing could be quietly arranged. It was horribly devastating advice: both were unthinkable options to consider.

With our turmoil magnified to oceanic proportions, we scrambled to find alternate information …… and another doctor. Our new pediatrician, who had been my own up until eight years before, gave us simple advice: *"Take her home and love her!"* We did. We named her Shannon Marie. She brought to our lives unconditional love, a bond of family, a purpose to our marriage and the challenges of raising a child requiring unique care.

Finding appropriate services for our "special needs daughter" was extremely difficult in the early part of the 1960s. Yet, when Shannon was about four years old, we finally located an impressive foundation that provided highly focused services for Shannon, and assurances for us.

Fast forward through a period of about seven years. In that time, working to support our little family and realizing our educational goals, we managed to survive. Our psychological incompatibility in intimacy resulted in little activity that might result in another child. My career was doing well, though there were burgeoning developments in my field that took me traveling around the world, sometimes for extended periods.

We had in the meantime contracted with a special genetics research group at UCLA to learn if either of us were carriers of the defect that caused Down's syndrome, a condition almost unheard of with younger parents. We were not. Our first child was a genetic accident. That finding, though it didn't soften the blow, at least let us know that future sexual relations between us would probably not lead to a second child with the same affliction.

Then, our lives changed again. Something magical happened. I have no idea why or what happened, but our marriage became intimately active. After an interlude of eight years, we gave birth to our second child, another beautiful daughter!

Madeline was born on Thanksgiving Day, healthy and active. We were very thankful.

Our marriage compatibility lasted for about two years, and we gave birth to our third child, our son Cameron, only fifteen months after Madeline was born.

In between their births, we learned we had to bear yet another cross: Shannon Marie contracted leukemia. The survival rate for childhood leukemia in that period was about two percent, according to reports. Despite that dismal statistic, we compelled ourselves to do our best every day to nurture her and try to save her life.

After Cameron was born, we learned that Madeline would need surgeries to correct a "lazy eye" condition. One surgery resulted in another, then another. Eight in all would be required, with only minimal success. These operations overlapped our travails in dealing with the emotionally trying cycles of leukemia, remission of the leukemia, then failures of the remissions, on periods of about three months.

Overlapping the same time, two of my wife's (whom I'll call Jocelyn) elderly aunts contracted cancers, one after the other, and a third, her grandmother who raised her with her two aunts, fell, broke her hip and suffered a stroke. Neither of us had any siblings, so the responsibility fell solely upon us to arrange for their care and to manage the affairs of her family. For an extended time the events compounded with the leukemia of our daughter, the surgeries of our second daughter, and the maladies of Jocelyn's family, we attended different hospitals and medical regimens every day and every night – consecutively – for five years.

We had become used to the unrelenting cycles of chemotherapy, remission, followed by reemergence of the leukemia. Each cycle was shorter than the one before, yet we were wishfully hopeful that somewhere, there might be a magic medical breakthrough to save our child. During the cycles, we did our best to live our lives as normally as possible.

Shannon was in the hospital – again – for medications and tests requiring another indefinite stay. This had become part of our routine of life. One morning, I was at work walking down the office hallway. Our receptionist called to me, *"You have an urgent call from the hospital!"* I was already in motion to get to a phone as it rang on my desk.

"Mr. King," said a very dry voice from the charge nurse at the hospital, *"I regret to have to tell you: Your daughter has passed away."*

"What happened?" I exclaimed as my voice broke, almost in a screeching tone. *"We were taking her down to extract bone marrow, and she just slipped away. There was nothing we could do."*

"Where is my wife? Does she know?"

"Mrs. King is waiting in the room for Shannon to return from her tests. We have not told her. She doesn't know."

"DO NOT tell her!" I said, "I need to be there with her! I'll be there in a few minutes."

Everyone at work knew what was happening in my life, and my screeching had drawn attention to me. I raced out the office door, almost unable to speak. I saw my boss and coworkers staring at me, and I managed to turn around just long enough to say, "It's over. I won't be here for a while." I barely heard my boss say and ask: *"She died?"* I barely found the strength to only nod "yes" as I raced to my car.

The drive to the hospital of about ten miles seemed interminable. My focus was on my wife, what to say to her, and how to say it. Would she know what happened before I got there? I hoped not. After everything that we had gone through, we had done it with mutual support, and this had to be something we worked through together.

When I entered the hospital room, she was surprised. I was supposed to be at work, and this stay at the hospital was supposed to be like many others. She seemed happy to see me, brightly smiling as I slowly walked into the room, and she said *"Glad to have you visit! Shannon is down having some tests. Why did you leave work?"*

I paused, solemn in what I had to say. I looked into her eyes as I held back my tears, then gently embraced her, softly saying in her ear… "It's over."

There was a moment of stunned silence. Her eyes drilled into mine, and then she said, *"She's GONE?"* as her voice broke. Tears flowed down our faces. She shuddered, and I said, "Yes," as she collapsed in my arms.

I helped her up, held her tightly to my side as we walked out of the room. I noticed that parents of other children in the ward were watching us…. with respectful silence. We found a quiet place to be together in our sorrow. Leukemia had claimed Shannon's life about two weeks shy of her eleventh birthday.

After our emotions calmed a bit, we wanted to see her. The nurses directed us to the morgue. On the way, a priest whom we had often seen in the corridors of the Catholic hospital passed us and said, "She is with God, now. We gave her extreme unction."

Incredible, I thought! Even the church taught that our child, any *retarded* child, *was incapable of sin* in God's eyes! At this incredible moment, en route to see our daughter in death, I just politely nodded at the priest. Internally, though, I was nonplussed! What a hypocrite to give this ritual to this child of innocence.

About two months after her death, I responded to a page when I landed at Los Angeles Airport from a trip to the Navy Department in Washington, D.C. I looked around and found the "white courtesy" telephone, and the voice said, "I have an urgent call for you."

With all the medical problems of my wife's family and our own, I was emotionally numb. Whatever the call was, it would not be good. It was my wife.

"Your mother suffered a major stroke! She is in the hospital. You'd better take a taxi directly there."

This was a surprise. My mother had been in good health, though she had discomfort with phlebitis (blood clots in her legs). Immediately I left for the hospital.

Arriving there, I looked at my mother. She was in a coma, my father at her bedside. A blood clot had broken loose and struck into her brain like a bullet. My father said that she was lucid as she collapsed around 2 a.m. that morning, about eighteen hours before the time when I arrived, and she had asked him to call a priest to perform extreme unction.

I carefully studied her body. Her energy of being was gone. To the best I could determine, there were no striations of color, or hues, nor any activity. She had already departed.

I clearly remember my emotional reaction as I approached her comatose body. I dryly said to my father, "What else might go wrong today?" We looked at each other, hugged in silence, and left the room together.

Fully immersed as we were then with the prolonged illness and death of Shannon and the surgical events of our daughter Madeline and also with Jocelyn's family, I swear to you that confronted by my mother's coma and death, I never shed a single tear. I had no tears left in me to shed: None at all.

All who were going to perish in our family in that five-year span did perish. The last death, the last of Jocelyn's immediate family, occurred about two years after Shannon's death.

We tried to save our marriage, but our incompatibility had once again roared furiously to the surface. We had met our responsibilities to others. We had survived: no more, no less.

Despite our efforts, our marginally functional marriage soon became fully dysfunctional and we would not survive as a couple for much longer. Consultation with priests only affirmed that marriage and "God's cross of incompatibility" we had to bear, was supposed to be life long while offering no solutions. The dysfunction of the marriage contributed to my internal conflicts, a trap with divorce prohibited because it was against God's will. Even society of that time considered most sexuality taboo and stifled discussions on the subject, leading to increased repression with no obvious avenues open for relief. I even gave up one of the few remaining joys in my life, playing the piano. I moved out of the survival mode and into depression, often into despair.

I reflected back upon my travails, starting with the motorcycle crash about sixteen years before. My belief system offered no consolation and provided no answers to the deep conflicts that eroded my soul. I desperately needed to find a way out of an incredible crater that was getting deeper and deeper. Occasionally, I had flashes of inspiration from the impressions gained during the near-death experiences surrounding the motorcycle crash. Contrary to years of religious instruction, I slowly began to have a new understanding of my personal role and responsibility, from the seeds of thought planted during those moments *within the light*.

These inspirations were very valuable since they offered some subtle hope that I might survive the current impasse. All considered though, between the inhibitions caused by the instruction from the exorcist and the personality-altering effects of the motorcycle crash, I recognized that I faced a daunting challenge – one of the most difficult challenges I have ever been compelled to engage in – to untangle my confusions about who and what I really am.

Religions, as belief systems I have learned, cannot yield to logical thoughts or explanations of reason. They must explain away any incompatible observation or experience in terms of *God's will that works in mysterious ways* or in other terms that the religious institutions will accept. If a person only functions through training in a belief system, self-determination, volition outside that belief structure, would be a fearsome proposition. It follows that if a person is captive to blind beliefs, he or she might not have sufficient objectivity to pry him or herself out of captivity and into the freedom of knowledge, which is the wellspring for individual beings to thrive.

I was such a person: immobilized in a prison of embedded beliefs, trapped in the turmoil of conflict between reality and the tenets of churchianity, adherence to which was demanded by blind faith. Faith could no longer come to my rescue because I, myself, had been rendered impotent, entrapped by the conflict between reality and my beliefs. The mantra that *God works in mysterious ways* no longer provided comfort or answers.

While in my early thirties I seemed to exist in a state of confusion, cyclically interspersed with frequent withdrawals and depressions. The turmoil of my confusion caused a sort of disassociation in which my technical skills were on firm ground but my self-esteem plummeted into depths, like a vortex swirling me into an abyss.

My technical consulting business became my refuge from my internal temblors, and at least the business was prospering. Nevertheless, the focus of my engineering activity only provided transient respites from my pervasive and lingering issues.

I became determined and committed to reach into what I then called my soul to find myself as an individual. The problem was that I had no idea how to accomplish what seemed to be an impossible, and substantially frightening, daunting task.

Increasingly I began to understand, or suspect, that prayers, "faith," and blessings from others for me would not show me the way to attain my eternal evolution, yet that was something I could not bring myself to fully accept. I learned in a tentative way that I must find my true self, though my lack of acceptance continually tripped me up on my task. In fact, so great was my quandary, even my physical health was undermined through my embedded and seemingly intractable conflicts! My internalized conflicts were tearing me apart in a torturous and stressful tug of war between what remained of my shattered belief system and what I suspected instinctively was my true destiny. My apprehension, pain, and fear were swirling in constant turmoil of conflicted emotions!

Issues with my health were increasingly surfacing, often with unresolved diagnosis and excruciating physical pain. So great was my self-imposed torture that at one point my body displayed the symptoms of a stroke. The left side of my whole body became numb and semi-paralyzed. I was experiencing an excruciating headache, my pupils appeared unequally dilated, I was having difficulty walking and my speech was slurred.

Weeks of diagnostic tests found nothing, though the neurologists said: "If 1,000 people came to us with these symptoms, in 999 we would have found a brain tumor, aneurism, or meningitis. With you, we have found nothing. Stress in your life might be causing your symptoms. We suggest you might work with a psychologist!"

"Psychologist?" I said in an incredulous tone.

"Yes," the neurologists insisted. "We in medicine are beginning to understand that the mind can influence the body in ways we never thought possible! Think about this: Have there been times when your health declined during depression?"

That question seemed to suddenly resonate with me. I stared at the two doctors attending my condition, and they stared back with a look of concern.

Then I remembered. "Yes," I responded, "I was very depressed in the sixth grade. I almost failed the school term because I was out sick for many days."

"Did something happen to cause the depression, some kind of stress? Something that emotionally bothered you?" they persisted. I remembered the humiliating incident with Father McCarthy. I remembered that I was feeling sick after the confrontation and that the sickness was painful. I remembered that my health had degraded with fevers that would come and go with symptoms of colds or flu that would linger. I remembered also that I was loath to go back to class.

"Yes," I said. My voice was trailing off as I reflected on that humiliation. "There was a horrible incident in class that I didn't know how to deal with, so I wanted to hide from everything."

"Okay. Since your history implies a pattern that your mental condition can hurt your health, we urge you to see a psychologist. We can find nothing medically to explain your condition, so your condition might be psychosomatic."

"Psychosomatic? Symptoms that are not medically real, caused by fantasy in the mind?" I asked.

"The symptoms caused by the stressed mind can become real illness if they persist for long periods. When you almost failed the sixth grade, your depression became pain and the pain became illness that kept you out of school. We assume you had a measurable fever and other indications of some sort of flu. True?"

"Yes. Clearly I felt sick, sometimes very sick."

"That's because you probably were ill," they offered. "We're not sure why, but depression, which we used to write off as psychosomatic symptoms, can become real illness. We urge you to see a psychologist, and soon, because of the severity of your symptoms."

With that, they handed me a business card for a psychologist who had an office in their medical building. I stumbled as I turned to leave the doctor's office when their assistant informed me: "Mr. King, Dr. Morella, a psychologist we work with, can see you this afternoon. We asked him to prioritize an appointment for you."

That was that. I would see the psychologist they had recommended to me that very afternoon. I dragged myself down to a snack shop and waited for the time of my appointment.

"Dr. Morella?" I tentatively asked. As I shuffled into his office, I saw a bespectacled man, slight in stature, about 45 years old with curly grey hair, standing behind a desk that was part of the lobby area. He was very casually dressed with a loose Hawaiian print shirt.

"You must be Michael," he offered. "Doctor Noel's office described your condition to me, and their diagnosis – or lack of it, I should say. Please call me Bob, and we'll get started right away." He opened the door behind him to his inner office. He could see my struggle to walk, shuffling my uncooperative left leg along. He came over and said with emphasis, *"Let me help you."* I welcomed his support.

The inner room was unlike any office I'd ever imagined for a psychologist. Rather than the stereotypical "couch" and wing-back chairs, there were large pillows cast about on a large oriental rug. There were few other furnishings. He helped me ease myself onto a large pillow, and I adjusted myself into the softness to be comfortable in a semi-reclining position. He picked up and fluffed another pillow, then sat down facing me, slipping off his sandals.

He said, "Take your shoes off, if you wish" but I declined. This was already enough of a foreign experience for me, and I felt vulnerable.

Bob Morella explained that he was a holistic psychologist, working on a broad approach not limited to the "talk" therapy that most therapists used at that time. "My approach is to raise my client's awareness of himself in the broadest sense, incorporating mind, body, and spirit."

I was intrigued, to say the least. There was something about this man, a calm, a feeling of peace combined with energetic fields. Those sensations resembled some of the intensity I had experienced during my encounter with the exorcist. Haltingly, my feeling of vulnerability changed to a feeling of hope. He seemed to reach into me, to touch something that I had not been able to feel in a long time.

He said, "Please close you eyes and breathe deeply." I readily complied. I instinctively felt that I could trust him. We were silent for a few moments and in that period, I swear I could feel and hear his breath interspersed with mine. Something seemed to stir that I could not explain, and in a very soft tone of voice, he broke the silence: "Who are you?" he asked. Startled, I opened my eyes and stared at him. *"What?"* I snapped.

In his soft baritone voice, he simply repeated, "Who are you? It is a simple question." as he gazed at my face. I was befuddled, even flustered, as I attempted to respond. The question was so simple that I started babbling, "I am a father, a husband," Bob slowly shook his head back and forth, signaling no, that's not it, and so I continued with "Michael," only to receive the negative signal again.

I paused. I started to grope for an answer that he would accept. "I am a manager in engineering," I offered, only to get the no signal once again, as he cast his gaze downward.

I asked myself, "What answer would gain his acceptance? How could such a simple question meet with such rejection?" He raised his gaze back to my face, and excitedly I pleaded, *"I am a servant of God!"* He held his hand up as if to signal *stop.* I stopped.

He said, "Those are all titles, functions, or labels that you have been taught to believe you are. They do not describe who you are but rather what you do, what you feel you are obligated to do, roles you feel you must play in your life." I stopped to dwell on his words when I realized, I have no clue who I am, and I don't know how to even start to define myself.

Surrendering, I said, "If these labels and titles and even my name don't accurately describe me, I have no way to answer."

Bob replied, "People tend to live their lives in the character roles, functions, and labels that others have assigned to them, never asking themselves that very simple question. In effect, they might go through much of their lives living for the acceptance of others, in the roles prescribed for them. If you are willing to commit to the quest of discovery, in time you will learn who you are."

It was an astonishing statement and an astonishing moment. I had been living my entire life meeting my responsibilities, carrying the burdens that I believed God Himself had assigned to me. I was not living for myself, not seriously questioning whether my purpose in life was other than to serve.

I rattled on to Bob about the travails of the past years, my failing marriage, the stress from feeling I had failed to meet the expectations of others, and God's burdens. In meeting the needs of others, I had lost my sense of myself.

Bob asked me to recline fully on my pillow, and he said, "Close your eyes, and imagine a place of peace and tranquility you would love to be in right now."

I allowed myself to imagine myself sitting by a stream meandering through a meadow, with a gentle current burbling against a few rocks, and a small waterfall in front of me. Bob asked me to describe every detail of my imaginary environment, and I readily complied. He asked, "Are you alone?"

"Yes," I answered.

"Is the sun shining?"

"Yes. It is brilliant and there is a cool breeze that is invigorating and beautiful."

He asked, "Are you visiting this place, or are you a part of it?"

I felt that I was wistfully dreaming as I replied, "I feel at one. My place of beauty is a place of myself." Bob offered, "Then you must BE beauty."

I was stunned. Then I understood and said: *"My God! I am!"* as I broke down sobbing in tears.

Bob gently soothed me and guided me out of my meditation and back to normal reality. When my mind was back to the room, he said "You are extremely perceptive and sensitive. See if you can hold onto the feeling you have just experienced, and learn the beauty of yourself. I am part of a group of holistic psychologists that specializes in working with individuals such as you. We're having some special programs at our mansion that I believe would benefit you. The next program is in two weeks – a weekend retreat. Hope you will join us."

He helped me up, handed me a paper describing the program he mentioned. Though I was still hobbling as I walked, somehow I felt lighter. As I opened the door he said, *"See you there!"* I nodded "Yes" as I said, "Thank you."

The symptoms of my physical maladies that had lingered for about two weeks simply disappeared within a day. I find it fascinating to this day that the body can provide incredibly proficient signals about disorders of the mind, that the mind does not want to acknowledge let alone accept! The terrifying incident of *the stroke that was not a stroke* finally was sufficient to capture my attention. I could no longer ignore the signals, the excruciating pain from my body that my mind sent out screaming for help.

In a previous time, I would have attributed my decline to *God's will,* and increasingly lambasted myself with guilt for my inadequacy to bear His crosses. I realized on an intuitive level that this was the very process that had transported me sliding down through my river of life, into the whitewater of class seven rapids with a plunging abyss just ahead. All of my self-imposed ploys failed because I simply did not have sufficient faith to deceive myself any longer. To survive, I had to finally confront – and address – my conflicts with impressive compulsion.

The guises of the character roles I had been exploiting came to the limit. They (and I) became wholly dysfunctional. The roles were now as un-shielding, as irrelevant as a paper bag shield would be against a point-blank muzzle blast of a shotgun!

The conflicts between my nature and the blind beliefs instilled in me had taken away the reason and objectivity I needed to learn, know, or reassemble myself. The roles no longer worked, and neither did the admonition that I did not have enough faith.

The truth is that, because of my programming from youth was that my only role was to please my "God," I never really had the tools of objectivity or reason to use in the first place. Because of this, my inner conflicts went unresolved and unaddressed for so long that they had literally crippled me.

I was churning in the whitewater, the roiling rapids of ignorance and self-deception, fast approaching the abyss. The glimpse of beauty that I experienced with the psychologist gave me a brilliant flash of hope, a branch poking out of the riverbank in the current of my life, that I grabbed and tenaciously clung to. With one slip at this critical point, I intuitively knew I would be gone.

To survive, I had to develop the tools I could use to emerge from a very, very dark and deep crater of my being. I had to slay the dragon of death that was surfacing with increasing force within me, yet I had few weapons available.

In sum: I desperately needed help.

I hoped to find that help with a group of holistic psychologists.

Questions

Events in life can pile up slowly over time, layer upon layer, into the psyche of a person so deeply that the light of reason is no longer seen.

Have you experienced a sequence of traumas, tragedies, and events that spin your life out of your control?

Have you found tools to regain control without blocking reality?

Are there beliefs instilled within you that you accepted as a child turned out later to be incompatible with your true nature?

Do you have the tools of objectivity to extricate yourself from negativity to reconstruct yourself, and find your true nature to move forward in your personal journey toward your fulfillment?

CHAPTER NINE

THE RETREAT: DISCOVERIES

T he descriptive flyer Bob had given me describing the retreat lay on the table in front of me. I was fiddling it around with my fingers. Should I call and go to the re-treat? What would happen at a retreat? Would I be vulnerable? Should my wife go with me? Should I withdraw? Would it be bet-ter to just see Bob privately again? At least I had some idea of what might happen in a private session.

Then there was my wife's response to deal with. I had re-turned home after my session with Bob, feeling euphoric. My physical malady had disappeared within a day! Her response to my excitement was to be incredulous: "You imagined you were in a peaceful place and this healed you? What deluded fantasy." My pleas to the contrary went unheard, typical of how our rela-tionship had deteriorated. I withheld further expression of my emotions from her, but I was churning internally, trying not to allow her naysaying to dissuade me, frail and caught as I was in between anticipation of the unknown, and ecstatic at the pos-sibilities for my future.

Only two days before, I had met Bob, and my experience with him was compelling. I had to meet Bob again, no matter what. At least this much seemed certain. Committing to a full weekend retreat, though, filled me with anxiety. Yet, thanks to my session with Bob, I felt like an excited wide-eyed child that had just discovered a candy store for the first time. The next moment I was tortured with doubts and fears, unsupported by my wife. The flyer seemed to beckon me to make the call - to reserve my place. Despite tumultuous internal arguments over a couple of days, I decided to make the commitment to myself. The retreat was to take place in two weeks. I made the telephone call to reserve my place.

During that time, I was emotionally oscillating between a sense of purpose and the reflex to run and hide. What kept me from falling was restoring my memory to the enlightened moment, when I discovered, *"My God! I am (my own beauty)!"* Those few words and the experience with Bob conveyed a profound sense of hope: a ray of light shinning into my dark abyss of depression. I tenaciously clung to those beautiful feelings whenever I started to fall – which seemed often. I fought not to let my wife's negativity influence me to surrender to her opinion and negate myself. I fervently tried to do what Bob had implied: hold on to a sense of positive energy, my feeling of beauty, and a shimmering ray of optimism that I had blocked for years.

As the time for the retreat approached, I was brimming with anticipation – or nervous anxiety – that was difficult to quell. The mansion was more than an hour's drive away. In my eagerness, I left early to avoid any possibility of being late and arrived almost two hours earlier than planned. All of a sudden, my timidity kicked into gear and I avoided knocking at the front door by wandering a bit around the grounds of the facility. I was trying my best to look nonchalant. As I walked by a large window, a woman waved at me, motioning me toward the front door. I forced a smile, then turned and reversed my direction back toward the door.

She greeted me at the door with a cheerful, "Hi! Are you here for our retreat?"

"Yes," I responded, "I'm Michael, and Bob invited me two weeks ago!"

"Welcome," she said, "I'm Susan and I work with Bob and the others. Bob was delighted to see you had registered! Please come in."

Susan's welcoming was so ebullient, so reinforcing I started to relax. Even the nuance that Bob himself, an important figure to me, had noticed my registration seemed affirming to me.

"We're having a meeting before the retreat starts. Please come in and join us!" Susan said enthusiastically as I walked into the massive entryway. It was difficult for me to believe. This openness, this warm acceptance, was marvelously embracing compared to the aloofness of my normal life's environment.

My first impressions of the mansion were about the very high ceilings, the large spacious floor areas of the main rooms, the sweeping clear view of well-polished light oak floors, the almost total lack of normal furnishings save for a few small tables here and there, and floor pillows everywhere. Bob's austere floor-pillow office was a diminutive version of this large house.

We walked upstairs through a very wide corridor to another large room where Bob and two others were chatting.

Bob saw us approach and said, "Glad you decided to join us. I had hoped that you would," as he walked up and took my hand gently between his. This was not a handshake. It was a warm greeting. He noticed that the left side of my face was responsive and I was no longer dragging my left side along like a bag. As his eyes scanned my side that used to be limp, he said with a large grin, "I'm delighted that you feel better!"

"Yes!" I acknowledged, "I magically recovered within a day of our meeting."

"That wasn't magic," he corrected. "That was the power you allowed for yourself."

"You've already met Susan, I see. Please meet our partners." He turned to look at the others as he said, "I met Michael at our satellite office about two weeks ago by a special request of

Dr. Noel's group. Michael was very responsive to a guided meditation experience we had together." Bob turned to look at me, smiling a bit sheepishly, as he reported, "I suspect that Michael is very sensitive, and probably perceptive."

The others, introduced to me as Kayla and Morgan, broadly smiled. They seemed to exude a confidence, an aura of fore-knowledge that caused me to also feel confident, and at home. Bob explained that he and Kayla frequently worked together with Susan in sessions with groups of clients. They would be con-ducting the retreat that weekend. Morgan, Susan explained, had a position of greater distinction and usually worked privately with clients. Susan spontaneously smiled, then made an offhand comment, "If it turns out that you have the chance to work with Morgan, you'll need all the preparation that Bob, Kayla, and I can give you. You'll have to be prepared, because working with him will be challenging!"

A moment of quiet happened in the wake of Susan's com-ment. Maybe her comment had overstepped her bounds. Morgan seemed to feign a smile, said nothing, and then walked away. This pause gave me an opportunity to express what I was feeling about participating in the weekend retreat.

"Bob, thank you so very much for inviting me so I could have this opportunity! My session with you gave me a positive glimpse of a beautiful feeling that I haven't dared myself to have in a very long time. I must confess: I was very tenuous about coming here, and anxiety almost turned me back. I clung onto your words, in multiple repetitions, and brought back the feelings I experienced with you. I often started to wobble and slip back into a crater of depression. I feared coming here to meet with you today. At the entryway, Susan's delightful greeting was infectious! Her greet-ing gave me the push I needed to come in."

I noticed that as I was speaking, I was becoming annoyed – even edgy – at myself that I had to expose my failure and incom-petence and the mess entangling my mind. The intonation of my voice revealed my annoyance and discomfort.

Dr. Bob Morella had a steadiness, exuded a competence, which is hard to define. As I was speaking, he was studying me with a gaze that felt nurturing and understanding. He quietly listened and watched as my edginess increased. With a soft smile, he gently lifted his hand, palm toward me as he had during my feeble attempts to answer his simple question, "Who are you?" This time, when his palm lifted to signal me to stop my rattle, I felt an energetic field and glimpsed a hint of aura that reminded me of my encounter with the exorcist. That *really* grabbed my attention.

Bob sensed my distress and responded, "Michael, please pay close attention. Emotional craters are like funnels, flowing with swirling voracious acid that slowly etches down into the vital tissues of life and being. The acid is the denigration of self, and gradually, painfully, it dissolves away a person's self-esteem. I have learned, through working with many people, that extricating oneself from a deep emotional crater requires a prodigious, and very personal, commitment. It also requires a commensurate level of intent, and energy along with the commitment. Make no mistake, Michael, it is your effort and commitment that is required, not mine, not Kayla's or Susan's, and certainly not Morgan's. This is something you must do for yourself. It is your personal quest. We can help you find tools of objectivity that you can use in your quest."

Bob went on to say, "My efforts with others have clearly shown that prolonged periods of existence in personal craters of depression will transition the crater to become a belief reference of how to live and feel about life. This negative state of being simply deflects a person from facing reality even to the extent of dissociating a person from their true nature. While in the crater, there is little clarity for objective reason to prevail, and hence the person locked in the crater, cannot move forward with life. Michael, it is clear to me that over many years, this is what has happened to you. You surrendered yourself to the will and needs of others, subverting yourself and your true nature."

"Bob, everything you say all makes sense to me – on a logical level," I said, "Yet in an instant I'll vacate my sense of logic and yield to negative feelings telling me that I'm worthless, even to the extent that I question if I deserve to live."

Kayla chimed in. "Please understand, Michael, that this has been a long-term decline. If you were a building, the destructive forces of control that influenced you by circumstances and by actions of others, weakened the walls of your building, and started to disassemble the building itself. It was not just those factors, but also the way you submitted yourself to their influence that caused the destruction. I am quite certain a foundation of self-esteem remains below the rubble you are carrying around in your mind. Your task is to clear up the rubble and rebuild, reassemble your sense of yourself in the brilliant light of acceptance, trust, and love. The disassembly required time. The clean up will require effort and time, and so will the reassembly. When you were impacted by a negative and allowed it to permeate your sense of who and what you are, that negative took on a personality of it's own – and it's still in your consciousness. You can think of these as tyrants in your mind."

Susan seemed to be absorbing Kayla's words, occasionally glancing back and forth as if she were studying my reaction as well as Bob's. She then went downstairs to greet others who had arrived for the retreat.

Kayla continued. "Think of this metaphor, for a moment. There are concealed tyrants lurking within the crater of deprecation that have taken up residence in your mind. Tyrants such as depression, anger, fear, and the ego of self-importance can invade in an instant to thwart off the threat of change and your personal renewal. The tyrants are determined to hold on to their territory, and negative feelings, self-denigration, calls them up into vicious service. When they respond to the call, they'll stand ready to inundate your mind with the acid of self-loathing, a feeling of surrender to worthlessness."

Bob added, "They can take you off guard, whenever an attempt is made to climb out from the darkened shadows of your mind, beating back your quest for freedom. You must become aware of your reflex emotions, so you can learn how to take action to rebuild yourself. This is what we mean when we say that you must increase your self-awareness. We hope to provide you with the tools to awaken and explore your inner self."

My mind was whirling – racing between glimmers of hope, and anxiety about the magnitude of my task ahead. Would I be up to this task? How could I reassemble myself from the shambles of my self-value? How could I deal with my wife's reticence, even refusal, to work on these issues with me? How could she not grasp that she, herself, had been living with negations implanted in her early life – that these people might help her? Bob's words and Kayla's words were trying to sink in, and though my confidence was quite frail, for the first time in years I desperately grasped onto the support that this holistic group could offer me.

I was on the cusp of understanding that I'd fallen into a *pattern of deluding myself*. I convinced myself that craters of deprecation *are safe* because they appeared to build a defensive wall around my self-being. The crater became a place to hide from the continuing, unrelenting pressures of life. That self-deceit caused me to *believe* that the crater *would protect me* from outside harm as a *normal place as a reference* of my daily life. When negative emotion seized me, fear of leaving the crater pressed me back time, and time again. I sank deeper and deeper into withdrawal, emotionally addicted to my crater, convincing myself of my *worthlessness*. As a crater of depression offers to protect a person from outside harm, it promotes and perpetuates *inside* harm.

In an interesting twist of fate, through my psychosomatic pain, my body became an ally. By screaming in excruciating pain and displaying malady, my body grabbed my attention in a blatant way: alerting me to the peril of maintaining disassociation from myself. By directing me to *Dr. Bob Morella*, and to his holistic group, a small crack had opened in my armor of disassociation. Through his guidance, I saw a shaft of light that illuminated beauty in me! That beauty proffered hope, hope set up inspiration, and inspiration became a mission. It felt *almost* like an impossible dream.

On our way downstairs, I asked: "Do you assign yourselves to specific clients or would I be a client - student of your whole group, if I stay with you?"

Kayla smiled, then explained: "Each of us, as psychologists, has diversified abilities and approaches to use with our clients, and there is considerable overlap among us. We align our varying methods toward a client's specific needs and we devise a sequential and incremental process. As a client develops, attains a higher state of personal awareness about what has occurred to cause the problems they wish to overcome, we will move you from one teacher and experience with us, to another, until you attain your goals."

"What goals?" I tentatively asked, pushing through my nervous timidity.

Kayla gently placed her hand on my shoulder, stopping us at the bottom of the staircase. I responded to her reassuring touch, faced her to greet her soft smile, as she said: "Why, the goals that you define for yourself *as you evolve,* of course." Her words *as you evolve* seem to linger in the air as I mused through the implications while we continued walking.

As we came to the main room of the mansion, I noticed that about twenty people gathered around Susan. She was explaining how the weekend retreat was organized. There would be four sessions, one each morning and another each afternoon. I noticed that there were mostly couples, and a few individuals attending the retreat, with the number of men and women about equal.

The psychologists asked us to arrange ourselves on floor pillows in a circle. Bob, Kayla, and Susan positioned themselves at the center of the circle, also on floor pillows, with their backs against each other. Symbolically, we all looked like a wheel with rules of structure, they advised us, the psychologists forming the hub. We would be required to respond when one of the psychologists pointed to us. Otherwise, we would raise our hands to speak, analogous to the spokes in our wheel connecting to the hub. We would not comment on something said by another client unless requested.

After brief first-name introductions, Kayla asked, "Do you all believe you live your lives objectively?" The majority said yes, they thought they did. A few said they didn't understand what that means. I could not bring myself to admit that I didn't think so. Most of the time, I felt that my life in depression *was objective.* Actually, my emotional struggle was that I wanted to conceal my frailties. I wanted to appear confident to the others of our group.

Bob then asked, "What expectations of this weekend did you bring with you today?" The responses varied, such as expectations to be motivated; learn about attaining higher consciousness; become more sensual; better communicate with and trust my partner; and, gain knowledge of myself. When Bob pointed at me, I honestly responded, "I've never been in a program like this before. I don't know what to expect, so I have no expectations."

Susan asked the gathering, "How can you claim to live your lives objectively when you have brought in expectations of what might happen? If the weekend does not provide what you have already decided you want, will the weekend be supportive or disappointing for you?"

I thought this was very clever, because those who said they had expectations responded with either *supportive or disappointing*, they would again be demonstrating a lack of objectivity. *How can objectivity prevail if the outcome is already predetermined?* Objectivity implies that a person really does not know an outcome and is willing to do what is necessary to find out.

After much discussion, to bring the point about objectivity across, Kayla asked that we all respond, one at a time, to "Do you feel you are equal to us, or do you view yourselves as being higher or lower in the social order?"

I was the first to respond, and my response was that we have balance and symmetry, as a wheel would be. A few noticed my description. Others said they felt they are students, under the scrutiny of judgment of teachers; therefore *lower* on the social scale. Some said they were *higher* because they were *paying for the service* of the psychologists.

Then, in unison, acting on some unseen cue, something uniquely fascinating happened. All three of the psychologists abruptly stood up. They placed their hands behind their backs, and walked around our circle looking down at us. "Now how do you feel about us in relation to you?" Bob assertively asked.

Everyone had something to relate, some intensely. Many felt intimidated, even threatened. One person said she felt that Kayla was menacing! Some said they felt embarrassed because they didn't like anyone studying them. Another person said, "You are judging me and I don't like that!" My mind jumped back to the incident with Father McCarthy in the sixth grade, as if Bob's face had been replaced with that of the angry priest, admonishing me, challenging me – and I related this in some detail.

They returned to their positions as our hub on the floor pillows. Kayla explained, "We are exactly the same people as we were before we stood up. To be neutral and non-threatening, we had our hands behind our backs. Emotional reflexes cause your intense reactions. Triggers cause the reflexes from your pasts; memories recalled of someone standing over you, looking down on you, maybe menacing you. Memories stored in the younger years are not necessarily faithful to the real events, but rather the way the emotions impacted us, how we felt at the time. Emotional triggers are not objective thought-through views of reality. When they occur, you can challenge them as you work to reassemble your perspective – provided you are aware of them, stop, think, and do not automatically respond.

"We hope that this demonstration expanded your awareness of yourselves. This exercise was to demonstrate how invasive reactions might be. Why allow emotional responses to control your life without a basis of reason?"

The discussion that followed was very lively, revealing, and inspired. When my turn came, I exposed my emotional reflex to run and hide, to do anything to avoid confrontation even if that meant giving up on me.

The morning session was nearing an end. Most of us needed a break from the intensity. There was an announcement, *"This afternoon we will meet back here in our circle. Do you all wish to continue? Are you all committed to seeing through this weekend no matter how intense it might be?"* Unanimous: "Yes!"

"Good!" Susan exclaimed. Kayla immediately followed, "There is a condition we require for you all to participate in the session this afternoon. Regretfully, we inadvertently omitted the condition in the flyer you all saw. It is best that we alert you to this omission so we can discuss it now. Remember that the core of our effort is for you to gain increasing knowledge – awareness – of yourself, and that requires being open, free of concealment. *For the session this afternoon, you must all be nude."*

"What?" someone shouted.

It seemed that time stood still. This condition was shocking. No one seemed prepared. Then several people let loose an outpouring of emotion. Some jumped up protesting, loudly proclaiming they would leave immediately and demand their money back.

Bob, making good use of his soothing baritone voice, urged everyone to settle down into our circle, back onto our floor pillows. "Obviously, we need to discuss this," he said. He implied that the condition might be changed.

"Please settle down and return to your pillows," Kayla urged, and with a bit more prodding, everyone did.

Bob said that it was necessary for them to understand the objections before they made a decision to continue with the planned session or not. One by one, they asked each client to report what they experienced when they made the announcement about the nude condition.

Four people simply objected because they were not aware about the requirement, and didn't have time to consider exposing themselves to that extent. One couple said that they were members of a naturalist's resort, and had no objection. A woman, Andrea, exclaimed, *"This is against my religion. It is obscene to be nude in public!"*

About half admitted that they were not satisfied with the way their bodies appeared, with faults ranging across the gamut of deficits that they each felt their bodies displayed. Susan suggested that people hide themselves in many ways, putting on costumes, not just in clothing, but also in the way that they want to conceal their frailties from others. She added, "Many people are not faithful to themselves in the way they reveal their images to others in society. In different ways, people can disguise their authentic nature, all in the attempt of gaining acceptance from others, but with expense to themselves. This can be difficult to manage, because it takes energy to put on different roles for different people. The problem is that when people do this, they really just assume what the other person wants to see from them. Assumptions can be self-defined delusions, so the roles and guises people play might be for naught because they are founded on expectations from others and illusions."

I realized that I had spent considerable energy trying to comport myself to gain the acceptance of others, especially trying to strive for compatibility with my wife and my religious beliefs. I began to realize that this had taken a tremendous toll, pounding on my self-image and natural personality, racking me with guilt for my failures. No matter how much I tried, I continued to fail and this had to stop. Now with the interchange among this group of people, I realized that many people contorted themselves in different ways, to different extents, all to gain acceptance.

In the most nurturing and soothing tones imaginable, Bob addressed each person, followed by Kayla, then in combination, to show the follies that occur when people emphasize others over themselves. Bob and Kayla used a clever dramatic approach. They would role-play with each other, taking a statement or a phrase from each client, and then playing it back between themselves. Sometimes Bob would use the statement to seek Kayla's imaginary approval, and sometimes the reverse. When exposed openly in this way, the follies were obvious, sometimes excruciatingly.

Eventually, they got back to Andrea. Bob asked, "If God created your body, how can your body be obscene? Certainly, we didn't ask you to do anything obscene with your body. Please stay with us for this discussion. We really want to understand." She protested, *"I can't do it! My religion prohibits it!"* Bob asked, "Do you know how to dress yourself?" *"Of course!"* She cried out. "Then you must know how to undress yourself, yes?"

Her emotions were frantic. *"Don't condescend to me like that!"*

"I'm just picking up on something you said," Bob continued. "You said that you can't be nude here with us. You can undress yourself, so what you are actually saying is that you won't do it, not that you can't do it. True?"

Andrea started to say something but became quiet. She seemed to be contemplating what Bob had said, her eyes darting back and forth, working to figure out what next to say, and then Andrea calmly replied, "True. I won't do it. I can, but I won't."

Then Bob added, "Why not? Please tell us again." Andrea responded, "Because my religion." Kayla interrupted before she could justify her statement. "Are you certain that your religion demands that of you, or are you fearful of doing anything that might offend others in your church? Would you like to change your reason?"

Several minutes of silence passed as Andrea gazed at her feet. Then Andrea thoughtfully and softly said, "Yes. I can disrobe, but I won't because I need approval."

Bob addressed Andrea, and all of us, with something to think about by saying, "This teaches us all two things. People will often conceal something they don't want to do, by saying they can't do it, not that they won't do it. The other thing to think about is held in Andrea's last statement, 'I can, but I won't, because I need approval.' When the word 'but' is used in the middle of two phrases, it resets the phrase that went before the 'but' to zero, leaving us with the real message, in this case that she needs approval. Andrea, I am not trying to be harsh. This suggests you are living for the approval of others, even to the point where you don't allow yourself to take an action without approval. Do you really want to continue to live like this, or would you be willing to try and find the freedom to increase your awareness of what you are doing?"

Andrea nodded *"Yes"*, then said, *"I'm here with you because I want to be free. I want to learn how to be free!"* Many in the room smiled, and two women asked to hug Andrea, and did. It was a wonderfully emotional moment, joyous in the tears that all of us shed.

When these emotions had settled down, Kayla addressed all of us: "In case it is not obvious by now, in telling you that you would have to be nude for the session this afternoon, we exceeded your expectations. That means all of you expected that you would have clothes on, that even the possibility of being nude had not entered your minds before now. All expectations, or the lack of them, have some boundaries and we were exploring those boundaries. I can say – now – that you are not required to be nude this afternoon. I admit that we never intended that to be necessary. We intended to provoke your reactions, to cause your emotions to surface, and those reactions will be the subjects of our session this afternoon. Please stay with us, and perhaps you will attain a higher awareness of yourselves."

What a profoundly powerful process! Gather a few comments, ask a few benign questions to gain a preliminary profile of each person, and then become increasingly provocative in proportion to the client's responses. Then, stimulate introspection, and when the client responded with non-rational emotions or conclusions, act as mirrors to reflect the responses and ask the client what they saw in the reflections.

During the next sessions, they expanded their technique of acting out the dramas from the responses they had pulled out of us, their clients. This approach allowed us to view our foibles, guises, and inefficiencies in an enhanced and dramatic way. We became, in effect, *outside observers* of our own dramas, with amazing results. Heavily concealed and veiled issues within others and me became extraordinarily obvious when observed from a position outside of self. We also learned the benefits of group meditation, and of openly sharing our experiences with each other.

I left the weekend retreat profoundly excited at the chance to alter, to change, my negative patterns. I doubted myself, then elated myself, in a back and forth sequence.

I arrived home, and my wife was confrontational. *"What do you mean change?"* she aggressively said. *"If you change, you won't be you! Are these people trying to brainwash you?"* After the elating, enhancing, experience of the weekend, I felt as if she was beating me into submission – or trying to.

"Please go with me to meet them," I begged in a low and con-cerned voice tone. I approached her to gently reassure her with a gentle embrace. We had been through so much together, I was so bound and loyal to her, and it was worth another try. This time, her reaction was surprisingly violent. As I neared her, she struck out at my chest with both her hands, sharply pushing me away, screaming *"Are you crazy?"*

After I calmed down from her stunning reaction, I pleaded sorrowfully: *"Please…they can help us…I feel it…"* only to receive *"You are a maniac! YOU need help!"* from her. She stared me down, and as in so many other times, I just turned away from her, down-cast and defeated – again. By capitulating to her, knowing and not quite wanting to accept that this was a lost cause, I quickly became withdrawn, then depressed – seriously depressed. As in so many times before, she deployed her weapon: the hostility of silence, the hostility of denying not just support or affection, but of all conversation itself.

The contrast between the experience with my wife and the exploration of the retreat weekend was incredible, and it flipped from peak to crater in less than two hours. My body started to react, and I thought *not again* - remembering what happened to my body just before meeting Bob Morella. Emotionally crushed, I repeatedly tried to talk to her, plead with her, fighting my tendency to surrender. She would not respond. If I could not quit the marriage, I would have to quit myself. I realized that depression was a way of life that could kill me and I seriously considered - maybe it should. This time my crater was not like before. It was much more severe, more desperate. Death seemed a viable option, a logical "business management" decision.

In this morass of emotion, I had a very faint glimmer of hope. Something beckoned me, a flickering light that carried a message, I should, at least, try to live. I realized that unlike before, there could be a safety net. Maybe I had resources. Maybe I was not alone.

I picked up the phone and called. Kayla answered. I explained, choking through my sorrow, that *ending it all* would be better than living like this. I explained that ending it seemed like the logical thing to do. Kayla urgently responded, *"Get here as fast as you can. We will get through this. We can do it together!"*

Fighting through my pattern of life to hide and give up, I returned to the mansion. Kayla met me at the door in somber and warming tones, reached out for my hand, and led me upstairs to one of the smaller rooms. I told her the details of what had happened. I explained that I was in a trap, imprisoned by my religious beliefs that I could never divorce, and an environment that was crushing my soul. *Ending it* seemed like a management decision. It was not emotional. It was logical. She soothed me, not with her words but with the intonation of her voice just by saying *"I am very concerned."* At that moment, I didn't believe that anyone had been concerned about me since my childhood with my mother.

Kayla said, "Despite the severity of what happened and what your response has been, your report sounds like a business presentation. That means you have crossed a line when the decision to end-it-all, unemotionally expressed, has a grim determination of logic to seek a solution from pain. Michael, please believe me, there are other solutions than the ultimate one you are considering. If you choose to end it, you will never know what else is possible. Please give yourself a chance – please give us a chance to resolve your issues in partnership with you. Please rest for a moment. I have to do something. I'll be right back. Can I trust you to stay here?"

She held my hands, looked deeply in my eyes until I nodded yes, and left the room closing the door behind her. I felt bewildered. She seemed to be offering concern and support I hadn't experienced in decades. Maybe, just maybe, there was an option other than death. Maybe I just didn't know how to find it. Though tentative, I adjusted myself on the omnipresent floor pillows, and stayed.

Kayla soon returned – with Morgan. Kayla quietly retreated toward the back of the room, as Morgan approached me and settled into floor pillows with me. Kayla said, "Bob, Susan and myself, have already given Morgan our impressions of you from your meeting with Bob and during our retreat."

"Hello", Morgan said as he extended his hands. I reached out and gripped his hands, realizing then I was feeling cold and trembling. Morgan's touch, like Kayla's, was warm and in Morgan's grasp, I felt support. Morgan's deep baritone voice was smoothing like listening to velvet tones framed through his graying beard. His hazel eyes seemed to carry a power, first to nurture and inquire, then to penetrate for an answer as he said: "Michael, you have chosen to make depression a way of life. Your decision to stop living is not new. You have been declining for a long time. Today is just the most recent extension of your decision to extinguish yourself."

"How did you know?"

"Bob told me about what was happening to your body when Dr. Noel's office called him. You have been internalizing yourself, withdrawing from the light of your own love for a long enough time that it has become your way of life. I know your dark crater has been your hiding place because it takes a long time of inwardly directed pain for the body to develop those physiological symptoms."

"My wife's rejection brought me to the decision, to the conclusion, I shouldn't "be" any longer.", I responded feeling defensive.

"No, Michael. That is not sufficient. Somewhere in your life, you made a decision to hide and it became a repetitive pattern. Those decisions do not happen by accident. The choice to hide, to be depressed, was your solution to problems you did not know how to deal with in other ways."

"Morgan, no! I've been compelled to withdraw and accept my inadequacies."

"Who, or what, could possibly compel you? You've been hiding in depression much longer than your wife's rejections. Your pain is much more enduring than your marriage – I can feel it. Was there an event that provoked you to hide? What inadequacies do you believe you have? Why did you make the decision to degrade – to deny – yourself?"

"No! Goddamn it! NO! He commanded me! The EXORCIST…!" I stopped dead amid sentence, just barely beginning to grasp the significance of what I blurted out in my angered defense – something I thought I had buried forever. The room was hushed, and now I was trembling with heat, not cold. Tears were streaming down my cheeks. Morgan's eyes were penetrating my soul, and in the background, I could see Kayla's tears trickling down her face bringing a sort of shared pain, empathic compassion, between us. He reached out and held my hands, clasping them between his and holding me for what seemed to be a long time. Then he said with his deep voice in almost a whisper …..

"What exorcist?"

That did it. My anger, my veneers of staunch resolve to maintain my poise, to end my being, all crashed away. The shards of my life, the shrapnel that had been swirling within me spun out of control like a tornado had consumed my destiny. I broke down into a blithering, disheveled eviscerated mess of slathering tears, of sobbing emotions, to let it all out. I didn't care any more about what my façade might be. This was my "decisive moment", and I just let it all happen.

CHAPTER TEN

RECONSTRUCTION

My body and mind could no longer contain the conflicts that had built up, and there were limits to the pressure that the vessel of my being could sustain. I had reached my limit, not realizing it intellectually, and the pressure burst out in open emotional release. Once the shattered shards and swirling shrapnel had settled, I felt completely exhausted and open because the blast-force pressure release brought the aftermath of calm. I had deconstructed myself into fragments.

"My mother forced me to see an exorcist." I responded. "I had powerful visions and precognitions that seemed to frighten her and she needed reassurance that I was not possessed of evil forces. Those visions, those perceptions, were so overpowering that I realize that they frightened me - though I didn't admit that to myself."

Tearfully, I described the events and feelings I had with the exorcist. When I got to the point of seeing and feeling energetic fields, Morgan asked me to describe them in detail. I did, tentatively, halfway anticipating a "you're deluded" sort of retort. Instead, I could detect a soft smile as he heard my story, as if he understood the meaning of what I was saying. I felt Morgan's acceptance, and I glanced up at Kayla. She was dabbing dry her tears, and our eyes made contact. Her sadness seemed to melt into delight as she stood up to leave the room. She crossed her hands over her heart, held my gaze, and in hushed words I had never before heard, she uttered with a slight bow to me as tears trickled down her cheeks again, *"My God...*she gasped ...*We're the same."* as she turned and left the room.

As overcome as I was in emotion, the connotation of what she said barely registered yet her gestures and tears reinforced my feeling of acceptance. Morgan's voice snapped my attention back toward him.

"How do you feel about having abilities to see, to envision, to perceive in ways that are different?" Morgan probed.

"Isolated...cursed by God's crosses I have to carry." I responded as my feelings captured me and softly trailed off, and I thought about trying to hide.

"Hiding is not acceptable here – it accomplishes nothing!" Morgan insisted as if he already knew what I was inclined to do. "How can we work together if you're hiding in your shell?" I looked up and tried to stare into his eyes – and failed. His eyes penetrated my attempt to conceal myself.

He continued: "How can abilities, talents you hold, be a curse?"

I haltingly said, "Society doesn't understand empathic perception, precognitions, visions and the ability to feel and understand beyond words."

Morgan questioned my conclusion: "Why not accept yourself and develop your abilities? Has it occurred to you that these attributes are gifts you can use to develop yourself? Talents like music are developed because they are acceptable by society and necessary for your own fulfillment."

"Music? Strange you would mention music! Piano sustained me emotionally through private expression and my original compositions when everything else failed.", I reflected my feelings to him.

Morgan had an uncanny ability to bring up details locked within me, seeming to have just the right question ready to ask, even while I was working on responding to his questions. I related how my history of musical abilities had become interwoven into my fabric, and not even allowing myself pleasure at the accolades others would heap on me.

"Now that you have linked your musical composition and piano to abilities, why make any distinction from that to any other ability? Have you considered that if you developed your perceptional abilities you might free your soul to attain your ultimate achievement? Think about reconsidering your position about responsibilities. It is your responsibility to change society?"

"NO!"

"Could it be your responsibility to develop yourself – for yourself and NOT for society, or even God?"

"I've never considered that. I wasn't programmed to do it. I've just hidden…"

"How do you feel when you hide?'

"Isolated, fear of being discovered, pain."

"Then why hide?"

"To be safe.", I weakly responded.

Morgan continued to press forward despite my weak responses. "How can isolation, fear, and pain be safe? How can withdrawal from yourself and depression be safe? You hide and have pain! How can PAIN be SAFE? Those practices have almost cost you your life! THINK! Your approach only led you into conflict with yourself!"

Sheepishly, I said, "Yes. I suppose that's true."

Morgan did not let up. "The exorcist did not teach you to hide – you must have already known how to hide. WHEN did you start hiding?"

I looked up into those penetrating eyes, and I realized that I could not escape his call to responsibility. I wanted to run. Something in Kayla's utterance as she left the room had captured me, though I didn't quite understand what. I had to make a choice: stay here and respond; or flee and fail. Morgan again snapped my attention, insisting: *"Well, when?"*

I struggled to think back. The pressure Morgan was exerting was unfamiliar, discomforting; yet it was clear, and clarity felt good.

"When I first started school."

"Started school?", he queried.

"I felt terrible fear. I had never played with children, never been away from my mother. I was incompetent at social interaction with children. I felt worthless, trying to make myself acceptable to others and not succeeding. I had no interest in sports. I knew nothing about sports, and every one else seemed to be active in sports. The intellectual concepts my mother taught me offered no basis to build friendships with other children, leaving me isolated. I made the decision to become invisible to them so I hid in my own depression."

"How is that possible?

"World War II isolated my parents from each other, and me from society in my very early years.", I responded. I began to recognize what patterns had been set up in my life so incredibly long ago.

"I spent my first years on my grandfather's ranch in isolation from children." My response blathered out the detail of my early years, about not knowing I had a father until he showed up – a stranger to me – and doing my best to explain my incompetence at social intermixing with peers of my age, and my terrors with bullies that culminated in being kidnapped and thrown into the ocean.

When I paused, he said: "Do you know how to do brain surgery?" The question struck me as irrelevant, completely out of context of what was happening, and that irritated me.

"No! I do not know how to do brain surgery! What has that got to do with anything?"

"Everything. Do you feel incompetent, guilty, worthless, or depressed because you don't know how to do brain surgery?"

"NO!" I responded harshly! "I've never learned it, don't want to learn it, and I can't be incompetent at something I've never even been inclined to learn – let alone practice it!"

"Then why do you feel incompetent at dealing with your peer group? Your family kept you safe. You were in isolation from your peer group your age, and were not taught or prepared for social interactions. Why would you feel incompetent for something you didn't learn – and even didn't know HOW to learn?"

My first reaction to this exchange was befuddlement. Morgan was throwing things at me that wholly caught me off guard, and I struggled to grasp the point. Then, I got it: "Oh my God. Not only had I not learned, I hadn't learned how to learn."

"Why have you carried this burden for so long?"

I paused and thought deeply, and started to tear again at my own folly…. "Because hiding was all I knew to do. I thought it was safe." I broke down again, sobbing, realizing what had happened.

I took a deep breath and dumped out all I could gather in my thoughts, no matter how turbulent my emotional responses were. If my response even vaguely hinted at being negative to me, he assertively would stop me and get me to *think*. Morgan would not allow me to hide in failure or to replace reason with unthinking emotion.

Morgan left the room, and reappeared with two glasses of water and a fresh box of tissue. After we drank and chatted about unrelated things, like the mansion's history and the landscaped grounds, he started again – taking me a bit by surprise.

"What have you based you life on?"

"Responsibilities to be in God's grace – that I have also failed – trying to shape myself so others would accept me."

"Since when can you speak for God?"

"Throughout my life, I've been taught and instructed about what God expects of me! I've accepted that He forces me to carry crosses of burden to follow his will. If I lived up to His demands, I would be in His grace and go to heaven. When I failed, I would go to eternal damnation, and on matters of sexual thoughts, I would often fail. My guilt has consumed me. I married young to be in His grace. God sent me to an unresponsive wife as punishment for my failure to expunge sexual thoughts. No matter what I tried to do to meet God's goals, I am condemned because I've failed to carry the burdens God has given me."

Morgan held up his hands, and then reached down to touch my hands. He took a deep breath, uttered a comment that sounded like *my heavens*, and looked away from me. Turning back toward me, he locked his eyes into mine. He had a sorrowful expression on his face.

"Did God tell you these things?" He asked with a sigh.

"Not directly. God speaks through His priests, His sisters who are Brides of Christ, and an order of Brothers from Ireland in high school carried His message through his Church. Once I humiliated myself in front of my class because I asked a question of Father McCarthy."

"*Father McCarthy?* What humiliation?" Morgan asked.

I related what had happened in my encounter with Father McCarthy, and how I reflexively learned to pile that experience to the heap of events that I had hidden in my life. My story extended to the corporeal punishment we received at the hands of the Brothers. My conclusion was that even my continual fear of even entering the schoolyard was also punishment for my failures. I told him about the motorcycle accident that almost claimed my life, and that probably it was punishment for my sins as well. I smiled and said that at least the extreme unction I received had helped wash away my sins to that point. The smile didn't last because I admitted to again having impure thoughts and unrequited love in my marriage.

Morgan paused as if he did not know what to say. Then, in the velvet tones of his soft baritone voice he said: *"And you believed them in every literal way…………."*

"Yes, of course. What else could I do? Their message is all I know." I started to tremble as if lighting would strike me down at any moment as though it would be God's will.

Morgan again touched my hands. That touch comforted me as we sat in silence. I started to introspect and relive the dreadful experience with Father McCarthy, and my tears were flowing again. As I reached for the tissue box, Morgan said:

"Now I understand why we're together. When you entered school, you came from isolation into situations you did not know how to handle, so you withdrew and learned to hide from others and from yourself. The exorcist tried to help you understand that your abilities were natural for you, but that you'd have to conceal yourself because society would not understand. The admonishment of the exorcist validated your decision to hide. Father McCarthy's condemnation added emphasis to your decision. The unbendable rules of the church, as you understood them, added eternal damnation into the equation of controls foisted upon you. The only glint of light you saw to be yourself happened while you were in the field of foggy translucent light after your nearly fatal motorcycle accident, and you didn't know how to deal with that. I'll bet it wasn't an accident. You recently concluded that you needed to leave your marriage, and were willing to suffer eternal damnation for that, or commit suicide and suffer the same fate. Your history and religious training have given you few options."

Morgan's statements rang true, and I responded, "Yes, my death is logical because it simply brings the inevitable to the point. No reason to drag this out any longer."

"Michael", Morgan said with tears forming in his eyes, "I can assure you there are options other than death. Are you willing to consider that what you have been taught to understand, that you have used as tenets of your life, are incorrect?"

"How can it be incorrect?" I pleaded, trying to grasp his meaning.

"What would happen if you learned that the messages you've believed in all of your life, doctrines against your nature, are not messages from God? What would be the result for you if those messages were from humans seeking to control you for their purposes?"

"My God. Everything would change, I exclaimed. I would have to learn who I truly am and how to live for myself. I would have to find my own path, not the path dictated to me. Can I do this?"

"Do you need permission?" Morgan gently asked.

"Yes."

"Then you have my permission, and I'm very confident that you have the support of everyone here as well. Are you willing to try and learn to not just live but to thrive?"

The prospect offered a hope that truly captured me. I had no clue about what it would take, but I thought that Morgan's guidance could give me a new perspective on life. I broke down – again - and cried, this time in the tears of hope. Emotionally drained, it was comforting that someone actually seemed to care about what had happened to me, and better yet, I gained a sense of confidence that holistic psychologists could help me.

Morgan seemed concerned when he asked: "Can I trust that you can leave here today, and you'll come back as much and as often as required to learn who you are, to open your mind and reconstruct your philosophy of life?"

"I'll try."

"No. That is not good enough. I want your commitment." Morgan moved to the door and called down the hallway to Kayla. I could her the patter of her bare feet against the oak floor as she jogged toward our room. As she entered, Morgan said, "Kayla, Michael is struggling with making his commitment to alter his life as he engages with us."

Kayla said, "Michael, maybe for the first time in your life, you have found others who are like you. We have struggled to find our own identities as individuals, and we have learned to help others do the same."

"Kayla, when you left the room before, I heard you say 'we are the same' but I don't understand what that means."

"For now, please be assured that it means we have sought the tools of objectivity that are required to learn who we are. Remember your feelings during our retreat. Remember your feelings when you first met Bob. Beyond that, we have attributes that you will find in yourself."

"I feel I can trust that." I said, "I have feelings of belonging here and acceptance, that I've never had before, except with my mother."

"We can do this together if you will consider that we are partners, not controllers, and if you will commit to yourself. Do we have your commitment, which is to yourself?"

I halted for a moment, and suddenly realized that this might be the only opportunity I would have to change my life.

"You have my commitment. I really don't have a choice, other than ultimately failing."

Kayla opened her arms, and the glistening in her eyes with her gentle smile felt like love as she approached me and said: *"May we embrace?"*

"Yes." The emotions of acceptance and warmth seemed to light up the room and I bathed in that glory.

It was a very long, intense, and utterly exhausting day. Yet, they had sown some seeds of change in me. Clearly, in just a few hours, I had lifted from the depths of horrible despair to a light of possibility. As I left the mansion that evening, I began to envision that I could turn my life into something more than it had ever been. I was determined to find the resolve I needed to deal with my wife, and not sink myself into the depths of depression, but it still felt like I was perched on a slippery slope.

There would be many more days and sessions similar to the first one, working through exchanges of pointed questions and my responses, then more questions probed out of my responses. Morgan, or Kayla and occasionally Morgan with Kayla, would not accept even a nuance of my return to hiding. When I attempted to degrade myself, a sharp retort would soon follow. Naysaying, victim mentality, or concealment of my emotions was never accepted.

Sometimes I would leave a session with Morgan with deep appreciation and affection for him. Other times my emotions would furiously rage when he prodded something out that I did not want to admit, acknowledge, or deal with. When I made a breakthrough of recognition and understanding, I would rejoice in the wonder of my self-discovery.

I gleaned a sense that my malleable human mind was initially stuck in a routine of self-directed negativity that was working like an addictive drug! The addiction was a preconceived or preset routine of emotional patterns or behavior that had taken years to establish. Breaking out of *an addictive mental chemistry pattern* even though it is a self-imposed loop, can be a tumultuous task.

In a way, the oscillations that cycled my emotions between elation and withdrawal expressed during this phase of my development, seemed to be yet another pattern of addiction. With continued intent, I applied myself to delve into the deepest recesses of my mind. I became determined to pry out memories of events, inadvertently established early in my life. Morgan would not let me off the hook for anything. He would persist until reason, not self-degrading excuses, prevailed.

Each event that I could identify took determination and often courage to bring to the surface to recapitulate them, no matter how emotional my reactions. Recalling and inspecting my embedded memories with the help of Morgan's probing, enabled me to learn how those events imprinted emotional reactions in me that scattered my mind into needless emotions. I accepted that my reactions that led me into self-negations were consequences of not only events, but also how I had imprinted emotional responses within my mind. My primary issues seemed to fall under the categories of fear, angers, withdrawal and ultimately depression, all of which hammered down my self-esteem. I came to understand that the concept of learned responses, many that I had taught myself, were not authentic to my natural core of being, causing much conflict and confusion.

I gradually learned how to make my self-interrogation take on a pattern: Why am I reacting in a particular way? Why do I have the reflexive need to react? Can I recall when I first experienced the reaction, and what caused it?

By working through each response, I was increasingly becoming proactive for my evolution and *each point of self-discovery increasingly began to form a pattern of knowledge about myself.*

I must admit that in gleaning a sense of progress, emerging out of my crater, at first stirred up old tornadoes of fear and consternation. When an emotion of elation would temporarily occur, I would intentionally subdue that glorious feeling by covering it with uncertainty and fear.

Morgan and Kayla had an arsenal of methods to use with me. Guided meditation tended to help me set up what I'd call an intensely directed focus. For example, by guiding me to imagine a light source directed toward one part of the body, my mind would "feel" the warmth of the light, and connectivity between mind and body was elevated. With practice, the mind-body connection developed to be very specific. As these skills developed, I could focus my will and make temperature changes in my body that were measurable (with a thermometer) and felt at a specific fingertip. With practice, I could direct my meditative focus and cause a fingertip to become measurably hotter or colder. I found these focusing skills very easy to develop: they seemed simply "natural" to me.

As I progressed toward changing the way I viewed life, nature, religion, and God to reconstruct my sense of myself, it became obvious that I was replacing my view of passive religious precepts with proactive concepts. The blind-beliefs of churchianity were being replaced with belief in myself, in my use of reason, in my innate ability to trust, love, and be myself – for myself – not to distort myself to gain the acceptance of others, or of religious or social authorities. I increasingly realized that I had distorted my natural self to worship not God, but impossible tenets of religion itself. When I studied history not offered to me all the way through high school, I was aghast to realize what had happened in the name of "god" during the "inquisition", the crusades, and in the persecution of able men of reason such as Galileo Galilei and even my ancestor. I was surprised, now removed from parochial school, to learn how, when, and who assembled the bible. I increasingly distanced myself from any form of churchianity.

During my time with Morgan, he would occasionally gather groups of his clients together who were at compatible levels in their processes as they gained knowledge of themselves. For some of us, as our development ascended, the meditation experiences within the specific client group advanced to become empathic among us. We could empathically feel each other's internal sensations and emotions. At the height of these gatherings, a few of us could participate in each other's experiences as if we were in the same dream state together. These experiences and sensations combined to become simultaneous, mutual, and profoundly intimate among ourselves, even though we were strangers to each other in our everyday lives.

It was during a retreat one weekend with Bob and Kayla, during a sequence of guided meditation experiences with other clients very well aligned with my personal progress, that I began to experience a beauty in nature that I had not realized before. In my mind, I projected myself, my conscious vision, into the molecular level of plants, of animals, and eventually to others in the room with me. I could easily envision the molecular movements, the flow of blood and chemical interactions, and the electric field structures that bind all matter together. Once projected into the structures, I would slowly zoom myself out to view the surfaces, then the whole of the being or object, and then view the entirety of the surrounding environment. While enjoying the beauty and probing into the detail of my own body one afternoon, something incredible occurred to me – like a news flash. A deity was not required for this magnificence of nature to happen! It could occur through natural processes and dynamically adaptive interactions: evolution.

My technical training revealed ample evidence that the structures of the universe itself provided the ingredients of all matter, whether organic or inorganic. Maybe, just maybe I thought, "god" was actually the energy and movement of nature, maybe the forces of the universe itself. If that were true, "god" exists within me, in all beings, and in all life and matter. At first, this was a frightening thought. How dare I defy the "god" I had so long served? I faced this formidable emotional challenge with courage, and eventually came to decide that "the god" that had so controlled me was a figment of my religious indoctrination.

At one point, still seeking to close the gap that was growing wider and wider with my wife, I did manage to persuade her to join with me to meet Morgan. Though she was polite initially during our meeting, when it came time to engage with Morgan she just sat on a chair, crossed her arms, and became silent. As she sat down, she said, *"If I changed, I wouldn't be me,"* the same comment of defiance that I had heard before. Morgan, to his credit, tried to reach beyond the emotional barriers that my wife had set up. He probed her to learn what had happened during her childhood, and she claimed to have no memory before about 9 years of age. That something, or things, happened to her before then became obvious. That her memories were so incredibly buried they were inaccessible also became obvious. She would not permit even attempting to learn about herself - wholly closed to exploration.

The ever-widening gap of incompatibility between us could not be closed. I realized that it might not have *ever been* closeable and when I finally accepted that, I knew the marriage had ended. We were now two very different people, and the tenets of our beliefs could no longer bind us together. My compulsion became to learn who I am by removing the vestiges of the religious beliefs and denigrations that trapped me. After almost two decades of effort, I realized that this was still a formidable task, and that I would have to leave the marriage, to not only continue this work, but also simply to survive.

I decided to accept Morgan as my mentor. I eventually learned that he was also a practicing Episcopalian priest. With his understanding and knowledge of religious and church teachings, what I have come to call *churchianity*, he helped guide my way through my confusion and conflict with churchianity and religion. Morgan's approach did not fall back on the fables of *faith*, or unreasoned blind beliefs of a faith-based system. The replacements for those ideologies were reason and epistemology, not dictum or dogma.

The energy of life, the spirit of being that churchianity, as I understood it, ascribed to God, was already within humans, seeking to be released. Increased awareness was the key to this release: first of the events that happened; then of my reactions; then of the consequences of my reactions, in a process of evolving knowledge in place of inadvertence. Throughout my history, I had learned to disassociate myself from my true nature, even before I could fully grasp what my authentic nature was. What might have started out to be trusted love of self under nurturing circumstances slowly became loathing and distrust. As knowledge of myself increased, I began to learn how to love without dependency and that slowly developed my trust in my of my ability to use reason and think things through, and trust my decisions.

As clients of the psychologists, we learned that as we attained awareness of our reactions, not merely accepting them on face value, we could work through processes of crosschecking any emotional response to our experiences with whatever stimulated the experience and then understanding the consequences of these responses. We were gaining knowledge of ourselves, which is a deeply abiding realization because we had become very aware of what worked well to promote positive results, and what failed. Knowledge of self through elevated awareness, opened up our objectivity to monitor our reactions, and compare those self-discoveries to our histories, allowing me, allowing us, to move forward in my (and our) development.

This significantly gave me the one permission I desperately needed, previously denied, or had hidden from myself. I needed to openly proclaim: I am an individual; the advancement of my consciousness, my attainment of awareness and spirituality is solely my responsibility! The sowing of the seeds in my mind for this concept happened during my first clinical death experience as a teenager, and now I had a mentor to help me actively understand that responsibility.

Morgan rarely worked with groups. When he did, it was when we reached more advanced levels of attainment. These groups were intense forms of Gestalt sessions, in which Morgan would direct inquiry and challenge to each person individually. The remainder of the group would simply perceive and observe.

This arrangement carried a strict discipline. He would start engaging with an individual, then probe and inveigle until whatever conflict or emotional inefficiency within that individual became exposed, sometimes explosively in emotion. If one member wished to communicate with another, he or she would make a request, and allowed only on a one-to-one basis and only by mutual consent. From our interaction with our mentor during these sessions, it was obvious that he was an incredibly perceptive individual. He could detect things and responses before anyone openly disclosed them. It became obvious that he was an empath, and my personal identification with him became profound.

We called the permissions to engage with each other, or for that matter with our mentor, *contracts* to communicate. This process is drastically different from that of a *group encounter* that can degrade into a noisy chaotic situation.

The energy and emotional releases during these sessions were unequivocally magnificent and profound. One member in the group might sense high or internalized emotion within another person. That person, with mutual consent, would stand and physically touch the one with perceived internalized emotional blocks. Almost immediately, that emotion would burst forth, released into an envelope of expansive and empathic compassion. We, as clients, had learned that it was sheer folly to try to conceal our internalized components from our mentor: his empathic ability could easily probe through the foils of our silly guises. We also eventually learned it was folly to try to conceal ourselves from one another. As our awareness expanded, so did our perceptional abilities.

I am quite confident that no one participating in these processes remained unaltered. The mansion, Morgan, the holistic psychologists had become a safe environment for us to explore and expand ourselves. This expansion was the very antithesis of my crater. I found the process of expansion to be simultaneously intriguing, elating, stimulating and emphatically challenging. Eventually, with increasing attainment through self-knowledge, my internal feelings positively energized, increasing to the state where I dropped my defenses and allowed myself to feel euphoric. The more unburdened I became from the entanglement of the negativity I carried, the more my mind opened to embrace concepts of my evolution. Allowing myself more freedom to feel, I became open to the thought that I could evolve to be emotionally released, as if I could connect to all of the universe as a spiritual form with no connections to my physical being.

The raw and basically shared human exchanges that we experienced as a result of our effort with Morgan, were above and far beyond those found in only verbal exchanges. As we progressed over years, verbal conversation per se as the base of communication became less and less significant, giving way to sensing empathic feelings that are included in what I call *perception*. It was a phenomenal experience to be that undefended, and that exposed, yet confident and secure.

My sequentially revealed layers, over time, displayed my authenticity. I began to recognize the systemic traps to which I had fallen prey. I dug deep into the core of my being with the guidance of the holistic group over several years and uncovered the influences that brought me perilously close to self-annihilation. From these illuminating sessions, a new fundamental psychology emerged. I began to reconstruct myself to encompass and embrace an acceptance of my true nature. Although frail and faltering at times, I increasingly began to believe and trust in myself.

I learned to love the fundamental essence of who I am and to respect and have conviction in my thoughts, abilities and my moral precepts. I would no longer allow guilt to control and manipulate my actions. I would no longer substitute faith for reason, or delude myself that fulfillment was found in service of others or god. I would not sacrifice my love or my values to any other person's control. My life belongs to me; I would no longer submit my independence for acceptance in the view of others. I had reached a point of my expansion where I was comfortable with my volitional choices.

I learned to choose to live my life as a thinking being: a life of rational comprehension, no longer following societal and religious doctrines. I discerned that the lowest morality was to preach that mankind's existence has no value, that I had no value, unless in servitude of others. Accepting the truth about myself became recognition of reality and that led to reason as my path to knowledge.

The tenets of my life became to think and reason before I act, to trust in my purpose and to love my self unconditionally, and that set the bar for my ability to love and trust others without dependency upon their reactions to me. Although emotions are inherent in humanity, I would disarm involuntary emotions to control my responses to life. Their content and their origins and causations are explicit in my mind, and I now determine my choice of reaction by volition.

With the burdens of my mental torments understood I was released to explore and discover the beauty that was the essence of my being, and that, to me, is expressed in one word: freedom.

After several years of gradual progress, Morgan setup a private session with me. The events of that session would alter my life, attitude, and state of being: *Forever.*

CHAPTER ELEVEN

COMMENCEMENT

T hrough the years of working and interacting with the holistic psychologists, I learned to wholly open up myself and release all of my being into the trusted environment that they provided for me. I had finally overcome my automatic reflex to hide.

Those of us who attained this level of development had no need to protect or defend, even within ourselves. We called our state of being *freedom,* because we had freed ourselves from the burdens of fear, defense, angers, dependencies on automatic responses based on blind beliefs, and the conflicts they caused. We could be open to explore whatever and wherever our conscious and unconsciousness minds would take us.

I must emphasize that all of our processes had to be natural and volitional. We *totally prohibited,* and consequently never used, mind stimulating or mind-altering substances of any kind. Looking back, I can see that we had been losing our dependencies in order to become open to the universe.

While driving to the mansion on one fateful day, I knew only that Morgan and I were going to have a more advanced session. I had no idea how advanced or profound the session would be.

Morgan indicated to me that he believed I was ready to take the next step: to fully release myself. At the time, of course, I didn't know exactly what that meant, but we had been connected to each other for years, and I trusted him, not in blind beliefs but based on proven experience. We had peeled off many layers of impediments and obstructions that had ensnared the core of my being, as I described in the last chapter, which religions would say is my soul. By that time, given all of the other experiments, explorations, and experiences of self-exposure, I had some vague idea of what *full release* might mean.

I felt energized, but with mild anxiety about what might happen – specifically about what transitions might occur. I also had some minor, but persistent residual doubts, wobbles in my self-esteem. I knew that if doubt surfaced, it could be very distracting and therefore counterproductive. I reflected upon what I had learned during my first weekend retreat: Do not carry expectations; be observant; and live in the moment, free to learn by exploration. Because of my years with Morgan and the group gathered around him, there was sufficient trust and self-confidence to simply allow it all to occur, whatever that might be. I knew that I had already experienced various transitions, including one clinical death during the motorcycle accident. Despite any doubt or anxiety I might have had, I was determined not to permit fear to inhibit my evolution, which was now my ultimate commitment to myself.

I entered the mansion to find Morgan downstairs, in one of the larger rooms. Morgan motioned me to position myself on the surface of a cushioned and elevated table. It had the general appearance of a massage table. When we had originally set up the schedule for this appointment, my mentor had explained the ideas and concepts of Wilhelm Reich, which related to what would be happening today.

Morgan had asked, "Have you heard of Reich, who had worked with Freud?" I admitted that I had not. In fact, I had read very little about any psychological concepts, though I had studied some philosophy since it was the backbone of early science.

Morgan continued, "Reich had the idea that humans could connect to the energy that permeates the universe."

"That would suggest energetic spiritual connection," I commented, "and many others, including philosopher-physicists through the last several hundred years, held these concepts. The implication that 'God is within us' could be a metaphysical form of energy that is spiritual – of the spirit."

"Reich erred though," Morgan continued. "He believed that only sexual release could connect the energy of self into the universe. Reich became very controversial and largely discredited, partly because he believed that without that sexual connection, neuroses would develop.

"We are going to invigorate your mind-body connection, as we have before, and explore what may occur if this is advanced to a highly energetic level. It could be called neo-Reichian, because your mind is your consciousness and your spirit could be magnified using the energy developed in your body."

The adventure that day started with a form of guided meditation. The idea was to focus and then connect my mind to the molecular level of my body and alter it. *Altering* meant redirecting energies produced and held within the body. We started into a deep breathing ritual that increasingly became deeper, more frequent, and consciously under control. My abilities, from years of guided mediation, had become well honed and developed. As I connected with my energetic flows, I could feel changes in my body.

During the patterned breathing, Morgan asked that I focus my mind first into the lower extremities of my body, my feet, to attempt to grasp the life force flowing there. Morgan was standing by my side. He extended the palms of his hands above my feet. We, as clients, had learned to use energetic projection from our hands as our normal method to start up connection between us. By directing my focus to feel Morgan's energy, first as warmth and then as a sparkling electric exchange, my mind-body link occurred easily. When my link was secure, Morgan moved his hands away.

The feeling became intense to the point where I could connect with the heat I felt in my feet, and redirect it upward toward my torso. My feet became colder, and the area above my ankles warmer. The temperature then could be gathered and moved toward my knees. The goal of this gradual process was to bring my physiological sensations away from my extremities, then into the core of my body, then toward my mind. My feet, then legs, then torso, became very cold as the thermal concentration moved toward my mind.

Over a period of perhaps half an hour, much of my energy became concentrated in and around my mind. My body started to tremble, feeling cold, because I had shifted my thermal balance; yet, the room was its normal temperature. I started to question what I was doing. I had never experienced this magnitude and power of my mind-body connection before. "Morgan?" I called out, needing reassurance.

"You're okay." His voice said from behind me. "Keep your rhythm. Hold your focus. Don't stop now – I can see from your aura, you're doing well."

I hadn't noticed that Morgan had relocated to a position behind my head and seated in chair. I arched my neck and my back slightly so I could look over my forehead and clearly see him looking at my face. His eyes locked into my eyes, and in one extensive and protracted moment looking toward him, I had an amazing vision of aura emanating from both of us. I can clearly recall the color striations and the intensities. They were breathtakingly beautiful. I had lived through these effects decades before – with the exorcist, and at various times with my mother. This time, it was incredibly interpersonal between Morgan and me, wondrously phenomenal. *It felt as if my body had become a launching platform for my soul.*

I realized that my consciousness was being altered, ready to move away, even launch from my body shell. My attention returned to

Morgan's aura because I wanted to capture all of this experience: fully aware, fully involved. On the immediate boundary around Morgan's body, there was a foggy-looking layer of bright white. Circumscribing that was a striation of cadmium blue. Then came a comparatively thin layer of bright red. The outermost layer was an incredibly brilliant mantle of gold that seemed to electrically stream itself out as corona into the universe. Interspersing with Morgan's field was my own, which appeared to be primarily striations of blue, like a deepening blue gradient on the distant horizon at sunset.

Most of us have seen artwork of religious figures with halos. The visions that I was experiencing were similar in appearance, though the expansion and brilliance was far greater than anything I'd ever seen portrayed by artists.

As a child, I had often perceived color auras around others as noted in my description about my encounter with the exorcist. The auras of most individuals, when there was any aura at all that I could detect, appeared as a fog of aqua-white. The aura that was around my mother, though, was usually royal blue migrating to lighter blue, with red striations and filaments.

In contrast, the sheer brilliance of Morgan's aura was something I had never witnessed before. Empathic feelings developed as these events unfolded. Our fields felt as if they were permeating all of my being, and his, to the extent that an interpersonal merging was happening.

I uttered, "Wow!" He smiled gently at my utterance! I felt his joy.

Then, in an instant, my consciousness suddenly flung out of the confines of my body. I suspect, though I really don't know, that Morgan had used a fraction of his energy to add to mine. The only thing that matters is that it catapulted me out of my physical confinement! My very first feeling upon the launch of my consciousness was simply that of a surprising thrill. This, though, settled into fascination, followed by realizing I had moved from being entranced, to being amazed, and then to a level of unprecedented elation.

I soon found that I could navigate around the room though at first, I would overshoot my intended position, and had to work to stabilize where I wanted to hover. I could clearly see the details of the room from a position near the vaulted ceiling, which was quite high in the mansion. I watched my mentor, standing near my body. I could see that he was following my movement, which was responding to my will. The motion was slow, like a scene studied through the lens and careful motion of a panoramic camera.

As I adjusted to my new state of being, I experimented with using my will to navigate around the room while I continued to observe my mentor. He seemed to be a kind of *lighthouse* for me, a signal-beacon that I could use as a reference point. There were red and gold filaments of his aura linking to me, dancing and twirling in the space between us. "Magnificent!" I thought.

Unlike my first experience of clinical death during the motor-cycle crash, the view now was very clear, not diffused in an image of white fog or light. Now, in contrast to the crash experience, I also sensed my own aura.

Eventually, the experience seemed to have run its course. Morgan attempted to persuade me back into my body.

I had become enthralled with my state of being, I must confess, and did not want to return. The freedom, the expansion of peace, was a very powerful incentive not to return. I had never before experienced this magnitude of feeling: unconditional love of self, of the powerful magnificence of being, as I did during that afternoon with the help of my mentor. The thought occurred to me: "Having attained this state, why be confined in an organic body with its illnesses and structural hardships?"

As I experimented moving myself about the room, the filaments interconnecting me to my mentor captured my attention. I noticed that when I repositioned myself, my end of the filaments would tenaciously swirl and snap around, adapting to the change I had willed. As my confidence grew, I worked to try to reposition myself at different speeds to see how the filaments would react! What fun!

After my playtime with the filaments and motions had satisfied my curiosity, I relaxed and my mind drifted toward expansive thoughts!

"What were the possibilities for this new ability? Do I possess this ability all by myself or do I need Morgan's support? Wow! I love this feeling!" I deliberately lingered in this state of euphoric splendor. I wondered: "Could a temporal crack in the universe open to show me the potential of my energy and mind? Are space and thought actually separate energetic forms? This experience may be only the beginning, the first step to learn how to open that crack. How could I extend my being beyond the confines of this room? Could I gain greater control? What was my ultimate destiny?" As these questions surfaced, I became inspired to commit myself with renewed exuberance to further exploration.

Years later, during my spiral into a new death sequence in Yellowstone Park, I would finally find the answer to that question, but now, I had no desire to leave this *safe environment with my mentor,* of my projected consciousness, my state of free being.

At some introspective level, however, I had the presence of mind to realize that I was still a novice. Reason prevailed over elation with one logical thought: "An experience of one event, aided by a mentor, does not an independent expert make."

I noted the clock on the desk. I was learning that I had complete control over my state of being and of my decision-making, but I could sense that my mentor had an increasing concern. He was still gesturing for me to return. The filaments that connected us were tugging at me, but I was still reluctant to let go of the experience. My freedom from confinement in the body, my new state of being, lasted 30 to 45 minutes before I reluctantly made my decision to return.

Then came the shock! It occurred immediately as I reentered my body. My body was quite inhospitable, seeming to be freezing cold, and having spasms. My heart rate was quite low. My reaction was: "I'll fling myself back out!"

"No! You're not ready!" Morgan said as he detected my thoughts. He was hovering over me, his hands above my chest, like a guard to protect me from doing anything impulsive.

"Be patient. There is much more for you to learn. You have to earn this ability for yourself."

Reentry required considerable time, perhaps half an hour or more, probably because of my reluctance. The state of my body reminded me of the temporary paralysis from the motorcycle crash two decades before. As was the case then, the immobile body is a very small prison for an active and impassioned mind. (And an imprisoned mind, locked into a crater of self-deprecation, is an even smaller prison cell of solitary confinement.) It would require more than a day for my metabolism to rebalance and stabilize.

On that afternoon Morgan had orchestrated the projection of my consciousness into a state of free being. That feat represented the ceremony of my attainment: my commencement. I strove to dedicate my life to learn and earn that attained state of being for myself.

In the time frame surrounding my commencement, my clients synergistically provided opportunities for me to expand my development through mentoring many protégés, and marvelously, Rosy and I started to develop our relationship. Exploring and embracing our evolving partnership worked perfectly in synchronism to support my growth attained through the inspiration and methods learned from the holistic psychologists. My life became exhilarating, and forming an extended family with her children dynamically added even more depth and experience to my development and to hers. As we worked to understand and resolve the emotional triggers historically set in place by our interactions with previous partners, Morgan and Kayla continued to be touchstones, references upon which we could rely to help us resolve our frailties when needed.

About three years into our relationship, Morgan donned his priestly attire and gloriously officiated our marriage ceremony, which represented the culmination of our most recent evolutionary ramp of attainment.

Plateaus frequently follow ramps of personal growth and in the plateaus, individuals and couples (in our example) learn to integrate and balance the experiences gained during each ramp into their lives. During the plateau, an individual builds a new foundation for life, often through tests and trials that challenge, stimulate, and inspire a person to apply what they've learned in a process that demands constant self-vigilance. If vigilance is neglected the individual may wobble before the foundation solidifies, and regress to some level below the plateau.

Approximately five years after our marriage (and fourteen years after I first met Bob Morella) I wobbled and reinitiated my reflex to hide, to withdraw with emotional stress, conflict and tension, and my body responded once again - this time with cardiovascular-symptoms. Rosy insisted I visit a specialist, and again the medical analysis showed no reason for my blood pressure and heart rate to have ascended to threatening levels. Perceptions, and my renewed unwillingness to deal with them, were partly responsible for my deterioration through conflict, and I had reverted into self-denial: old habits are hard to break.

I realized that mediation and peace of mind are keys to balancing the mind and body, and I had to faithfully apply the methods attained through Bob, Morgan and Kayla to my life. As I moved through life over the next few years I maintained my vigilance, and increased my sensitivity to using my body as a "signal flag" alerting me to bring purpose into action: lesson learned. In those years, I managed to live my life in a delicate balance between accepting my abilities to perceive, while suppressing my reactions to precognition - until that fateful day in the shearing forces of the hot desert wind, when standing on the rift precipice of the Canyon Muerto in the Defiance Plateau.

Observation

Extrication from craters or from automatic responses to belief systems is not effective if the person simply substitutes one "blind belief system" for another. Knowledge about what has occurred to cause a person to be the way they are comes through an incremental sequence. The sequence starts with an acceptance that one's emotions and reactions are causing issues that degrade one's feeling about oneself.

With that acceptance, a person next would make a decision to seek solutions. Solutions are found through introspection and the resolve to change. Yet, if negative self-image or emotional reactions are pervasive enough, outside assistance may be required. The goals are to replace one's automatic responses with introspection and reason that, in turn, builds up trust and love in oneself. Trust and love, the ingredients of self-respect, together form a new belief: the belief in oneself. With that belief as a foundation, an individual can learn to be free of the tendency to live for the acceptance of others or of institutions, rather than the acceptance of self.

It is said that every action taken, every thought and decision, all have consequences. To this, I would add that for every action not taken, for every decision not made, for every exploration avoided, and for every missed opportunity to use reason, there are also consequences. In my personal history, those consequences were the failure of myself, by myself, to myself.

Do you accept, trust, and love yourself enough to open your door to realities that are broader than what your belief system may have confined you to with limitations? Are you afraid of what you might find if you open that door? If you say that you "can't" overcome any negations or impediments you hold inside yourself, that get in your way, are you really saying, "won't" because you are clinging to whatever is familiar to you?

CHAPTER TWELVE

TRANSFORMATION

I n contrast to the serenity experienced when I faded to black, even knowing that my body had entered the condition of clinical death, my emergence from the black was invigorating, energizing, as if I had awakened bright and refreshed after a great night's sleep.

I emerged to find myself enveloped in a field of brilliant white light. Time seemed to suspend for a moment, which gave me pause to gather my thoughts and recall what had happened. I clearly remembered my last moment of consciousness in my body. I remembered telling someone in the hospital that I knew I was dying. I remembered the feeling of serenity, my acceptance, and all fading to black into what might have been the ultimate sleep. I had no idea how much time had passed since that pivotal moment. Now, my primary instinct was a sense of curiosity: "What has happened to me since that moment? Where am I?"

All I could see was the brilliant white light field. It fully engulfed me and was like a very dense but bright-white fog with a few swirls of subtle texture hues, without any sensation of motion or temperature. Everything else that might have been in the light field was obscured, everything but white brilliance.

Gradually, I adjusted myself to this altered state of being. Reality check: I could do nothing about it. It was whatever it was, and I was accepting of whatever was happening to me. There was no pain, no tactile sensation of any kind. Slowly, I became more alert, more focused. I tentative questioned: "Surely there must be some action for me to take or something to do?"

Something undefined grabbed my focus, something in the texture, and I directed my attention into the light field. I felt a compulsion to *try to see something – anything*, as you might if you suddenly found yourself in an opaque fog bank. "There must be something here other than light," I thought. "But then, where is here?" I didn't try to move.

Peering into the haze of the light field, that without eyes was a matter of conscious intent, I could detect some gentle movements, like swirls in a cloud. The more I focused, the more the haze seemed to part – as if a channel were forming. Then I realized: it wasn't just a channel forming! The light field as a whole was diffusing and becoming translucent! Clarity improved and I realized where I was! Though the view remained hazy, I was in the ER! From an elevation and at some distance away, I could see my body and the medical staff working to save my life. My curiosity took hold. I felt compelled to gain some confirmation about my body's condition. I wanted to inspect what was going on, so I positioned myself to get a close-up view using the skills I had learned with Morgan, my mentor, when we had projected my consciousness.

I saw my body tethered to fluids, blood I.V. bags, probes, and monitors. The monitors were flat-line displays, no heart beat registering. My complexion was pale, actually ashen. There was no motion in my body apart from the activity caused by the physicians as they frantically worked to save my life. The reality of the drama in the ER was compelling and fascinating as I realized my body looked like a mannequin.

Imagine that just for a moment you had a *direct communication line* to listen in to my thoughts just after I had exited the state of black that I call *non-being*. In imagining this connection, please keep in mind that it was clear to me that I had been predisposed toward this event, and had accepted that my body and that I myself was dying even as I collapsed in the ER in Yellowstone. By listening in to my thoughts, I offer you an opportunity to essentially share the experience, because my thoughts now are essentially all that I am, my consciousness itself, absent my body.

The following account is, to the best of my memory, an accurate replication of my experience.

"Wow! My body really is in the cycle of death! The doctors are doing their best to save it! If I'm correct, I should be able to navigate and position myself as I have before with Morgan. Yes! This works. I can move myself by my will! I know how to do this!"

"My experience here and now, maneuvering myself to view my body and the ER, is essentially identical to the feeling I remember experiencing when I viewed Morgan from the ceiling in the mansion - a plane above my body!"

"Magnificent! I still exist!"

"Before, Morgan orchestrated and guided me to launch my consciousness beyond the boundaries of my body. This experience is very similar, particularly in the manner that I can maneuver myself. My feelings of being un-tethered and free are the same as before. Oh! Un-tethered! That's different! There were filaments that connected me to Morgan! Oh my! This feeling of being free - I remember! This is incredible: Wonderful! I feel more powerful than before! If I could sell this feeling as a potion on Earth, I'd have many people addicted in a moment!"

Seeing my body dying, I realized that this has not occurred by my intent, as it had before. Pondering my situation, a feeling of concern took hold: "Uh oh! I might not be able to reenter my body at will! It really might be dead and yet I am fully continuing as myself … a sentient being. What happens to me *now*?

"Interesting! I in a sort of sphere, encased. This looks like a translucent fog of white light (as I panoramically scan around my environment). I have seen this white fog before! That happened during my first sojourn into clinical death with the motorcycle crash! My conclusion just might be correct after all: Have I really been prepared for this experience? So much of what is going on now is very familiar. What now? Something is happening to me. I'm having a surge of anticipation. What's this feeling? My feeling of comfort is evaporating! What's happening to me?

"I have a compulsion, an inspiration: I suspect that I cannot be in this position for very long. What do I know? What am I really feeling? What is the compulsion? Motion- motion is the compulsion. In my life, I learned that stasis might seem peaceful, but it can also mean confinement. Motion can change stasis and break confinement.

"This situation doesn't feel safe any longer! What is it that I must do? Something is challenging me not to stay in this situation! What is motivating me? It feels like I'm supposed to do something." The feeling of anticipation was overwhelming. I needed to stop emotionally responding to this flurry of reflective thoughts. I needed to allow my reason and trust to guide me.

"What am I supposed to do? I think I know. This is no time to be distracted. My very existence might depend on it. I have to explore this environment. I have to explore the realm of light.

"The translucent light-field is changing! My field of perception is changing quickly and dramatically. I'm not in control of these changes! What a startling reality –I have no direct control in this environment, other than my movement! It's becoming increasingly dense! I am not in a cocoon at all! It's starting to look similar to a sphere, but it's much more elongated. Incredible: The ER has disappeared! All I can see is white! The brilliance feels like it is somehow beckoning me. The density change is happening much faster now! This is familiar - familiar yet very different.

"What now? … I think I can make out a shape. The light field resembles an elongated spheroid and now it seems indeed to have boundaries.

"Michael, think about this - lose uncertainty, trust your abilities! Draw on your familiarity from the past. You've been almost intimate with this wondrous, embracing light before this moment - almost!"

Reading the above, I hope you have gained a sense of what was occurring. I was using thought and reason to deal with my reality, doing my best to be coherent in my thoughts.

The density of the white fog was increasing as it progressed away from me. That density seemed to become an opaque boundary. I wondered whether the light-field spheroid that surrounded me was what others had reported after near-death experiences as *the tunnel of light*. At a distance, it was becoming sufficiently thick to look like a white wall – a boundary – with swirling fog as its texture. "Am I being confined?" I wondered to myself.

Because of my training in systems engineering, underpinned with studies in physics, a physics lesson regarding nature's order came emphatically to mind: *Nature abhors stasis; Nature embraces dynamics.*

I concluded that if the spheroid of light with the implied and perceived boundaries signified a stasis condition, then the spheroid could be a confinement structure. If that were so, I surmised that it could imply the end of my being. Why would I have come to that conclusion? Energetic confinement, in that context, represents stasis – that's why. I was acutely aware from science that trapped and confined fields can become absorbed or even dissipated into the vessel of confinement.

From decades of professional training, I surmised that the *sphere* of brilliant, enveloping, and embracing light, could be a boundary condition. Would the translucent light-field continue indefinitely, or did something exist beyond this confining sphere? If that were the case, it could actually be a test of my will power and my belief in me!

Insofar as I could tell, I was no longer occupying my body. There were no tendrils of connection. My sentient consciousness seems to be all there is of me, and that sentience feels energetic. So, I thought of myself as a being comprised of energetic fields. Since I realized that fields confined in a vessel could be absorbed into the vessel and cease to exist, it was logical to react that I did not want to cease to exist! If my body was dead, and I could not return, I had no option but to take action: But what action?

My thoughts continued to explore possibilities. "Should I retreat and try and find a way back to my body? NO! My body might not be able to sustain my life! The last moment I could see my body, it didn't seem viable – it was a mannequin."

A myriad of other thoughts sprang up automatically. My first responsibility is to me, and that involves the use of reason, not emotion. It seemed momentarily like many lab experiments I'd participated in, that demanded technical reasoning, in the form of questions: "What do I know for certain?"

"Michael, you know that you exist. You know this because you are sentient, cognizant of things going on. You are able to explore and maneuver about this environment. Perhaps you can explore this realm of light – if you will yourself to do it! You probably do not have a viable body, or you would be in your body. You are composed now only of energized sentient fields. I do not want to exist as a spiritual form, locked indefinitely in a vessel of light! I will not take that risk! I do not want to risk being isolated in a boundary of confinement! Years of discovery and developing the fundamental essence of who I have become, provides me with conviction to trust in my intuition. There must be more!"

Somewhere, I concluded, there must be more involved for a being that was composed only of sentient, energetic, fields – true spirituality that I call "pure being." Simply being comfortable in the light no longer felt so comfortable. It was now a feeling that seemed threatening.

More questions sprang up. "What if this is a test? What if this is a test to determine if you have moved beyond fear? It might be safe here. Should I hide in this light field? I don't know for certain if there is existence beyond the light. If this is a test, it's meaning is huge. Why would I be tested this way? Who would give me such a test? No. It does not matter. Don't speculate. Work with what you know. It only matters that I have the will to continue as a being, and to prevail for myself. I must explore – but how?"

I reflected that this might be a situation set up to learn if I would have the drive to venture beyond this realm of a light-field, *if there even is something beyond this realm*. I continued to ponder possibilities and options. "I wonder what will happen if I push myself into the dense boundary? I feel that I cannot stay here in this spheroid shell, so I have to move! It doesn't make sense to me that eternity would be this confining, this limiting, IF this is my eternity!"

I thought I could possibly move beyond this threat of stasis by taking action, at least attempting to explore, and just maybe, find more than *just the light*. My intuitive impression was that possibly my sentience itself, which now meant all of my being – was *imperiled*. If that is real, then I could have nothing to lose by experimenting and exploring: *flourish or perish!*

Instantaneously, as if compelled by instinct and motivated by that concept, I drove my intent into purposeful navigation by my will to continue.

"I wonder what will happen if I gather my force of will, and fling myself into the boundary," I considered as my courage built up. "Nothing is happening anyway, so I might as well make something happen. What do I have to lose? Something unde-fined seems to be driving me, inspiring me, and I might never learn if I don't at least try something! I'll go for it!"

Accordingly, by force of my will power I projected myself as intensely as I could into the boundary of the sphere.

You've probably seen police dramas where the policeman throws his body against a locked door to break it down. My self-projection into the boundary was like that, though the impact was quite different. At the point where I would have collided with the boundary of the sphere, there was an *instantaneous* change. The structure of the spheroid immediately elongated into the general shape of a large conduit: a tunnel. Was this the oft-reported *tunnel of light?*

"What a rush this is! I'm moving at high speed! The light is extending itself and moving with me! There is nothing vague about this! It's fantastic!"

Then troubling doubts surfaced. At the far end of the tunnel, there remained what appeared to be a continuing, elongating, boundary.

"What? What is this? Is the end of the tunnel closed? The boundary changed shape by my force before. Maybe the closure will change with my velocity! You've gone this far, keep on going! This isn't over!"

Driven by my will and firmness of purpose, I made an instant decision – ignore the closure, keep on going. With that decision, the next transition occurred. Amazingly enough, the off-white, sparkling, swirling tunnel actually vanished as if it had been shattered into tiny particles!

Immediately, I experienced an incredibly high velocity – the equivalent of a catapult. I felt wonderfully energized, even electrified, like a child seeing fireworks for the very first time. The visions and the energy of this experience were powerfully fascinating.

What remained of *the tunnel* now appeared as a dazzling stream of photons, some as small individual clumps of light particles, with others appearing as waves. These appeared to fly or swirl around me, moving generally in parallel with me. Maybe I was moving at light speed! The sensations were magnificent, exhilarating, and wondrously beautiful!

This was incredibly profound as I was now in motion and wholly in a state of energetic exhilaration. My immediate and triumphant thoughts were: *"I was correct! Nature does abhor stasis! I made the right decision to explore!"*

These thoughts led to a premonition that I was being propelled or pulled by unseen forces and that those forces were catapulting me into interstellar space. Later, I would learn the significance of that premonition.

For now, though, the surrounding particle or photon stream appeared as a swirling color-flow of blue, lighter than navy blue, and embellished by brilliant white particles that looked like sparklers. All of this activity interlaced into the black background of space, through a sort of translucency of the *particulate channel*, that was accompanying, enveloping, or surrounding me.

There was also a *physiological* sort of feeling: an intense sensation of interaction with the stream of energetic particles and me. I felt as if these particles were randomly streaming through me, around me, and propelling me. It was as if I, myself, was now an electric field spheroid, generally translucent, and partially defined. Expansive in size, the spheroid was two to three times the dimension of my previous physical size. There was a shimmering of a cobalt blue surrounding the spheroid of my being.

I felt as if I was somehow surfing a wind-stream of subatomic, charged particles moving at high velocity! I had experimented with charged electron flows and energetic coronas in laboratories, and I surmised that the electrically charged particles were providing support. (Later, much after my return to normal life, it dawned on me. There is such a wind known in physics: the solar wind. There are also vast streams of electromagnetic energy: macro-strings.)

Then quietly and without any warning, my movement stopped: not by my decision or direction. I just stopped without any physiological sensation, and I became suspended, floating in what seemed to be the energetic vacuum upon the fabric of space. The *electrified feeling* of the energetic particles had ceased when the motion-stream, stopped. There were no temperature sensations of hot, or cold, and no sense of a boundary or of any structure I could define.

"What now? Where am I?" I thought as I surveyed my surroundings. The scene before me, encompassing me, was *not* that of a black void of space or the non-being of black that I found immediately after my physical collapse. I don't know why, but it seemed obvious to me that I had projected myself *well beyond* the tunnel of light.

There were dots of light at large distances, looking like stars or clusters of stars in a clear desert night sky. The dots appeared to be intermittent! "Intermittent", as I use the term here, does not mean *twinkling,* as stars appear to do because of the atmosphere around Earth. It means wholly visible or invisible – on or off! The dots surrounded me in every direction and every once in a while I saw a much larger image – like that of a galaxy.

What was I seeing? Light sources in space should be more or less constant, and these were shifting on and off and never in the same locations. My impression was of multiple, yet invisible, overlapping *sheets or planes in the fabric of space.* If so, then the sheets were in continuous motion. They seemed to have apertures of different sizes in each of them. Randomly, the motions of the *sheets* would allow the apertures to align! When they aligned, stars, star clusters, or galaxies would appear in various locations. When they did not align, the location would be a void of black.

Whenever I observed something that was unfamiliar to my technical mind, I usually groped to find a hypothetical possibility. "Incredible!" I thought. "This resembles the hypothetical descriptions of inter-spatial phase interference! This is fantastic! Just maybe I'm directly observing the overlay of planes that are interspersed or interleaved dimensionally, as they interfere with each other! I could shock the science community by writing a technical paper about these phenomena! But no, I couldn't prove it even though I'm observing it directly."

At all times I could view in any direction I chose by focus of my will. I was being prudently careful and generally motionless, but with a high sense of curiosity and intrigue. Through I didn't know what was going to happen to me, I was exhilarated!

Waiting for something to happen, I wasn't in the mood to try to force anything – after the catapult I'd just experienced. During this time, I contemplated what possibilities might be in store for me as an inorganic being. I was greatly reassured that I could feel and see in a physical sense, I could think and reason, and my ability to choose and to make decisions, as well as the strength to act on them, were all intact!

I had one concern at the forefront of my realizations. It felt as if any uncontrolled thought or emotion, any instability in my sense of myself as an intact and coherent being, would amplify as motion into an uncontrolled oscillation, resonance, or even chaos. Emphatically, that recognition seemed threatening and that caused a moment of anxiety. I needed all of my self-discipline to quell this anxiety, to prevent it from escalating into terrifying fear. I felt that if the field comprising myself became perturbed, or worse, dissipated – *I would cease to exist!* I had essentially no doubt that this whole transition into a being of spirit was going to be an *all or nothing* experience. Without access to my viable body, even if it were still viable, I had no backstop. In other words, I was simply being careful - *very* careful.

I concentrated to stabilize myself, to avoid the *oscillation effect* that seemed threatening. After a brief period of adjustment, I gained renewed confidence and ability to maintain and control my positional stability. Then I noticed that something was approaching. A single luminescent field spheroid had appeared at a distance. At first, I thought it was another blip of intermittent light, but this sphere was different in colors, and it was drifting toward me. I guessed that my stability might have signaled that I was ready for another event. I didn't know what this meant in truth, but whatever was happening to me seemed to involve forces - not all of which were in my control.

I suspect that in the state of existence as *pure sentient being*, all dimensions, distances, and time itself may be irrelevant. For purposes of your visualization, however, scaling from the size of a physical body, I am able to suggest some possible dimensions to help describe what I was observing.

The spheroid drifting toward me appeared partially elongated, in what would have been the vertical plane on Earth. It was perhaps two to three times the size of an average human form. It had a translucent surface of color, interlaced with striations. The hues ranged from a moderate blue at the core, graduating to a cobalt blue toward the circumference. Layered upon the circumference was a gradient of sparkling gold.

The gold layer formed a haze that radiated outwardly into space as a corona. The entire surface appeared to sparkle with swirling, metallic (reflective) flecks. (To get a better idea, imagine a grainy photograph where the granulations are reflective metallic flecks, and are in continuously stirring and swirling motion.)

There were also floating striations throughout the translucent form. They seemed to stream from the core and become increasingly active as they migrated toward the surface. These appeared as tendrils or filaments – wisps of color ribbons. Most striations appeared to be cobalt blue threads in a darker blue field. A few striations took the form of a burnt gold or amber.

The approaching spheroid halted away from me at what would have been three or four meters on Earth. This pause provided, for me, a quiet moment to study and observe, and to continue to balance myself. I was silently observing the image with an intense curiosity.

While I was attempting to study the detail of the form, the image began to gradually display a change in appearance, some kind of metamorphosis.

"Now what?" I mused as both my thought and my concern.

Observation

Fear is often based on having insufficient self-esteem. Self-esteem yields trust and confidence in one's decisions and actions, and it gives a person permission to explore beyond known boundaries. One's knowledge of self, buoyed by experience gained incrementally over a period of time, can provide a sense of self-esteem that is the opposite of self-importance or ego. A high sense of self-esteem elevates objectivity, and that as a tool allows a person to examine, explore, and consider alternatives using the sequential thought process of reason.

Do you have sufficient self-esteem so you don't feel you have to prove anything to anyone?

If not, is your lack of self-esteem causing you to be controlled by or emotionally dependent upon others?

Do you have sufficient self-esteem, with adequate trust in yourself, to evaluate your circumstances, prudently alter your references, and even venture into the unknown?

CHAPTER THIRTEEN

THE TEST

Something astounding was happening, stirring in space immediately in front of me! However, I recognized that the spheroid's metamorphosis, a stimulating and dynamic change, was occurring gradually and because of that, it wasn't threatening. I studied the image and thought: "Here I am, before this apparition and I realize that whatever is going to happen is happening, and it is beyond my control. I have no responsible alternative but to remain calm and observant."

Besides, I had enough to deal with! I had to hold my focus. I had to remain calm and learn how to keep myself stabilized without oscillating within the fabric of space. I comprehended that fear itself is a threat because with fear, I could lose coherent focus and risk scattering my energy - and scattering might end my being. So, with deliberate and tranquil patience, I quietly watched as the field sphere hovered and developed before me, gradually increasing its sparkling activity and intensity moment by moment. My attention grabbed onto something striking: the approximate size and shape of the field seemed to be similar to my own field! That conclusion increased my comfort level because, at least, it wasn't larger than my own shape and that seemed less of a potential threat.

Captivated by this apparition, I searched for hints about what the nature of the image might be. I felt again like a child seeing something amazing for the very first time – wide eyed with a sense of awe.

As I calmly waited during the changes as they progressed, I honed in, studying all of the details to glean information or some concept that might be valuable to me. In particular, the varying colors and striations exhibited by the approaching field of light intrigued me. My impulse was to compare what I was observing with what my personal field sphere appeared to be. "Am I the same sort of being as this luminous form?" I wondered. While I could find similarities in size and shape, it was not immediately apparent to me what this really implied about the nature of the apparition. The nuances of royal and cobalt blues, like a haze at both of our boundaries, were where the color and striation similarities between us appeared to end.

I increasingly found it comforting, though, that my own form approximated that of the other sphere. Because of the vague similarities observed, I considered: "This spherical field has a structure similar to mine. Since I am sentient, what I'm seeing is probably sentient. That would make this an energetic being! I have always thought it isn't logical that humanity would be unique or alone in this vast universe.

Moreover, I had been enjoying a journey at incredible velocity up until now. My thoughts focused on unknown factors: "I was halted and not by my own decision! Some other force halted me. What force or forces launched my travel, then halted it, and for what purpose?"

Another thought dawned on me as I studied the apparition: "Similarities. That must be it. We seek similarities among ourselves. We are comforted when find something in common and by recognizing similarities, maybe a connection can be constructed - and maybe an implied understanding. I'm actually seeking comfort by trying to find and identify commonality between this entity and me. Interesting: the changes in the apparition now seem to have stopped. Good, I can use this as an opportunity for further study."

As I waited, another idea surfaced: "I wonder if possibly the color and striation hues exhibited by any sentient field spheroid has something to do with the characteristics of that individual – assuming this field before me is sentient! Perhaps all beings are as unique and individual as energetic fields, as we are when in human form! It that's correct, and if the energetic spiritual forms are eternal, then individuality is eternal: a component of immortality!"

The distance separating the apparition and myself was about what would be normal conversational distance in society. The field sphere started to increase its activity again, and as the field increased its rate of metamorphosis, it gradually changed appearance. The new appearance initially retained many of the color hues that I had previously seen, but it then began to take on a human form! My attention seized on the image as it emerged and became clearer and remained held within the field! What I recognized in the image, took me by surprise!

"Clergy?" I thought tentatively, as the clarity of the image became sharper. I felt like I wanted to shout: *"Clergy? What in the…"* - My question quietly trailed off, pondering the possibilities. Stunned at first, next I was dumbfounded, then I thought: "Fascinating – this is incredibly intriguing! Why would an image present itself to me as something resembling a member of the orthodox clergy? He looks like a priest - maybe a bishop."

The form appeared wrapped in a long flowing cassock. I could clearly see that a black miter adorned his head, outlined in something that appeared to be gold beading. As a human image, he displayed gray hair, a bit unkempt with nuances of curls at the ends. This tended to suggest from appearance: he was maybe 60 years old, giving him a mature and stately countenance. To complete the effect, there was a vague image of sandals on his feet. All combined, this seemed very peculiar and even incongruous.

"*Whoa!*" I thought. *"Okay, you've seized my attention! Now what?"* The image remained silent. The apparition, immersed in a field of translucent haziness seemed to be studying me, slowly tilting its "head" from side to side. There was a pause in activity, and I took advantage of it to observe more details of its features. Then it dawned on me: "Eastern orthodox clergy? Why would this apparition have taken on the representation of some orthodox sect of clergy?"

Fascinated and captivated by this manifestation, my intrigue sharpened my focus as this image of a cleric came into even sharper clarity. Suddenly I recalled the pompous image of Father McCarthy, bombastically admonishing me – the intimidation from clergy was a focal point lodged in my memory. If the goal had been to capture my attention, it had certainly succeeded.

I really don't know why, but I had a premonition that this being was going to present a challenge to me, that there would be a specific attempt to test or tempt me through some sort of pretense. "What could be the purpose of this image, this presentation? Clearly there has to be a purpose or it would not have taken on a human-like form and specifically that of a cleric."

I still did not feel anything threatening. As much as I was intrigued, I was not fearful of the apparition. Its slow approach toward me, the gradual metamorphosis displayed, the change to a humanoid form, all gave me some sense of identity with the image that allowed me to adjust to its presence without trepidation.

Lingering questions were stirring in my consciousness. I mused: "This must be some form of a messenger to greet me for some purpose!" I permitted myself to engage in a farcical question: "Could the individual of this apparition even be an angel, a saint, maybe some form of god?"

Despite not having answers to these perplexing questions, my consciousness whirled around with the fascinating possibilities.

I seemed to be able to easily view myself from within my own structure. The more intense my thoughts and feelings, the more active were the motional, energetic stirrings in my field, including the color filaments and striations. My thoughts were rapidly, very energetically, exploring possibilities: "Okay. Maybe this is another test, a challenge. The boundary in the tunnel of light seemed to be a challenge, and I prevailed through that. Maybe this is set up to see if I will fail myself through fear."

My stirring processes paused for a moment as I contemplated the word fear. "No. Not fear. The apparition has presented itself carefully, giving me sufficient time to adapt to this new experience. If not a test of fear, maybe 'the cleric' is here to instruct me. Explore your perceptions, Michael. What do you feel? Challenge, yes, I'm feeling this is a test." I was contemplating: "Should I initiate communication? Or should I just be patient and observe?"

I decided on the latter. I was not directing this experience. My intuition was that the best course of action was to observe and respond if indicated. For now, there was nothing to do but watch and monitor the situation. "Maybe this is simply a test of my patience to learn of my reactions."

Now the form moved closer to me and I continued to scrutinize it, thinking "what now?" with a high degree of curiosity. I increasingly sensed that communication would soon occur.

Once again, my history seemed to have provided partial understanding for what occurred next. In my experiences with my mentor, Morgan, and previously during my first experience of clinical death and even for that matter with my mother and the exorcist, I firmly knew that sentient communication can and does occur through an empathic or telepathic form.

As incredible as it might seem to you, this being before me began a conversation that seemed very simple, even natural, to me. It was as if we were not strangers to each other. I was astonished at the ease of the exchange.

He issued a soft smile. A gentle motion of his head added to his gestures of swaying movements of his arms suggesting a direction he wanted me to see. There was nothing to see in the direction, so I concluded that his gesturing was an invitation for me to move in that direction. "Is he wanting me to follow or go with him where I would be his companion, and he my guide?" I thought quietly to myself.

Then he issued a statement, and the message was powerfully stunning for me because it carried momentous significance. The message simply said was: *"Come with me. I will take you to God."*

My thoughts raced around, searching for truth, and the significance of his offer: "He's implying that he can take me to meet God. What does this really mean?"

I paused and carefully considered my options. "I've evolved my philosophy to understand that god doesn't exist as a singular deity. For years I've discerned that god is composed of the forces of the universe itself, and that we are composed of those same energetic forces! What if I'm not correct? Is this an opportunity to confirm my conclusions if I'm correct, or condemn me if I'm not?"

As an adult, attempting to evolve myself, I had questioned and blown away the concept of blind faith and with that, the traditional version of an omnipotent monotheistic deity. This visual representation of my old belief system invoked how much power the clergy had previously held over me, and been as an integral part of my early life.

I exclaimed to myself: "I once believed that I was obligated to reflexively follow their instructions, without questioning the authority of their commands! This is a command to follow, and that has failed me before!"

Then in what seemed to be an instant, it dawned on me. "Whoa! This is smack in the middle of my most sensitive vulnerability! To fail this might be ultimately to fail myself! Think, Michael, think! Be very cautious: take the time to think it through and apply reason. Do not react. If this is going to be a test, it might as well be a defining test!"

I was certain that this was in fact a challenge, a test of my character and the decisions I had made. I could contemplate no greater defining moment, for me, than to be provoked on the subject of a church-defined deity. I felt this experience would be an intense, even pivotal, test.

Moreover, insofar as I knew, I no longer had a physical body to contain my consciousness and I had no responsible option but to continue. The thought surfaced: "This may indeed be an *all or nothing* process." I felt this and felt it very strongly.

Images arose from my childhood instruction: "To offend 'god' would be to risk eternal damnation. If I exclaim that there is no god, and there is a god, *will I be condemned?*" The words *eternal damnation* had been resonating within me for a long time – and maybe, just maybe, the moment had arrived to resolve myself to make an unconditional decision.

"Michael, do you trust yourself or not? Do you trust in your ability to decide what is valid or invalid for yourself? You have spent much time and effort to pry into the events of your youth to understand the core of your being – to learn who you truly are. You have thoroughly explored the questions about your perceptions and sensitivities and learned to accept and trust these abilities. These are your building blocks, the foundation of your trust, love and spirituality. This cleric is inviting you to challenge your convictions. No matter what you do, you must be true to yourself and adhere to the convictions you have developed. Nothing new is presented here that merits reconsideration!"

I quietly reflected: "Consider what you know. Explanations from the church were inadequate and unsatisfying, and this image implies churchianity. The tenets of churchianity were responsible for producing conflicts, frustrations, and doubts that you even deserved to exist. You lost your self-esteem and replaced it with guilt. Moments ago you accepted the challenge to find the courage and push yourself though the light boundary. You passed that test, and now this is another test – again! Don't doubt yourself now. You are already continuing beyond organic life. You've striven to optimize your evolution. Trust in yourself!

Your body is dying and maybe it is dead. This cleric might be testing you to make a decision that has consequences for your eternity!"

There was completely no doubt that whatever my decision would be, it would be once again, an all or nothing result and it might have eternal consequences for me. I had firmly concluded that one's evolution develops solely through personal responsibility: No one, or being, can save you – or advance you – other than yourself.

Humanities' tendency to invoke belief in a supernatural deity as a means to eternal life, instead of a rational process to accomplish one's eternal evolution, simply seemed to add unnecessary mythology. Mythology involving a deity became a diversion or confusion to the whole process of an individual's personal development of responsibility - because people would follow what they are told to follow, believe it – without questioning or having the tools of objectivity to allow them to question. Worse than that, I became convinced that proclamations of deity involvement in human affairs usually forced rules and demands set by sectors of mankind for their own purposes, even though they always have claimed these demands to be *in the name of God*. Those in control also can cause their followers to lose vast levels of personal power by being dependent upon the institutional beliefs rather than in the power of themselves. Formal religious institutions claim to be interpreting the requirements of their deity. To me, that makes *the deity* into an instrument through which humans can control other humans. That, in turn, implies a vast distance between the institutional approaches and my concept of personal evolution.

My personal exploration continued: "Michael, what have you learned? I've learned through personal experience that dependencies can squander personal strengths! Dependencies can redirect personal energy to others or to mythology when you need it most for yourself! The launch of my consciousness out of my body with Morgan inspired me to reach for more lofty goals. I've learned that continuing my being beyond the flesh and blood of life takes a prodigious amount of work, concentration and personal commitment. If I accept the cleric's invitation, a directive to go with him, am I not being dependent on him to take me to god?"

I had spent more than a decade in study, meditation, and rational thought all designed to prevail over emotional reflex. Significantly, these introspections included rebasing me from blind belief systems (churchianity or dependencies on others) to a rational foundation – the use of self-determination as personal volition. This new approach led me to the understanding that the entire universe and all of life – including sentient life – evolved through natural processes, from elementary particles. Nothing had to be created, per se, through some master plan by a deity for sentience to become a reality.

I began to experience significant anxiety. "You've got to commit to a decision! Is there a god or not? Can you subjugate yourself to another to take you to that god – if there is a god? Well, maybe there is an alternative. Maybe there is a way you can maneuver a neutral answer, not make a commitment, and play it safe. Maybe you can finesse your way through this challenge. What response might get you through this in some middle ground where you don't have to make a commitment? What would happen if you said there *might be* a god, when you don't believe there is? Would that attempt at safe-play result in the opposite – causing you to self-destruct and cause termination of your being? Would you end any hope that you could continue into eternity?"

Suddenly I had a surge of enlightenment. "If everything you are, if all of your being is made up of fields as you are now, then you have no backstop, no safety net! You could lose all of your being – all of you! You could cause your own oblivion by any distortion or attempt at deceit. You know that deceit shatters your impeccability to yourself, and you could become dismantled, with your energy scattered! *You must be impeccable* to yourself, no matter what."

The cleric seemed to be pushing for a decision. His gestures became more rapid, urgent, and apparently indicated the direction that I to take, and at first, they were compelling until I realized it might be an ultimate test. He repeated his simple statement that conveyed so much to me: *"Come with me. I will take you to God."*

Then, in a supercharged wave of intensity, I captured the reality of my situation: "There is no escaping this: no way out. I must make a decision. Given all that I have learned and experienced, it will be a violation of my very commitment to my personal evolution to subordinate myself, and submit to the invitation that he will take me to god. *Decide, Michael, reason this out!"*

Then in one powerful moment, I found the answer to resolve my uncertainty. "If there were a god, why would god send an intermediary? Why is this challenge presented to me through the image of a cleric?"

The old question from my childhood surfaced: "If there were a god he would be all knowing, omnipresent and with me. That god would send no one to take me to him! I realize that lack of commitment cannot be allowed to dictate my response – cannot!"

The intensity of working through this quandary continued: "Do not screw this up! Be true to yourself! Allow for no deceit and no distortions. You cannot manipulate your way through this, thinking you can take some vague position, and not commit. No matter what the consequences, I have evolved to this point in my life and being by learning through reasoned thought, and I have concluded that there can be no god. This cleric cannot lead me to eternal spirituality. My understanding embraces the universe, and I am composed of those same energetic forces. I am a child of the universe, and the essence and energy of the universe is god."

My refrain continued testing my decision again, and again: "I must stay true to myself! This is my test, of my convictions, of my fidelity to myself. This cleric is a deception asking me to follow an old belief I no longer accept as valid."

It became obvious to me that this communication, this presence in the image of a cleric, was a deception, a sort of "Trojan horse" tempting me to deviate from my true foundation I had worked to attain. My crescendo of intensity was building up to a fevered pitch! I had to know the truth for myself and there was only one-way to find out: "Commit! Trust your continuance as a being in evolution to your personal knowledge – your impeccability. Win or lose, this is the best you can do!"

Bolstered by working through my turmoil and uncertainty by *testing and retesting myself* using my rational and directed thought, I responded to the cleric by projecting my decision to him: "I believe you have been sent to test me, to test my strength of character and resolve. You are here to probe my fears with a false imagery and attempt to lead me away from what I have come to rationally understand and trust in myself."

I continued, possibly in over-intensification by then: "This is a test, even perhaps a trap. There is no god!" I assertively replied. "I am made up of the energy and particles of the universe itself! It moves with me, flows through me! My spirituality is myself!" I added for emphasis: *"How can you lead me to a being that does not exist?"*

Immediately my thoughts seemed to resonate loudly as if I had projected them throughout the universe. I was trembling, maybe shimmering, because of what I perceived to be the *all or nothing* consequences of my decision and commitment.

Then a profound pause of absolute silence happened. The cleric seemed stilled, frozen in time. I thought that I had entered the eye of a hurricane. I was anxiously awaiting any response, any signal that would define the consequence of my action. Then, in what seemed to be a momentary but brilliant flash, I received the first glint that my decision was correct. The image of the cleric before me – smiled. Even more surprisingly, in what I consider a wonderful gesture of acknowledgement, the image graciously bowed toward me with one hand across his waist, then arose holding his smile. When he arose, still facing me, he slowly faded back into his luminous form, and vanished as he drifted away from my view.

I wasn't certain what to feel or to think. Turbulent event horizons surround the eyes of hurricanes, and my awareness was on high alert for what might happen next. In that one incredible and indelible moment, everything seemed to pause and I felt that I was alone: *Truly alone.* I had a muted flash of anxiety, waiting for what would happen next, as I asked myself: "What just happened? Was this really a challenge – a test of my resolve? If so, did I pass the test? Will I even continue to exist – even after my response?"

In the solitude of that moment, I needed to cling to any confirmation or acknowledgement that I had met the criterion to pass this challenge. I relived the scene of the cleric's smile and bow toward me, holding onto those images for a feeling of comfort. "Patience, Michael – be patient. Whatever will happen is going to happen, and you did your best."

After that brief pause, it happened again! Once again I was instantaneously, literally catapulted into motion at high velocity. Something or someone catapulted me again, back into the particle wind stream, carrying me further into my journey! *I was continuing as a spiritual being!* Correct or not about the existence of *a god,* I was continuing. Somehow, given my continuing existence I had latched onto solace signified by the cleric's smile and bow, I joyously realized: *"You must have passed the test! What a relief!"* - I mused as I gathered my focus, relaxed, and began to enjoy traveling in the particle wind.

I carefully re-inventoried myself. Once again, I was moving as a field spheroid that appeared superficially to be light. I felt assured that my field still contained all of my being. I was flowing in a stream – or as a stream – of energetic particles, seemingly again at light speed. In terms of normal human awareness, this would have been *breathtaking.* In the state of pure being, it was wonderfully *exhilarating,* and the feeling of exhilaration increased as I relaxed.

Any anxiety remaining in me had melted away. My exhilaration was borne upon the joy of one phrase: *"I am continuing!"* I was so elated that it didn't occur to me to ask the obvious question: *Continuing to what?* The elated feeling happened because I had passed an extraordinarily impressive test. I felt that by demonstrating the strength of my convictions and commitment to myself, I might have moved across an important threshold in my evolution.

I noticed a significant change in my energetic form that seemed to accompany my feeling of exhilaration! The hint of the hue of cobalt blue striations interspersed with royal blue was *no longer* just a hint. The colors of my sphere seemed to be in an elevated state of intensity, swirling more vigorously, and the colors now more clearly defined. The depth of my hues changed to resemble those of *the cleric* who had just tested me. There was an exception, though. Marvelously, within the structure of myself, I now saw more filaments of gold and red floating about, as if they had been formed or released from somewhere within my being. *"Yes!"* I joyously proclaimed again, *"I have passed the trial! Wow! Progress!"*

Viewing the intensified color forms of my field sphere led me to recall the incredibly brilliant fields of color that I saw surrounding my mentor so many years ago, when I had launched my consciousness out of my body and into the room. Certainly, I realized, my mentor had attained a much higher state of being than I had attained at that stage of my development. Marvelously, now my color striations were getting closer to his! I exclaimed to myself: "These changes within my energetic being confirm that this is a process - and I'm evolving!"

I surmised that the colors either signified, or actually were the abilities or attributes that an individual attained. That possibility suggested that the very spiritual core or soul of a sentient being was indeed these radiant fields, imaged as forms of light and colors. My line of thought expanded, reaching for detail: "If the brilliance of illumination and the color forms represent abilities, then it's implied that they would indicate the level of attainment the individual had gained along the path of their evolution. Clearly, in order to engage in the test, I had to be true to myself – without deceit or conditions – and commit myself! My state of being seems to have perceptibly changed: I feel more confident and this feels like intensified energy! Maybe I have gained more ability by being true to myself. Maybe my evolutionary attainment has advanced!"

Through the premonitions at Canyon Muerto, then after transitioning from life on Earth and now into a state of sentient consciousness as an energetic field open to the universe, I embraced an incredible respect for the progressive forces in nature. Dwelling on what seemed to be an evolutionary process, I thought: "I have evolved to become an interactive participant with free choice and control or power over my destiny. One's evolution is volitional, and profoundly based upon personal responsibility developed through volition! This is a highly dynamic, and dramatic realization! What a marvelous insight! Given the intensity and clarity of insight produced in me, it seems to be a significant gain in my understanding."

These experiences and these images continued to bring back memories of seeing color hues around my mother and others in my youth. Back then I didn't question anything about the colors and the hues. I had thought they were just normal visualizations, that everyone experienced them in everyday life. Perhaps, I mused, everyone might see them, perceive them as children, and learn to ignore or deny them as they age! My mother reinforced this idea of normalcy. She confirmed, as normal phenomena, the visualizations that I reported to her – until the overwhelming experience with the baroness. The individual auras I saw surrounding some people were as distinctive as their faces. Now I had an increasingly clear understanding that these images were markers of the personal evolution attained by each individual. Many open questions remained: "What next? Were other beings besides 'the cleric' involved? If so, who?"

I concluded that I would likely gain new information in an intentioned way so that my development might continue. At that moment, I could not fathom any other reasonable explanation for the continuation of this journey. Since I was again experiencing the energetic particle wind, I explored the experience further as I counseled myself: "Take full advantage of this experience as you travel in the wind. You have no idea what will happen next. You have no idea how long this travel will last, or if it is the last experience you will ever have."

I reveled in the sensations of how the wind seemed to be interconnecting to and supporting me. I applied the methods I had learned with the holistic group to focus my attention, gathering my energetic forces and redirecting them. I recognized intensification to my feeling of a continual flow of electrical sparks permeating throughout my being, especially when compared to the initial experience before the cleric's test. The color intensities seemed to also change with some proportion to my feelings and thoughts! That brought up memories – the way I experimented and amused myself with the filaments that had tethered me to Morgan.

Directing my will to shift my position within the channel of particles surrounding me caused the red filaments to become more active, gathering and pointing *away from* the direction I wanted to go. My explorations replaced my suppositions with increasingly clear and delighted indication: "My being, and all of my nature, truly is the energetic spheroid field of light and color. This is all of myself, all that I am." I permitted myself the luxury of taking joy in what I now believed was my attainment: "My experience appears to be that of increasing energetic field activity, and it feels like more intensity. The sparks, the electrically charged particles, are exhilarating! I have no discomfort, no consternation, and no fear. I am content!"

After some period of travel in this incredible mode, feeling like flight at the velocity of light, I again came to a halt. Since the previous halt involved an immense test, my feeling again moved into high anticipation: "Would this halt be for another test? Pay close attention – focus your awareness. You are not responsible for your travel in the particle stream wind. You are not responsible for the halts! Something, or some one, is guiding you and there must be for an agenda that you don't yet comprehend. What will happen next? What purpose will this experience have?"

A note about telepathic/empathic communications

When you read text, or speak to another person, each syllable, word, and sentence sequentially projects from or within you. On the other side of the discussion, each word or syllable is heard, or received, in the same serial form by the other person or by you.

I've learned that telepathic or empathic connections can convey the equivalent of whole concepts, complete thoughts or images, all at once – literally instantaneous! The individual word does not have to be spoken aloud, or in a sequence, in order to completely grasp the communication and understand its full meaning. In other words, the whole message is simply exchanged or transferred at once, in one single "thought event."

The closest analogy I can relate to explain this would be that of a photograph. If you view a photograph, you'd probably know, almost immediately, what the scene was. You could then take time to carefully study the details of the scene. Looking at an entire photographic scene at once is what I mean by a parallel communication. Then, once the image is set into your memory, the details are available for careful inspection and review.

In my experiences, any information transferred telepathically is just *known*. Yet, there is nothing vague or confusing about the details exchanged through this method of communication. It becomes my emphasized responsibility to study the details to be certain that I know what I think I know!

Evaluation of my own personal thoughts internally, however, remained serial as if I were assembling an image one detail at a time, one word and sentence at a time. In some perhaps instinctual way, I seemed to realize that it was important for me to compile or contemplate the message that I wished to communicate before sending it away from my being.

I had learned by experience that private thoughts are not *released,* projected away from me, which would commit me to the communication, until they are completely compiled. My understanding is that once released, the message is committed as a reality of self, linked to my intent about what I want to say.

With that in mind, I was very careful not to *release a thought,* which means to commit myself to a thought, until I consciously wanted to issue it, committing myself to my communication. This concept, as a communication process, suggests that there is less noise of random thoughts floating around the universe. Actually, I suspect that a highly evolved and sensitive or perceptive being would have knowledge of what my private thought processes actually are!

Observation

There was a time in my early history when I absolutely believed in "God" as posited by the church. I believed in the concepts of redemption, salvation, and eternal punishment – damnation.

The previous belief in these external forces actually exonerated me from taking full responsibility for my own soul and my continuance beyond organic death.

Do you find yourself in control of your destiny, or do you yield that control to others to define your destiny for you?

Does your belief in your relationship with churchianity absolve or prevent you from seeking greater possibilities to evolve into a higher state of being?

Do your current beliefs cause fears, uncertainty, and conflicts?

Do you want to seek beyond the limits of what you've been told to believe, with the desire to bring knowledge to yourself?

Consider the possibility that eternal life in a highly attained state of being is not dependent upon a belief in, service or obedience to, a deity.

Consider the possibility that the whole of spiritual attainment is an extension of processes that originate as physical in the organic body, and with personal development through personal responsibility, can evolve into the metaphysical state – the realm of physics not yet explored.

CHAPTER FOURTEEN

CELESTIAL THREAT

O nce again, forces not in my control halted me and I was hovering in space. I was very comfortable, even tranquil, as I surveyed my new environment. The only sensations I had were those within myself. Whenever exposed to a new situation, my tendency was to be in an observational mode and that was serving me well. Although I did not know what to expect, I was confident that I could deal with whatever it was going to be. I had become extraordinary acclimated to this condition of my being, and this view in space. Hovering as I was, I did not notice anything happening that seemed significant enough to capture my attention. I was alert, readying myself for whatever might occur next.

I again noticed the randomly appearing dots of light intermittently scattered throughout space. They seemed to highlight the vastness of space – the black background with a few swaths of an indigo to royal blue, swirls of gray, and all were enormous in size. My thoughts meandered retrospectively about my experiences as I traveled in the particle wind: the exhilaration; the energetic impressions; the catapult into the travel; and, the halt.

Around the vastness of it all, something about the dots of light again captured my curiosity: "The intermittent dots – the light flashes. They resemble the effect of inter-spatial phase interference!" Then it dawned on me: "Flashes! Not dots - flashes! At each event that catapulted me into the wind, there was a flash in infinitesimal time! When I exited the wind stream, there also was a brief flash when the velocity halted! Why didn't I pay attention to this before? Maybe, the flashes signify passage in between spatial phases. The concept would be incredible as a manifestation of interspatial parallels!"

Interspatial parallels are a very wide set of hypothetical conditions, sort of like energy spurts that pop together. When they pop, they would cause energy transfers between spatial planes. My thoughts wandered off in curious speculation: "What could cause breakthroughs between spatial barriers? Maybe enormous electromagnetic energy strings that focus on dimensional weakness between the planes then puncture the spatial planes. Is this possible? This is not yet known physics but speculation – maybe metaphysics! *Stop this!*" I said to myself. "You're overanalyzing."

My contemplations had distracted me, and my position in space wandered about. It happened so gradually, I didn't notice. Then I saw it, and it was huge.

Directly before me was a physical object of massive proportion and irregular shape. The object was rotating at what appeared to be an interval of about one rotation per four or five Earth-time seconds. I had approached it gradually and inadvertently, or so I thought. The distance between the object and me seemed to pale when I realized the size. I intensely studied the object: it was brownish-grey in color with several large pockmarks of darkness that seemed either to be a very dark brown or something like a glassy obsidian black.

As I had come to expect, I found that I could navigate around the object, moving in any direction or orientation simply by intending to do so. The position that I was holding away from the object was sufficient for me to view its surfaces as it rotated. I found reassurance in realizing that my ability to control my motion and position had become very well refined. When I willed it, my movement easily happened. My navigational movements were similar to that of a slow panoramic camera, moving around while scanning a scene. I continued to be fascinated with how precise, how simple, the control of my movement actually was.

I must admit to you that I was somewhat wary of getting too close to an object of this massive size. I had no firm idea what influence or force might be produced through its mass or rotation that might affect me. Caution and prudence, then became my watchwords.

Before this pause in my journey, my ability to move seemed to be somewhat limited. Now, my ability to direct my position seemed not to have limitations. This was very different from what I felt initially in my confrontation with the *cleric* – when I felt instability in my skill to control my position and had to work to control my anxiety and focus. Actually, I'm not certain if this was due to my increased experience, or to an increase in my self-confidence.

Despite that confidence, I was determined not to press my fortune and get too close to this object. The object was a massive asteroid. "Perhaps if back away, I can see the whole thing from my position" I mused. "Size: the size of this thing! I'd guess that it's about a quarter-mile long and rotating on the long axis counter-clockwise. Its diameter is about one-third of its length!" I relocated myself to better observe details. The visual effect was extraordinarily clear, with every detail and shadow of the rock in clear focus.

On closer inspection, I saw sharply chiseled creases appearing as if large chunks had split off. I willed myself to drift away, back to my approximate original position. Apart from the asteroid, nothing else was going on, insofar as I could discern. Without any sense of other activity happening, my thoughts again wandered: "Why was I brought here? This is not a dynamic event. I'm not learning anything. Who brought me here? Why am I having this exposure to this asteroid? There has to be a purpose. I'm continuing as a being, but this is only a view of a huge rock and not an experience!"

As these idle thoughts drifted through my consciousness, a concept captured me: "Continuance! This might be about continuance." An inspiration struck me like an acknowledgement of something I've known for a very long time! The word *continuance* seemed to linger in emphasis. It formed a sort of echoing refrain within my consciousness.

Contemplating continuance, I searched for an answer. "No: that's not enough reason to bring me to this asteroid. Think harder. How does this link to continuance? I've got it! The probability is essentially inevitable. Some day, a large asteroid *will* strike the Planet Earth! The eventual strike may actually be from *this* asteroid, now positioned before me. The continuance of most biological and organic species will be imperiled, and that includes humanity!"

I continued to wonder about the meaning and purpose of my present situation: "Continuance. Somehow, continuance links this scene to me. Those who can project their consciousness and awareness beyond their bodies attain spiritual continuance. As a sentient, spiritual form of energetic fields, exposure to this asteroid cannot be about me - it has no influence. Why have I been brought here? Is this the information that I should relate to others? This is nothing new to science, nothing that hasn't been made public."

According to geological studies, there have been five extinction-level events on Planet Earth. These were all caused by impacts from asteroids. Each impact extinguished many life forms that existed on Earth at the time. The first was the Permian Extinction, about 250 million years ago. The most recent was the one that ended the reign of the dinosaurs. The implication of these events, when projected into the future, is that the human species, certainly an eminent life form on Earth, could eventually become extinct. Even though major motion picture studios have capitalized on producing asteroid-strike disaster films, the population on Earth does not routinely recognize the threat, having other (normal) priorities in their lives.

Realizing these things, my contemplations moved into other possibilities. " I don't think there is need for a clarion call because I have no perception of urgency about an impact. Besides, to whom would I issue the call? I have no indication that I will return to my body on Earth, and those who have highly evolved, assuming there are more than the cleric, would probably have no interest in what may happen to a little planet in the vastness of the universe."

I was contemplating this dilemma, rolling it around over, and over, rethinking what the purpose of my visit might be. I realized that I was not traveling, not going anywhere, just lolling around an asteroid. My Journey was paused: velocity zero and it concerned me. "Surely you have not traveled this far into this vast expanse to be stuck here indefinitely. You've prevailed through two all or nothing challenges, and by comparison, this seems like no challenge at all. What's holding me here? Maybe it's only my failure to figure out why I'm here that's the problem. Even the population of Earth doesn't grasp this threat as a priority!"

In a flash of inspiration, the word *priority* seemed to shout at me from within. *Priority* seemed to connect with the concept of continuance. "Priority. Continuance - continuance beyond my body is why I still exist, and I've made it my personal priority to evolve so that I could continue. This is my personal quest, which has extended from taking responsibility for myself, and it seems like I'm succeeding."

I paused for contemplation: "Maybe I've captured the point of why I'm here. Priority: it's about priority. Many individuals have not learned to take personal responsibility for their lives, let alone their independent spiritual being. They follow their leaders, be they for political, religious, or for other causes, waiting for instruction about what to do, even how to act. Human history is replete with examples where a leader, claiming to be the intermediary for their god, sends them to war to slay others that don't believe as they do. They don't question their directive: they follow and kill without mercy. They follow zealots for many causes, usually social issues converted to belief systems, and manipulated into action by their leaders, without taking responsibility to find veracity for themselves – let alone acting with independent, objective, minds.

"Oh, wow! This visit is not directly about the asteroid at all! It's about priority and continuance: the priority of accepting personal responsibility in every aspect of life and being. Mankind has a responsibility to use their minds and intellect, to develop and expand technological achievement, and not retreat in fear or guilt contrived by manipulators using specious data to form a belief system. Environmental and humanitarian efforts are best served by allowing the freedom of mind to thrive, to integrate humanity in partnership with the environment, not valuing one at the expense of the other. The preservation of the species, of human existence, requires commitment powered by reason, that begins with each individual's recognition of his or her role and responsibility in the preservation and quality of their lives, thereby committing to the preservation of all life.

"The asteroid is a symbol of the very real threat – humanity is oblivious to extinction and places its priorities elsewhere. Compared to energy stored in the mass and motion of this asteroid before me, anything that humanity might do to itself, and its planetary home, pale to insignificance.

"Why is humanity so truculently mired in issues that deflect responsibility away from themselves as individuals? Why do they play 'follow the leader' with leaders who connive to push them into states of fear, even many that are only based on speculation? Maybe the leaders contrive the fear and people buy into it, relinquishing their use of reason. To me, fear means stasis or decline, not attainment. If an extinction threat were in the public mind, perhaps personal priorities might move toward the advancement of self-awareness. Perhaps humanity on Earth could cooperate, sharing a sense of common purpose: the survival of the planet, the survival of the species. With mutual cooperation, they would develop the technology to continue their survival!"

It was reassuring for me to contemplate that those who evolve could continue as sentient beings composed of energetic fields. I even speculated that sentience could develop from other electrodynamic processes in the universe, as long as they could project as spatial fields and learn through adaptive processes. From Earth, though, continuance in the energetic state of being would only be available to those who directed their energy to continue.

More questions surfaced. "Will I return to tell the story of my journey? Should I report this journey to anyone, and if so, what would be the purpose? Would anyone use my report for his or her benefit?"

In my musings, it didn't seem to matter because I was here in a state of pure being, feeling enhanced beyond any expectations I would have thought possible. There was a high but not arrogant reassurance: my journey already had expanded my cognition, knowledge, and understanding further than anything that I could ever have once imagined. My nagging feeling was that this segment of my experience had happened for a reason that I had yet to grasp. Though the concepts of personal priority, responsibility, and continuance seemed to be at the core of that reason, I was struggling to apply these to myself, especially with regard to the asteroid.

Then I probed deeper to find more significance, seeking an answer for my visit here. "Responsibilities. In working through personal responsibilities, I cannot ignore the involvement of others. Others such as Bob, Kayla, and Morgan, had cooperated with me for my personal gain, and they benefited from their involvement as well. If I saw someone in trouble and knew that I could be of assistance, I would be failing myself if I did not even attempt to act. If I reached out to the person, and they rejected my outreach, then I would have met my responsibility to myself. This is incredible! By prioritizing my responsibilities and my continuance, I can extend my own energy unless it depletes my own resources. If my actions pervasively wasted my resources in deference to others, I would bankrupt myself through self-sacrifice and violate my responsibility! Wow! This can be a delicate balance."

As soon as I had derived this conceptual clarity, the infinitesimal flash occurred! Again catapulted into the particle wind stream: my journey was continuing! Apparently, I had completed the purpose of my (presumed) detour to view the asteroid by arriving at the conclusions developed during my introspections.

I was again traveling through time and space at an incredible speed, probably toward a destination that would bring more exposure and more experience. At this point, I still did not know the answer to the important question: *"Exposure and continuance - to what?"*

My intuition inspired my optimism that there had to be more to this experience than a challenge of my resolve to be true to myself, then to visit an asteroid to provoke my introspection! In the meantime, I enjoyed the ride in the particle wind.

Observation

It seems simple to observe that many in humanity are so engaged in the structures and routines of daily life that they easily neglect the possibility that some extraordinary event can instantly redirect the basis of their lives, out of their comfort zone of routine.

Serious illness, the sudden death of a loved one, or a cataclysmic event of nature can abruptly alter a person's attitude – and life – forever.

Emotional conflicts can also invade to cause serious consequences. For example, if you leave someone you love in anger, or with emotionally charged issues, consider that before you can resolve the issues, the other person could

perish. The survivor could be left with profound regret, unable to bring harmony into their memories.

It might be valuable for you to ask yourself each day:

What really is important to me in my life?

What is unresolved that demands resolution?

Am I wasting my precious energy in inefficient ways?

Am I living my life for me or am I being held in the controlling influence or dependency of others?

Are others co-dependent with me?

The most precious asset we have is the energetic form of our consciousness and with that the viability of our health. Cherish and conserve your energy, and when you use it, deploy it with the priority of responsibility to yourself.

CHAPTER FIFTEEN

MENTORS

Launched into this new segment of my expansive journey, I again inspected the characteristics of my field sphere of being as a sort of survey of myself. It seemed appropriate to check myself as I did after my encounter with the cleric and now after exposure to the asteroid.

My thoughts reflected on the events: "It's obvious – something or someone is again propelling me to another destination. What would the purpose be for this travel now? The cleric challenged my conclusions about belief in a deity and to be either a follower or self-directing. I must have passed that test. My reward is that I am continuing this magnificent journey, and my field sphere is manifesting increased numbers of gold and red filaments! I'm feeling more able, more energetic, more invigorated. Each destination point has been for a purpose. The visualization of the asteroid inspired me to contemplate the frailty of organic life, continuance beyond the Earthly plane, and priorities of life. What, I wonder, will come next?

"At least my consciousness, my sense of myself, is intact and both my awareness and sensitivities feel incredibly heightened – and, I think, related to the filaments and colors in my sphere.

Maybe, just maybe, these filaments relate to knowledge, aware-ness, understanding and abilities!

"I'm uncertain about the future. Someone, some force, or some being must be orchestrating this experience. Angels? Are there angels or spirit guides? Could it be god, intent on showing me my error? Ah, no, it would have been simpler to do that when I was with the cleric, and now I feel energetically more power-ful. That seems like a reward, not a punishment. Don't waste ef-fort, Michael. If you are supposed to know, if you have earned the ability to deal with the knowledge as it happens, you will learn soon enough."

The incredibly neglected question of who or what was in control had not been at the forefront of my experience. I had enough to deal with: thrusting myself beyond the tunnel of light was a challenge to my courage and self-determination; and, adjusting to the thrill of my first travel in the particle wind had enraptured most of my attention at the time. What was currently important to me is my magnificent journey! It has catapulted me into new levels of awareness, and into attaining more breadth in my per-ception. Emphatically, most importantly of all, I was not only continuing to exist, but my continuance was now beyond all pa-rameters that I could have previously imagined.

Then the brief flash happened again as I had seen on each change of travel when entering or exiting the wind, and I halted, suspended in what seemed to be the infinity of the universe. Although my awareness remained fully open, my familiarity with this situation allowed me to relax and be prepared for what might next be in store for me. I felt sufficiently empowered to handle whatever would happen in any new manifestation pre-sented to me.

About the point where I was beginning to settle into my new position, a new visualization began to emerge. The fabric of space was stirring, heaving a bit like the ebbs and flows of ocean waves. Something appeared to be penetrating through the fabric of black and indigo blue. The stirring took the shape of an aperture elliptically shaped like a very elongated slot. Around the elliptical aperture, there was a haze of multiple colorations, purples and blues, penetrating through primarily a swirling gray-white undulating fog. The aperture seemed to peal back away from me, and as it did, a wide and flat surface protruded in my direction. I thought: "It looks like space is *giving birth* to something! What?"

The protrusion penetrating the ellipse was a thin and wide structure similar to the top surface of a theatrical stage, a plane or a large platform. It had diffused edges on the sides that appeared to merge back into the fabric of space. In all of this sequence of magnificent experiences, I had not seen anything like this image before.

The platform surface appeared as a dark sandy color that diffused into space. There was no sand per se, although the surface of the plane was not perfectly smooth and flat. It seemed to be composed of low, broad, undulating waves like gentle wind-swept dunes or ripples along the shoreline of a beach. The ripples undulated very slowly in motion, like thermal optical wave distortions on a hot desert floor. If the platform were analogous to a map of the United States, I was hovering over Florida, looking diagonally toward the Northwest.

Four new luminous forms slowly appeared upon the surface of the platform. They were magnificent – much more intense in color and activity than the sphere of the cleric. As these new images of light and fields began to appear, I decided to improve my viewpoint. I repositioned myself using my slow panoramic navigational ability that I had become accustomed to directing, simply by willing it. My observation point now centered a little above the platform. The four luminescent apparitions were upon the plane immediately in front of my position.

I was dazzled a bit as I thought: "These must be sentient beings, but their field intensity and motions of filaments within the fields are much more dynamic than what I've seen with the cleric's spheroid, or my own. They are generally similar in structure and shape, but the colors are striking and gorgeous!

Their spheres are emitting auras of very brilliant and magnificent colors that extend across and throughout the plane in all directions."

One at a time, each spheroid began to faintly take on a human-like form, barely noticeable at first. I had the firm impression that these "human-like" appearances were for the purpose of my own psychological comfort level, rather than for any real necessity. I thought: "I wonder if these beings were once human and have now evolved? Strange, I didn't think to ask that question of the cleric." I dwelled on the magnificence of the glorious images.

The core color, so brilliant that it appeared dazzling white, was a comparatively small segment of the geometric ovoid shape. The core comprised only about a quarter or less of the actual image size. This resplendent color hue then merged and expanded into a brilliant electrified gold.

The gold continued across the shape until it reached the outer boundary of the spheres. There, the color and structure diffused in a sparkling way into space. It appeared to me that the whole of these spheroids glistened, with sparklers surrounding the periphery like a Fourth of July fireworks celebration. In my technical experience, it was similar to the expansion of corona surrounding a structure of high-voltage electrification.

The sparkling permeated the images and at the outer boundary, the sparkling caused the diffused appearance. I also noticed that there were wisps of filaments and tendrils of striations in motion stirring within each sphere. The striations were primarily royal blue, with impressively bright filaments of red, shimmering and meandering throughout. Combined, these auras were similar to artists' renditions of holy images, even divine and blessed. The human-like figures remained immersed in their brilliant field, seeming like the haloes or auras that artists attempted to capture.

Within the spheres of brilliant energy, the diffused human figures continued slowly to emerge and as they became clearer, I recognized that they were adorned with hints of robes from ancient times, similar to depictions in Renaissance paintings. I was reminded of the renderings of the 1531 apparition of *Our Lady of Guadalupe* in Hidalgo, Mexico, which coincidentally was only a few years before my ancestor returned to Spain after traveling in that general area (1528–1537). Renditions of *Our Lady of Guadalupe* depict the entire figure of the Virgin Mary in the foreground, surrounded in a vertical ellipse of golden and red aura.

The first three images appeared sequentially. As the first came into shaper clarity, I noted the image of a female, still diffused in the haze of her spheroid. A feeling immersed me as I was observing her image and I realized – *I know who this is.* Before I had time to react, the image within the second sphere became clear, displaying the form of an elder male bent slightly forward. Coupled with the first feminine image, I felt enthusiasm and glee. I knew with every fiber of my being that these perceptions were real, that the identity of these two beings had been made known to me. "I know of you!" I exclaimed: "I know who you are!"

I needed to slow down a bit so that my enthusiasm didn't overrun my use of reason: "Be careful, Michael. Does this feel right? Could your perception be right? Pause. Think." I probed into myself as deeply as I could. I learned that my certainty was assured and so solid that I projected my thoughts to the image with joy and excitement.

"Mary of Magdala! – Mary Magdalene!" As I projected her name, she turned and gazed at me. A ribbon of softly flowing energy, appearing like a sweep of magenta, seemed to flow from a gentle extension of her hands toward me, swirling around my sphere in the gentle sensation of embrace, and I accepted that as a confirming gesture. Then, her human image diffused back into her luminous field.

My attention then immediately focused on the image of the elderly male, and after taking a moment to recheck my own perception, I projected my thoughts with as much grace as I could. "Simon Peter." My thoughts and feelings paused as that image straightened up, turned to me without expression but with an affirmative nod, and then diffused back into his sphere.

Before I could grasp the immensity of what this visitation implied, my attention snapped around to focus upon the third sphere. This sphere tended to have more red striations, brilliant crimson, which morphed into flowing red robes (or a cape) surrounding a male, then converging back into the brilliant sphere. I waited quietly as the image of the male became more distinct. Then I felt a very familiar one-phrase refrain. It came to me as softly as if it were a whisper borne of vapor: *"Familia"* then…. *"Family."* My feeling actually was very similar to that I experienced as a child when I was in the presence of my mother and our relatives.

The image remained present in the luminescent form, as I thought this through. "There have been many occasions where my relatives from Spain and I would use the phrase 'familia es familia' as affirmation of our blood relationship. It's a warm and embracing phrase used to emphasize the common bond of family. For me, the only one of my generation of our family to have been born an American, distant from my family in Europe, this is a very reaffirming phrase. Now, in this state of being, that phrase with its implied reassurance carries even higher significance for me."

I returned the phrase with an assurance that I've rarely felt before: *"Familia es familia. Cabeza de Vaca – mi familia."* which was a statement that my ancestor Álvar Núñez Cabeza de Vaca would make as a greeting to his bloodline descendant. My projection was with a feeling of embracing appreciation. His image seemed to flutter like a cape in the wind as it diffused back into luminescence. Here, in the vast reaches of the universe, beyond time and space as experienced by humanity, images both from biblical times and from my own ancestry were being revealed to me: *Familia es familia…* after all.

My attention next directed toward the fourth sphere. The fourth luminescent field sphere appeared as brilliantly as the others, but sparkled with a deeper hue saturation of golden warmth, approaching that of an amber gold and swirling like energetic clouds. There were intense red and copper-red filaments and striations interspersed throughout. This entity not only appeared to be different, but its emanations *felt* different as well, with an underlying feeling of a powerful heat. As the fourth and unique image appeared in progressive clarity, I was awestruck. My feeling was tantamount to being spellbound and profoundly shocked. I felt numbed, paralyzed and overwhelmed with awe – incredible reverence and awe.

I knew now – instantly, instinctively, and clearly without any hesitation – for what and why – *and by whom* – I had been prepared for a very long time. All my years of seeking answers to my identity and my purpose for being, all my small strides that were stepping stones along a path, all now combined to lead up to this one momentous, magnificent, and pivotal event. There was and is no question, no doubt, that this moment and experience was *the critical juncture of all my existence*. I serenely drifted into a state of the deeply felt emotion of love, the embracing and unconditionally accepting power of pure and unconditional love, and I realized in every fiber of my being what the purpose of my preparation was. *Finally, I knew.*

A soft whisper came from within me *Yêšûà'*, first as a murmur, and then firmly: *Jesus.* Oh…my…. In my thoughts, all that I am composed of, I uttered the name, not in question but in reverent acceptance: *"Jesus"*… Which caused his reply in response to my utterance: *"Yes,"* first through a nod, then as his gaze turned to briefly settle on me, as if the reply were a both an acknowledgement and a greeting. The expression of his facial image was one of sincerity – relatively stoic, yet gentle.

There was a magnificent surge of intensity in his sphere. The intensity accompanied a swept motion of his field that seemed to be an embrace or outreach toward me. Then, his field expanded and immersed me in an incredible power that I can only describe as love – with a profundity not experienced before or since that time. If I then had a body, I would have trembled, even fallen, gasped, and cried.

Years of religious teaching overwhelmed me and reflexively surfaced as I dared to express my thought as a tentative, even shaking, projection: "Savior. My Lord."

His sphere briefly surged with activity, and his image extended, elongated itself in my direction as he intensely issued his response: *"NO!"* Carried on an electrified, directed, crimson beam that focused upon me, his response could not have been more pointed, or more specific. His gaze was stern. Then his crimson beam withdrew as he turned his attention back to his companions.

His human-form image diffused back into his brilliance, and I dwelled on what seemed to be a power that I cannot truly describe. "Why this rebuke? Had I not addressed him with his proper title? Was he displeased with my awkward response? Have I angered him? Will he punish me? All of my life I have heard of judgment day upon death. Is this mine?"

Yet, I had no doubts whatever about whose presence had *summoned* me to meet them. Compared to the intensity of their spheres, implied by their colors and brilliance, my royal and cobalt blues seemed to be rather dull and otherwise quite insignificant. Though I was continuing in evolution and consciousness, by comparison I was clearly not near their level of accomplishment.

Perplexed, I began to regain my composure recovering from the stunning realization of what was happening to me. Now, burning with curiosity, I again found that I was able to move about, study, and observe the group. They had directed their attention toward each other, not to me. It was evident that these individuals all had attained profoundly advanced evolution.

Balancing myself, my energetic form, I carefully and reverently closed the distance between us. I could easily ascertain that the four beings were communicating with one another. There were gestures as shown by the directional movements and motions of the striations and filaments within their spheres. Through the activity of movements and stirring of filaments and tendrils, it appeared obvious that the discussion among them was intense. My interest intensified, and I projected myself cautiously and tentatively into perceiving their exchange. I thought: "I've come this far. These advanced beings brought me here for some purpose. Is this my moment of judgment for all time?" Falling back on the old dogma of churchianity, I asked myself "Does the glory of heaven await me – or the horror of everlasting hell?"

The consequences seemed ultimate in magnitude for me, whatever they would be. I started to fall into my own trap, diminish and withdraw – my historical failure modes - probably triggered by the thought of everlasting hell. Immediately I felt my essence flood with fear! My blue striations started to dim! I immediately realized that I was losing energy. I stopped and caught myself: "Michael, stop this! This is no time to slip into your old failing ways and risk losing your very existence. You've worked too hard to get to this level! I know that I am responsible for my destiny that I am answerable only to myself. I need to continue on this journey. This will *not be the end of my being* – I will *not allow myself to fail*. I am accountable for whatever their judgment might be – if this is a judgment." An indelible moment was at hand.

Immediately my energy form had collected and re-established itself by the force of my reason and will to continue. I thought: "Lesson learned. I must be continuously vigilant. I must never degrade myself. I must keep myself collected and coherently together. Self-negation threatens ultimate failure – the cessation of my very existence!"

It was striking to learn by this experience how powerful or frail my being can be, solely determined by my commitment to myself. After working my way through that turmoil, I managed to regain my sense of myself and refocus upon those before me.

It is worth reminding you that communication in this realm is essentially instantaneous. Language, as humankind might define and experience it, simply does not apply. The communication or sensory transfers between or among those entities that have evolved to a transcendent form, occurs in a *flash*. As I studied their motions, I could directly feel and experience their thoughts in their communication. Then, with some surprise, I quickly captured the concept of their discussion. Jesus' energy flashed with filaments directed toward me as he said: *"He has used his reasoning. He has discerned our truth, our reality."*

Stunned, I thought: "They are discussing ME – Michael! Maybe this really is my judgment day! That is not exactly comforting. It implies they are trying to come to a decision. What happens if their decision goes against me? Clearly, they seem to be in control of my journey! What occurs if they decide not to allow me to continue? Maybe I can interject myself and participate in their discussion. Maybe I can influence the outcome. Why sit on the sidelines? This is the opportunity of all my life's work and quest to evolve. Don't waste this moment! Engage, Michael. Knowledge awaits you, maybe unequivocal knowledge - just assert yourself and connect with them."

As I now reflect back on this incredible experience, I realize how arrogant I must have been. I tried to thrust myself into their discussion. They did not acknowledge me. I had been muted as if a force field were confining me. My single permission was to observe.

Nonetheless, I repetitively continued to attempt to insinuate myself into their conversation. Surely, if they were involved in a discussion about me, perhaps I might have something to contribute. If this were a trial, I felt they should at least give me the opportunity to defend myself. If this were a test, I might at least try to promote myself! Although I might have thought of this as trying to contribute, that is inaccurate. I was attempting to insert myself to influence their discussion and potentially their decision.

I should have known better by then. They did not allow me to influence their discussion. They blocked all of my attempts to participate. I finally realized the foolishness of my attempts, as I thought: "Stop this! It's folly to even consider that I can inveigle or influence their discussion. These beings before me have evolved beyond my wildest dreams! They probably know every molecule of my being and all of my history. This must be another test. Anything I might attempt will come to naught. I have come this far, and there may be more. Be patient and learn."

As my curiosity stirred, and I outreached again to connect to them, their exchange halted, and the pause seemed to hold everything in suspense. I remained in reverent awe awaiting the continuation of their discussion. The stillness of that moment was broken with a surprising statement. Jesus said: *"He knows."* That statement seemed directed toward Mary Magdalene, which I inferred from the color motions in his sphere flowing toward her sphere. Jesus continued, *"What are we to do with him?"*

"What? Do WITH me? What do I know? What have I done?" My thoughts, though intensified, went nowhere, projected only into my own field. I launched my attempt to communicate, but my thoughts would not leave. I could not project my intentions from my sphere. I might as well have been whispering into a deep pillow in my bed on Earth. "Settle down Michael. I must accept that I'm not in control no matter what I might try. Don't waste energy and make a fool of yourself. This is a profound moment."

Jesus' question resulted in a response that seemed to come from Mary Magdalene and Simon Peter simultaneously: *"What are we to do about him?"* There was another pause. Was that an opening for me to enter the discussion? Was that an opportunity for me to make a suggestion? My thoughts went rampant: "Do with me? Do about me? I have to try to get into this. Please…hear…"

I'm not certain who issued the message. I had become so tangled in my thoughts, that I had lost my focus. I only could decipher two very clear and disconcerting words: *"No. Stop."* I stopped, quelled into my own thoughts. Then there was a stirring of ribbon-like red filaments issued from the field of Cabeza de Vaca. His message carried forth to the others:

"He confronted our emissary who tested him on his conviction to his knowledge. He overcame his fear of church authority. Even the

nuance of revenge from a god did not dissuade him from his commitment. He did not become a follower to a false image. Next, he viewed the object that would threaten Earth, used his reason, and reached the conclusions we hoped he would reach. Even before his death, his perceptions alerted him to review his past. His awareness, his preparedness has never been so evolved as now."

The comments made it extraordinarily clear to me that my ancestor was acting as my advocate. It might not be called *judgment day*, but it certainly seems to be *decision day*. My thoughts still would not leave my sphere, no matter how hard I tried, so I turned inward. "Okay. I've done my best. They must know that. Is this to test me again, or is this deliberation to decide my destiny? Pay attention and stop trying to change what I cannot change. I accept that I've done my best. Maybe this is just another test… maybe…"

They did not direct their attention toward me. Their attention solely focused on each other. Insofar as I could discern, they were acting as though I were invisible to them, so I continued my introspection. "My attempts to insinuate myself, to influence and manipulate the discussion are a human protective reflex. What have you learned? What do you understand? What a presumption of arrogance I have! They probably know everything about me. I've realized that attempting to influence those in a state of pure being, ultimately evolved, is a silly human folly. As fully evolved beings, they might embody all truth and knowledge of the universe.

"I know that I can trust what I perceive, that empathic connection is pure. It does not have an agenda. I've come to believe that: I cannot deny my true nature; I cannot inveigle; I choose not to damage another, but I can damage myself; I am accountable for myself, only to myself, for my evolution. I've also discerned that my ultimate responsibility is to self, to evolve to the state of pure being as represented by these luminous forms."

Then it struck me that I am a mere novice compared to these beings before me. I halted all attempts at interjecting myself, and moved into a state of acceptance and peace to the extent that I was able.

I deduced with certainty that if my destiny were simply going to be extinguished, with my sentient fields dissipated into infinite space, it would have happened already – and I would not be in the presence of those who had apparently brought me here. My rambling thoughts probed for more: "Are you being presumptive in your conclusions? No. There must be more. Maybe I can expand my awareness with their help! Have peace and patience, Michael. What they must reveal, they will reveal. Trust in your judgment, there is a purpose to this journey."

So immersed as I was in my own thoughts, I had failed to notice that their activity, the stirring in their fields, had become still. By the positions of the filaments in their fields, I could tell that they now directed their attention solely toward me. Yet, nothing seemed to be occurring.

"What has happened? They've stopped their discussion! When I tried to insinuate myself into their discussion, I was rebuffed. Now that I've learned not to try to influence their discussion, maybe they are waiting for me to open myself to them. That seems reasonable if they have finished their discussion. Could that mean they have made a decision about me? It must be my responsibility to find out."

My analytical intuition had been telling me that I had been under evaluation for this meeting and that my unconditional trust of these beings was appropriate, probably imperative. That trust made sense to me, I reasoned, because all that I am was here, my sentience composed as energetic fields and that my abilities paled in comparison to the abilities of those now before me.

I reasoned: "This stillness feels like a critical juncture. Maybe I can move across the threshold that's separating us, and take advantage of this magnificent opportunity. I feel humbled to be in their presence, and maybe the next move is mine to make." I cautiously moved closer to narrow the gap that separated us. Their fields remained quiescent as I approached. When I was satisfied with my position, I gently, reverently and carefully expanded my field in their direction. Filaments from my being extended outward from within the haze of my sphere, and their color intensified to a crimson red as I approached these incredible beings.

During my approach, their spheres expanded toward each other so that a form of combining occurred, though I could still recognize the individuality of each being. When they connected to each other, a magnificent event happened: they extended themselves across the expanse to me as I extended myself to them. I was convinced that this signaled the opportunity for me to communicate, and that I would be heard.

"I think that you have orchestrated the events that have confronted, embraced, and challenged me. I understand that you have brought me here to be with you – though I don't know why. My ancestor among you as much as said so, indicating I had met the challenges you presented. I understood your question, 'What to do about me?' and this was the point of your discussion."

The response issued simultaneously from Mary Magdalene, my ancestor, then Simon Peter in what seemed to be a cascade of communication. Jesus seemed to control the direction of the response as if they were constructing a consensus simultaneously while responding to me. Precisely which of these individuals issued what statement was not important: it was as if they expressed themselves with the harmony of a chorus. The answers came in such a gentle flow that it was as natural as a warm and soft breeze flowing through my being.

"You have used your reasoning and discerned that spiritual attainment is a natural part of an individual's evolution and that it is subject to personal responsibility. Each person must take that responsibility as a commitment to and for himself or herself. You forsook what was familiar to you and met the challenges with the courage of your convictions. Michael, we learned how to evolve beyond human form. The energy of the individual human spirit when gathered in coherence and focused into personal power can continue into all of eternity. Your conclusion is true. It is reality. It is

knowledge of yourself that brings the personal power that we call freedom."

Great peace flooded through me with elating energy as they confirmed my understanding, building my confidence and yet, I had to ask: "Is personal power derived from others or from a supreme being? Do you save souls? Jesus signaled 'NO!' to me when I attempted to address him as 'Lord or Savior.' What are you if not a lord or savior? What do you represent? I feel because of the challenges you've presented to me, this gathering must be about personal evolution. Am I now in my eternity?"

In unison, they responded, *"We are all formed from fields and the energetic matter of the universe."*

There was a brief pause that I took as an opportunity for me to seek further confirmation. I could think of no better time to ask a question made as a definitive statement. "I have discerned that there is no god, that our sentience, the consciousness that humankind accepts as our soul under the influence of a god, evolves through our focus in natural processes."

"Your body, mind and soul, all encompass the essence of the universe. By believing in yourself, and the power within you, your belief empowers and extends your energy to the power of the universe. God is your belief in yourself and the forces of nature you have at your command within yourself.

"Any individual may evolve, first by committing to individual responsibility for self-attainment, then learning how to use the power that comes from and flows through the self. That power of self is personal and may never be used in dominance or control over any other being, as that would make an individual into a parasite of another's energy. Parasites dissipate into oblivion unless they feed on a host. No one may utilize their power other than for self-evolution. No one is saved from allowing themselves to dissipate into infinite oblivion, other than by developing and using the resources held within. You, and the evolving power through your commitment, devised your own path to your salvation. That is truly your evolution into your spiritual destiny. That is the way we have attained our evolution. We cannot save anyone.

"You worked to break yourself away from the familiarity of the teachings that held you back, that suppressed your energetic form into withdrawal. You compelled yourself to strive and lose negative emotions, the familiar controls of tyrants and victims, of dependencies and co-dependencies, of self-importance that low self-esteem causes, and to bring your individual power into being. You were inspired to learn that trust and love of self enables the love of all. The love of self elevated to an unconditional state enables the unconditional love of all."

Carefully considering their words, I responded: "It is true. When I love, I have learned to love unconditionally even if my feeling of love is not returned. My choice to love is volitional, a state of freedom in my mind. I am unconcerned if another feels the same for me because that would limit my perception of love – placing a condition or parameter upon whom I choose to love or why I would love them."

"We know by observing you that you have conviction in your personal power from which you've gathered strength. We have brought you before us because you have qualified yourself by your actions. Words and intent are insufficient to qualify. We will not waste our energy with those confined in dependency of either seeking others to find salvation for themselves or impressed with their ego called self-importance. You have shown yourself by your progress to be a seeker of truth and knowledge.

"You have been searching beyond the confines of your human body's existence, and accepting the choice of continuing into infinity as your responsibility, and yours alone. You are correct. Your infinite continuance is solely your responsibility; it is not our responsibility or that of any other. You are experiencing an attained state of being. You have evolved by casting away what you once clung to as familiar, and found personal impeccability. An individual earns self-evolution and attainment through self-accountability, and that can only happen for and within each person. Each person must learn for himself or herself, using reason, to gain personal efficacy to attain this state of being.

"You cast off the dependency of pleading to be 'saved'. You have discerned that placing the fate of your destiny in the illusion that another may save you is sheer folly, taking that responsibility upon yourself. Your conviction and commitment to your personal control for yourself through reason has freed your energy to attain this state of being. You strove to develop freedom from dependency, reliance, and guilt, of using another's energy for your personal attainment."

I reflected on the events and decisions of my life, and realized that they know me intimately. I commented: "It's true. I lived in my early years trying to do what I was told "God" wanted me to do, yet it only defeated my attempts to learn who I am – and what I could attain. I realized that early teachings had diverted my personal power into the hands of others. These doctrines demanded my servitude and limited my ability to use reason and accept myself. Those early beliefs diluted my personal responsibility and with that, compromised the control I had for my own existence. I found that only the decisions and deeds of my life, through my personal commitment to evolve myself without usurping the energy of others, determined my ultimate destiny. Submitting myself over to control of a "god," as defined by those claiming to represent him and you, could not save me. My perception through the years has been consistent, that I have been both prepared and monitored. Is that true?"

"You have been monitored, tested, facilitated, and inspired. We know every detail of your life, and we know you have integrated the knowledge gathered from your experiences within you. You have worked to convert all the negative influences of your history into positives by learning the lessons we have offered, even through those negative events. Using your rationale, you defeated the tendency of clinging on to the familiar, breaking patterns of emotion and behavior. Through that action, you experienced, learned, and developed knowledge of yourself. You tested your knowledge repeatedly to be certain it was correct and without conflict."

I offered: "I attempted throughout my life to understand my emotions, what degraded me, and what promoted me to be more effective in my own knowledge and development. I was striving not to degrade myself by using dependency on others, or hide behind the protection of depression or anger. It seems on the surface as a simple quest, but I have found it to be a life-long challenge. By being summoned to be here with you, I accept that the learning and evolution of self might continue for all eternity!"

"Michael, the knowledge of self is the precursor for knowledge of the universe and your origins of consciousness within the universe. Your self-trust allowed you to correct errors by using reason without degrading yourself.

"You have discerned the correct conclusion, beating away your fears, passing our tests by being true to your commitment to yourself. Each person must hold these concepts, and hold them absolutely, to enable attainment of ultimate evolution. Because you have done well with the abilities you have, we have brought you here to this state of being as a candidate who merits our increased involvement with you."

Then, there was a pause. It was probably a very brief pause, but it felt at that moment like an eternity for me, and I was trying to formulate a question. "Merits? Candidate? Increased involvement?" I tried to ask, but before I could muster my focus, they continued as I struggled to maintain my composure, to absorb every nuance of their statements.

"We have brought you here, first to test you and now to be with us. When you arrived, we were discussing what to do about you. "We have made our decision. You have qualified yourself to be our protégé. We are your mentors."

If a gasp were possible, absent a body or breath, a gasp is what I would have expressed. Already laced by my fascination over this experience, my sense of myself was actually trembling, stimulated by my view of the expansively magnificent beings connected with me.

"Mentors"…I tested myself to feel my reaction by merely uttering the word, letting the breath and realization to sink in.

Resonances - I felt resonances – truths and reality swirling within me…. I felt energy and power growing within me. I explored the impressions captured in that one moment. My thoughts projected in appreciation of them contemplating the significance of what they said – what the term means in reality, thinking, "What would mentors do? Mentors would facilitate, but facilitate what?"

"Ah, perhaps to understand the ramifications of projecting myself into my infinity. I have more to learn –and mentors to teach and facilitate me. Incredible as it may seem, this makes perfect sense. My perceptions at the canyon, the events of my life, the challenges, all assemble here and now. I clearly recognize all of the mosaic pieces that are coming together to construct my evolution. What now?"

I had barely finished my thoughts when their direction continued…

"Your progress of evolution, and the tests that are required to verify your achievements, will become more intense. As you continue your commitment to attain your ultimate state of evolution, you will have increasing responsibilities. Your responsibilities will increase as your abilities increase, if your conviction to yourself does not falter. If you do not regress into human forms of negation, you will be at one with us, and continue so to be…into infinity. Remember you must be true to yourself and your purpose.

"Do not attempt to label yourself. There are no labels, nor titles, to partition or separate yourself from us or present us as different from you. We are only ourselves, as you must only be yourself."

Absorbing and contemplating their message, I queried: "If labels are not significant, why did you expose and impress on me your historical identities?"

"We claim no labels, titles or identity other than ourselves. We permitted you to temporarily see our historical human identities to confirm to you – by our example – what an individual's ultimate evolutionary potential can be. Separate yourself from designations that would define you relative to others, since such distinctions can become self-importance or partitions of protection. Be only yourself.

"If all you are is yourself, even your birth name has, as of this moment, no significance. In this manner of freedom, an individual will lose residuals of dependency and will attain our state of ultimate and free being."

"Mentors – yes, this must be true. I feel the trust and truth in you. Your statements collectively carry enormous implications for me. You have confirmed the validity of my conclusions. Eternal continuance is a high attainment of awareness and being, a natural extension of what individuals can achieve for themselves.

"Jesus, the Christian world and bible state that you have offered that 'I will be at one with you' and since you are only yourselves, then humankind has missed the point if they 'worship and adore' you! What a distortion through human follies has happened by deflecting their responsibility to attain their oneness with you - to others that claim to know and represent you! Independent reasoning and trust bring understanding, knowledge and oneness for all eternity. You do not 'save' anyone yet you are facilitating me. You have facilitated others like those standing with you now. Unquestionably, you began your quest and became a teacher, and have become highly evolved, much respected for your attainment. Yet few realize that the high level of your attainment is accomplished by each being's own commitment, by using their own direction and reason, not because of power from a deity more powerful than you are..........than we are." I tentatively, probingly, allowed.

His directed reply was: *"You are just beginning to experience the significance of your attained state of being."*

As I was working to contemplate how majestically profound this was, they offered what I felt was going to be a directive.

"Remember, and remember this indelibly – there will be increasing responsibilities for you. Remember that increasing abilities couple with increasing responsibilities, in direct proportion. You will engage with others who will be identified to you to advance their evolution and attain our state of being. They will become apparent to you. You cannot search to find them. That would be a futile use of your energy, which must be conserved."

In a model of restraint, they offered: *"Your sensory cognition is now heightened. Your heightened perception will further enhance, and that enhancement will help identify candidates to you. If you retreat in any way from your commitment to your impeccability, there will be consequences since, as we have said, abilities and responsibilities are inextricably bound together."*

The link between responsibilities and abilities seemed logical. Then I felt a wave of astonishment, and I enthusiastically blurted out: "Responsibilities to self, reason, evolution and the connection to abilities must all be a universal premise! Why are these concepts so elusive, so difficult for humans to grasp?" I probed to gain more understanding.

"When the seeds of life are first formed from the safe and familiar place of their mother's womb, people experience shock at their new environment when they emerge because the familiar state of the womb is lost. In every step of people's lives, they cling to what is familiar. They resist detaching from the familiar even if it holds them back, even if it is degrading. Human society devises groups that claim to embrace and enhance souls. Their embrace becomes captive yet familiar, and people will resist change because that means losing what they believe embraced them. It is the responsibility of each person to evolve themselves and this is an individual's most formidable quest."

"Yes. I understand from my own life the truth of what you say. Passing the test of breaking away from the religion that was familiar and so embedded that it held me back happened because I learned that the familiar was not safe or progressive for me and it was just the opposite by the way I reacted. I needed to find my own path to evolve, even if it was frightening. I committed to use reason and self-determination to accept the challenges that I would have to surmount in meeting that test. Retrospectively, it seems simple, yet fear of leaving the familiar and changing seemed so difficult when emotions were involved.

"Please, the profundity of all you have revealed is resonating within me. I need a moment to contemplate this immensity."

Thankfully, they provided a welcome pause for me to introspect on what was happening to me. Even in telepathic form, I needed to be silent and be appreciative of these beings. Every expectation that I might have had, or even vaguely considered, had now been exceeded. No, that is a vastly inadequate description. *Exceeded* doesn't cover it. *Supersaturated* would be more accurate.

Everything seemed stilled for a moment. Shattering the quietude of the pause they allowed me to have, in simultaneous chorus, they suddenly asked a simple question of me: *"Who or what are you?"*

"What? You already know... all about..." I sputtered. In an instant, I captured the answer, and simultaneously extended my energy to joyously embrace them, and responded: "I am only myself."

The brilliance of their spheres intensified and my form was drawn into their brilliance and I experienced an incredible all encompassing feeling of unconditional love. As our forms gradually separated, I found that after experiencing the power of their embrace, I had to compose myself.

Everything energetic then became utterly still. There was a short pause, equivalent to maybe a few seconds. I was gathering my thoughts internally when I sensed something changing. My attention returned toward my mentors, and I realized they were moving away and gradually fading. I suddenly remembered: my future remained not discussed.

"Wait! Is this my eternity?" I pleaded. My mentors and the platform-like surface upon which they had been situated, slowly vanished. I was alone, yet I continued to experience a reassurance that felt like unseen tendrils of connection to their energetic fields.

Then I emotionally stammered a bit as the realization hit me again. Essentially, I uttered the equivalent of a trembled gasp: *"My mentors..."* as my personal expression of unconditional and appreciative love, carried on the wings of respect.

Those words first echoed within my being and then seemed to build within me as a gathering crescendo of intensity. They seemed to burst out into space, projected as if I was calling after them, and I felt the words roiling throughout the universe searching out my mentors.

"Prepared for something significant" – as my perceptions and precognition had alerted me in Canyon Muerto – now seemed to pale as an expression when contrasted to the new reality of my being. With a sense of accomplishment, I had come to a condition of full acceptance. I trust in all of this experience. I trust in myself. To resonate in doubts would only waste my energy. I had another thought: "What challenges could I deal with now, in my current open and transparent state of being?"

It did not take long to find out as the flash occurred and I was thrust into the wind once again.

Observation

It is impressively valuable to inspect and evaluate feelings about yourself. The emphasis is to learn how you came to have those feelings.

> Are there issues that negatively hit your self-esteem?
> Are there issues that positively elevate you?
> Are you dependent on others to feel good about yourself?
> Do you exist in harmony or in conflict with yourself?
> If so, upon what personal history have formed your self-opinions?
> Do you think about them or are they compulsive responses?

Is it "okay" for you to die today? If not, ask yourself why. Imagine that you journeyed into and beyond the tunnel of light as your body entered the throes of death.

> What would you fear?

What is the basis of your fear?

Do you think you would have encounters with others who have moved beyond death?

If already evolved beings could engage with you, what do you think they would they say to you?

Would they, in your opinion, accept or reject yourself, or just be neutral? Why?

What do you think the significance would be to you, of what you've said by your answers?

Self-inspection could be used to learn if the feelings are based on impulsive reactions of automatons, or self-directed with objectivity.

Do you truly understand the foundation of any religious precepts you may feel compelled to follow?

Do you truly understand, historically, how the precepts of that foundation actually are constructed?

In that light of inspection, check out the reality in "the now of being" to you. Ultimately, can you detach yourself from what is familiar to you, confront the fear that may cause, and commit yourself to the personal responsibility of your evolution?

The knowledge of yourself is the foundation upon which your ultimate evolution is enabled to advance.

CHAPTER SIXTEEN

HUMBLED AND INFORMED

T his time my travel experience in the high velocity wind-stream felt more wondrous, more electrically energetic, than before. I was reveling in having learned that I have mentors, who they are as spiritual beings, that they are accessible and connected to me, and that they had orchestrated many events in my life – including this magnificent Journey.

Swept again into the dynamics of travel in the particle wind, I sensed a change. I could visualize it as well as feel it. While the prevalent color of my spheroid remained in hues of blue, there were many new striations of amber gold interlaced with red filaments. To my surprise, I enthusiastically recognized another change: a thin layer of amber gold was enveloping my core of blue. My mentors had embraced me, sharing their energy, enhancing me, and energetically altering me.

"Is it just that they embraced me, or is it something else that is altering me?" I wondered. "No. I had to earn this attained level, not receive it from others. I have learned to accept all responsibility and consequences for my actions, as the central feature of my commitment to myself. I am not a creature molded by my environment or in compliance with the dictates of others. I have

learned to advance my state of being by enhancing my awareness of myself, by intensely working to remove conflicts that inhibited my sense of freedom to be me!

"Consequently, my awareness of myself brought knowledge,
and that knowledge brought objectivity to evaluate my actions.
I have accepted the responsibility to introspect and alter my
characteristics that impeded my energetic flows. By accepting
responsibilities, I gained more abilities as displayed in my energetic form, just as my mentors had related that concept to me.
Congruence between information and experience is reassuring.
This is wonderful!

"Yet, even with the profundity of this connection with my
mentors, this journey, the whole of the experience is clearly not
over. I am in motion again. I have mentors who had brought me
to experience this sequence, and there must be more in store
for me!

"Michael! They advised that you are a candidate who merits increased involvement with mentors! Why didn't you think
to ask: candidate for what? This journey is clearly not subsid-
ing. Something else is going to occur. What could THAT be, after
meeting THESE mentors? Whatever it will be - I will be ready to
deal with it. My energy is precious. I must conserve it, and when
I use it, I must be careful to use it efficiently. The more I dwell
upon it, the more exultation I feel: the significance of meeting
my mentors is circulating through my being. I feel the elation of
their embrace, acceptance, and love. Nothing energetic seems
wasted in this energetic state of being."

The familiar brief flash occurred, and my travel halted. Again,
I was suspended in space.

"Okay, Michael. Check yourself out. Yes, there are changes.
My field of being is blue with swaths of cobalt blue, overlaid
with corona of amber gold set deeper into my field, and with
interspersed amber-gold and red filaments. My layer of amber gold is sparkling on the surface, which then diffuses into
space."

As I stabilized my position, I eventually noted that another platform was near my position and seemed to be there before I arrived. This platform or plane, unlike the previous one, was quite dark. The color was close to a navy or even indigo blue. There were highlights, though, resembling dark gray diagonal striations upon the surface. These striations took the appearance of gently moving ripples that brought an energetic and dynamic effect because of the motion. My location was immediately above the platform. That is, I was neither approaching it nor observing it from a distance.

The plane did not seem to have defined edges, though this might have been because of my viewpoint. The blue simply merged into the background of space. In truth, I have actually no idea what purpose the image or structure could have been serving. If nothing else, though, it tended to imply a positional reference for those situated upon it, including myself.

There were beings appearing as field spheres located upon the platform. They were already in place when I first stabilized my position, as if they had been waiting for me to arrive.

There were seven separate individuals present as luminous spheres. Their colors and striations were very similar to those of my mentors, with brilliant white cores; red filaments with red and blue striations; and brilliant electrified amber-gold throughout. Their white center regions seemed to be smaller, which caused the spatial distribution of amber-gold to seem larger, essentially approaching that displayed by Jesus.

I slowly navigated closer to them. As I closed the distance, I noticed that the amber-gold filaments in my own spheroid form were beginning to change. Some filaments seemed to metamorphose into red wisps that reduced the density of blues. In addition, my boundary layer of amber gold had become somewhat deeper, in effect penetrating and interspersing toward my core. Significantly, I had a sense of self-sufficiency and confidence.

Unlike my immediate recognition of my mentors, these individuals did not seem to present specific identifications for me to use as reference. My curiosity overwhelmed my tendency to simply observe, so telepathically I asked. "Who are you?"

When communication started, there was increased activity swirling throughout their fields. Although I did not have any indication of who these individuals were, I could discern where the communication was coming from based on the dynamic changes in field activity. Similar to my mentors, each could project an impression completely or in concept, in stimulating sequences with and from each other. As a combined effect, it seemed very communal or even conjoined as a chorus in its form.

They responded to my question: *"Throughout time on Earth, humankind has experienced our images, inspirations, and various other interpretations when we identify individuals with whom we have chosen to connect. We have gathered with you to answer your questions and advance your knowledge."*

There seemed to be a pause, perhaps to allow me time to contemplate and assimilate the message. I thought of many texts and many reports, including the bible, where specific people have reported various spiritual apparitions across the span of millennia. They seemed to know my thoughts as they said:

"Titles and labels and many various identities have been assigned to us by humanity as attempts to explain our presence, our appearance, or our influence. Some call us angels, spirits, or even guardians.

"We are a gathering of those who have learned to remove impediments that blocked the essence of our beings from full empowerment. We are members of a consortium of consciousness, extensions of those whom you have met as your mentors. We have evolved into a state where our sentience consists only of energetic fields. You have discerned that your own sentience is comprised of fields as well."

I responded: "I was able to identify those who brought me into this journey, those I know as my mentors. Do you have identities that might be useful for me to learn?"

"We function as mentors with the others. We do not designate ourselves with names or labels. These are not necessary as we are only ourselves."

"Yes, I have learned that I am only myself, and I have fully accepted that responsibility. Do you distinguish yourselves in any way from each other?"

"When you see someone you know in your life on Earth, you might identify that person with a name. If you know that person through direct experience, then the mere image of the person will define who and what he or she might be to you, including the nature of their personality. Names would not be necessary to retain your knowledge of the characteristic personality. Recognition and connection is sufficient to recognize each person, and each of us."

"Do you have gender?"

"Gender serves only the purpose of preservation of organic species. As evolved beings beyond organic form, gender would serve no purpose. We are only consciousness."

"On Earth, there are legends and myths about the existence of heaven and hell, and those are used to connote reward or punishment for those who obey of defy the dictates of people claiming to represent a path to an eternal reward in peace and everlasting life. Is this state of being I'm in with you called heaven?"

"There is no heaven or hell. We add that there are no divinities. Those are hierarchical concepts contrived by humankind, conceived and put forward by the social organization of the human race itself. Both myths of eternal rewards and punishments are techniques to cause behavior to conform to a social standard. Humans set those standards against the contrived rewards or punishments for purpose of gaining control. Some humans' standards or rules are set to cause others to respond in servitude, and for empowering leaders by the destruction of war or death as martyrdom."

"I was once taught that martyrs for what was once my religion were to be praised. Religious leaders taught me that martyrdom in the name of a divinity elevates the soul of the martyr to eternal reward."

"Religions have taught that the sacrifice of self for the church attains the ultimate reward. Martyrdom is human degradation. The folly of martyrdom is actually a statement of self-importance. Their belief in self-sacrifice for another through political or social agenda dissipates their energy. Martyrs actually believe they have accomplished something by destroying themselves. They actually have: they have accomplished their own destruction."

Understanding their message, and how logically precise it was, I replied. "Then that means that acting in blind belief and following instructions of another, they accept deceit that they can gain stature and importance by slaying themselves. Because of the delusion of eternal rewards, martyrs actually accede to the direction of those who control their actions, destroying the true essence of themselves in the process, relinquishing their energy to another's purpose!

"I have concluded that in tribal societies such notions are typically used for purposes of control and influence of people at the expense of their individuality, and rarely for mutual benefit, though that is possible. Do you have a hierarchy?"

"Most of humanity lives with and accepts distorted versions of reality as they project it into infinity, proclaiming that a god created heaven and hell. These distortions are impressed into humans, manipulated to the desired consensus by compelling myths or other social orders. The myths start as stories told by ancients as attempts to explain what they could not otherwise understand. The stories gradually mutated from generation to generation or revised in a deliberate and massive agenda to achieve group control. We possess our levels of attainment. Those levels are the attributes, our abilities that we have worked to gather during our individual paths of evolution. We, as we appear before you, have equally evolved. In our attained state of being, the concept of hierarchy would be absurd. We have no need or desire to control one another."

"Was your evolution based on developing knowledge and your responsibilities to yourselves?"

"Mankind often moves through life without adequate instruction to develop the ability to use reason – as their independent

personal authority to be themselves. Social mandates taught early on in life direct individuals to seek group acceptance over acceptance of self. That blindly causes followers to believe as the group believes, or risk emotional rejection, consequently degrading their self-esteem. The impact is pernicious: impressions of group control that demand group acceptance rather than acceptance of self often silence reason. Reason is the tool of all consciousness that defines the indelible right to evolve as individuals and when silenced, renders personal responsibility impotent."

"I've developed ideas using my reason that to many people might seem incredible. These concepts contravene an essentially assumed reality that humans continually live with, and accept – that all things must die. The finality of death without salvation causes fear of organic death, and that fear is the friend of the myth-givers! I have learned the reality that people *can* have free will to choose and claim responsibility for their own ultimate destiny: existence or non-existence; continuation into the infinite or dispersion; provided that they learn how to use their will."

"Collectively those who incite people to fear are using very human primeval concepts to gain control. Behave and act as those who seek control of others dictate, and they will bestow eternal rewards, so they say. Fail to comport oneself according to their rules, and there will be some form of punishment, through it might be as inconspicuous as imprinted guilt that reflexively call up negative self-emotions, or more obvious as an imposing threat of eternal punishment in hell. Those attempting to gain obedience to their precepts offer the reward of 'heaven' beyond normal life on Earth as enticement. 'Heaven' is an illusion foisted upon those who choose to follow. They use the concept of 'hell' to deter behavior they label wicked or evil. Morality is an inherent quest of independent, reasoning, minds that value life, all of being, and the lives of others. The knowledge of the power of self cannot use another's energy for gain without loss of cohesion. Using the punishment of hell, control results from conjuring up images of ever-lasting pain and suffering in the imagination of the followers. As you may well know from your childhood instruction, most would opt to be obedient to spare themselves in any way

from humiliation, and at any cost, from eternal damnation. Free will, reason and morality is subverted and diverted in the name of obedience to meet the need of those who would usurp energy and life force for their personal gain."

"Yes, my experiences in life coincide with your statements. I would do and say anything to avoid the eternal punishment of hell, no matter how illogical it was. I would tell myself any tale, distort any objective thought, and thwart any attempt to be me, all to obey the rules, as I understood them. I paid a very high price for these distortions, even to the point where I did not want to survive."

"Individual beliefs are embedded in a person through the persuasion and influence of others. Those they follow can manipulate through the pain of guilt, and by forcing conformance to their precepts, they absolve their followers of the guilt they themselves instilled. People typically, in order to confirm their beliefs, only see, feel, and hear what they wish to believe, or instructed and convinced to believe. Those in control often impart their beliefs, in rewards and punishments to people, as based on their own interpretations or illusions. This happens either by the consensus of their society or by ritual indoctrination. Beliefs, even beliefs in illusions, are confirmed if what a person does, how they behave or obey, yields the illusions of rewards or punishments even if these are founded on the myth of heaven and hell. Individuals led to hold these beliefs will yield sufficient energetic loss so they cannot evolve, and the inefficient can never attain their ultimate evolution.

"You have learned not to exist in sacrifice because that squanders your energy – the essence of your life-being. Beliefs that either discard justice in the demand of compassion and mercy, or that implore individuals to subordinate their authenticity, actually divert vital energy from those who could efficiently evolve to those who take without earning, transferring energy to those who are energetically inefficient.

"Self-esteem, the value of you for you, is not attainable by self-denial or sacrifice to others. Overcoming the admonishments from

the exorcist taught you that. Faith in a belief system that denies the use of reason was another challenge you had to overcome. You have become an individual of your own volition, not an automaton following the values dictated to you by others. The code of your own morality is a process of using your reason and volition to enhance your consciousness. That concept embraces the power of yourself without conscripting the power of others, or asking them to do so for you. Your morality teaches you to prosper in appreciation of your accomplishments. You have rejected notions that enforce guilt and suffering in conflicts over precepts that pretend to be values, but which only usurp your energy and give it to others who are not committed to their own evolution."

"You have clearly said that there is no heaven and there is no hell. I am here with you with only my consciousness, the essence of all I am. Since I accept there is no heaven and no hell, what is this energetic state of being that we are coexisting in now?"

"Of this be certain: There is continuance, or dissolution - which is the dispersion of one's energy. In continuance, the issue relates to the attainment level of one's abilities. In dissolution, there is insufficient energy of the consciousness to maintain the intact coherence of sentience, and the field dissipates upon the death of the organic body."

"Obviously, I am now continuing beyond organic form. Is my continuance in my current state of being now infinite?"

"Yes, if you wish."

"What do you mean by 'if I wish'? Does that statement mean I have a choice? Does this imply that my body may not dead?"

"This is not the moment to answer those questions. Understand that continuance occurs when the individual possesses sufficiently energetic coherent ability to hold consciousness intact, without a physical body to contain it. That sentient consciousness continues as fields, directed by will or choice to project beyond the human body. You have experienced that state of being during occasions before now.

"We observed you decades of Earth-time ago when you were a child. We watched your reactions to seeing visions, colors, and your

experiences of remote events. When you saw the airplane crash, you immediately found your mother to describe what you saw.

"It was not that you had the vision that was important. Many have the capability of those perceptions - yet deny them. It was that you allowed yourself to act on your vision, and your mother's nurturance of you, that mattered. These early events, when your initial energy was free and powerful, drew our attention toward you.

"We observe and we decide to inspire, if a candidate is known to have potential for their evolution. During your first deadly experience in the motorcycle incident, we brought you into our field that you saw as a fog of light. You were correct in concluding what the field of light was constructed for: a boundary that we established to protect you, to help you retain your field of being, and to meet with you for the first time.

"We were in our cocoon of light with you. We provided the inspirational seed for you to use: that you are an individual with the desire to discover your true nature. Your personality changed, and you were indelibly imprinted with this concept: As an individual, you are in control of your own being. It was your responsibility to use that information to reconstruct yourself away from your embedded conflicts, and evolve. Do you recall how you were feeling in your time immediately before the motorcycle incident?"

"Yes. I was severely withdrawn, actually depressed. My depression was causing me to feel pain in my body." I responded.

"Do you remember why?"

I had never admitted this sensitive question to anyone. I struggled to commit to my answer because it was something I wanted to avoid. Then, my present reality underscored my thought, "They know anyway. Don't try to hide." Therefore, I truthfully, and openly, responded:

"At that age, I was having intense thoughts and responses about girls. They lectured me, sometimes forcibly, that I must suppress these thoughts and feelings. A recent admonishment about what my teachers called 'Concupiscence is a sin that will take you to your eternal damnation!' was a lecture that instilled fear and guilt in me. My discomfort was so great I was trembling, rattled in a way that was incredibly uncomfortable. It was the first time I had ever heard the word 'concupiscence.' By simply representing lust, it carried a horrible connotation: eternal damnation. The consequence was deeply painful for me because of the conflict with my naturally developing sexual feelings.

"The conflicts between my natural feelings, that felt like an extension of my love, were flooding my body, and the instruction that having these feelings would eternally condemn me was more than I could understand or even accept. The only way I knew to deal with confusion and turmoil of this severity was to shut myself down into withdrawal and depression. The experience reminded me of what an exorcist had caused me to believe: hide who and what I am from others.

"I did not know at that young age how to interpret and prudently respond to this condemnation of my feelings. I forced myself to accept that my natural feelings were a sin unto my soul. I allowed my teacher's decrees to ensnare and subdue my natural expressions of love, because if love caused sexual feelings, then any love other than the love of god love itself had to be impure. Guilt controlled me because I was convinced my thoughts were impure and I was unworthy of god's grace. Oppressed with guilt I believed that my cardinal sins were so serious that they could be totally absolved only through the Sacrament of Extreme Unction – the last rites and blessing."

"We know that those personal and private denigrations combined together and almost ended your life. By example, this describes how pervasive the power of impressed guilt really is, and the havoc it releases as fear."

"Yes. I understand that now. My injuries, including the trauma to my neurological system, were so very severe that my memory was partially erased not only for the time of the crash, but also for the envelope of several hours before. I can only remember the day before the crash, the severity of my depression, and the time before that day. After the impact, I found myself immersed in the realm of light and those became my first new memories – as if I had started life anew."

"We recognized your turmoil and witnessed your crash because we had been monitoring your progress. That event signaled that for us to help you, you needed new inspiration, one that would allow you to find the strength and commitment to transcend the negative influences implanted in you. Your parents were told that you would not live, and while you were with us, your body received extreme unction, the absolution of sin you wished for."

"My energy swirling around my sphere of being is stirring in joy. I understand, now, that my joy arises by recognizing, understanding and placing truth for what used to be mysteries and blindly followed beliefs for most of my life through that time. The doctors told my parents that I would not live, and even if I survived, I might be paralyzed or highly impaired. They told me that I did receive extreme unction, though I did not inhabit my body during that sacrament. My being, my essence, was held in your embrace."

"All of these experiences stored within you are components of your continuance, even now with your body cycling in death again."

"Since I am continuing as a spiritual form with you, is there more you will offer about the nature of continuance?"

"You have learned, as we have inspired you to learn, that the quest of continuance is yours alone. Your volition is your primary tool for continuance. You and you alone, can actualize continuance for and by you, as an individual. It is and must be this way for each individual. Continuance is earned through self-determination, your volition and commitment to self."

"I fully accept your explanations because they match my conclusions and experiences. I'm curious about the colors and characteristics of filaments I see in our field spheroids."

"Yes. Your anticipation is correct. The colors relate to the intensity of the individual, which signifies the level of evolution attained. The filaments and striations are individual attributes and abilities. When there is a willed and volitional directive for an action, they are assembled into a focal point."

"Experiencing you and myself as spheres of fields with expansive dimension, compared to a human form, inspires me with an idea. In technology, I realize that electromagnetic waves from different sources can be interspersed into each other, yet remain coherently intact. This effect is common in broadcast radio frequency transmissions. Many frequencies, many fields, all are mutually interspersed, and these intersect with receivers such as radio, television, and mobile phones all at the same time. Each signal, though, is separately detectable.

"Since our form of ultimate evolution is sentience composed of field structures, it follows that the dynamics interspersing the fields together could intertwine sentience very intimately. Given that interspersed fields can retain individual identity, meaning cohesion and coherence, field spheres when merged together could imply or resemble the beliefs or myths of, for example, 'the holy trinity' – three separate beings as one! This implies that metaphysical, spiritual beings could conjoin and appear as one being. How have you distinguished yourselves from others? Are my conclusions true? Can you, as individuals, merge?"

"Yes, we may conjoin for mutual benefit, bringing ourselves together as energetic forms. Our histories, all of our beings, we share immediately when we conjoin. We then possess the most intimate of connections to and within each other while retaining our individuality. Conjoining expands our knowledge in a form of collective expanse throughout our consortium. The knowledge and experiences of one then embed as the experiences of others, even though we retain our individuality.

"You had a mentor, decades ago, who is connected with us. He taught you how to drop your protections and use the forces developed in your body to launch your consciousness beyond your body's boundaries, and just before you projected, you started to conjoin with him."

"Oh, my," I thought, allowing my recollection to trail softly into acceptance. There have been no coincidences in my life.

"How incredibly powerful, and wonderfully elating that experience must be! A form of extreme intimacy is established, exchanging not just information but of all experience in one parallel-conjoined event! Efficient, as an attribute, would be a vast understatement. In humanity, there have been rumors or myths about the consciousness of the universe circulating across millennia by intellectuals and astute thinkers. Is this what your consortium is, the consciousness within the universe? Can it be that simple?"

"It is." Their chorus resounded.

"Incredible. Not only are the myths of the trinity approaching reality, but connections of universal consciousness as well. It seems like a natural order of evolution. Energy or fields when placed into motion will yield dynamic result. Are there conditions to the process of conjoining?"

"You have observed the colors and striations of our spheres of fields. We have related the significance and intensity to you. These represent levels of attainment. Conjoining requires closely matched energetic levels of attainment between or among individuals, or intensity from the greater would be lost to the lesser and therefore the lesser could not rise to the level of the greater. That would be unacceptable since it would be inefficient for all. Causing a loss of energy or field strength would violate one's impeccability."

"That agrees with concepts I've learned in physics. Distributing field potentials among higher and lower levels of attainment would risk transferring energy of those who had achieved a higher form into those with a diminished form. When one earns enhanced abilities, the process of earning brings knowledge of how to utilize the abilities; so simply transferring intensity by itself would not accomplish anything beneficial. That would violate efficiency, purpose, and effectiveness, and could not be permitted if the efficient use of self, meaning not to squander energy, is a natural rule of order! Why would anyone want a system through which higher achievers lost energy to those that did not achieve and earn for themselves as individuals? That would be against a natural process of preservation – the conservation of energy. That means that the social concept of gaining grace through sacrifice is against a natural rule of order in the universe!"

"Precisely. The level of our individual attainment is the evolution of our energetic form. We must conserve our energy and our form carefully and use it only when it has efficient results. We will not expend our energy to save anyone because each must evolve individually through personal volition. We may inspire others to evolve, those who demonstrate open and independent thought, although great personal commitment is required to gain attainment. We have attained our levels of evolution by discerning we would progress through our individual efforts, as you have experienced through your efforts. Our impeccability to ourselves results in our attainment of pure being - occurring by our commitment, our will, and actualized by decisiveness.

"During the expanse of our existence, we learned to use the energy of our beings prudently, conserving it by removing all self-annihilating tendencies and other negatives that kept us from fully utilizing our resources. This required that we did not squander our energy on fruitless tasks or exertions of self-importance, and that we expend our energy only in proportion to our need. Considered together as a concept, this means we apply and direct ourselves with optimal effect. The efficient use of our energy means that there is no loss of levels among those conjoining, because they are conjoining as equals. We will show you. Be prepared. You will experience a portion of our combined intensities."

Before the significance of their statements could be garnered within me, there was a brilliant stirring in the fields before me as two of these evolved beings conjoined. The visual image was energetic, brilliant, and very impressive! The two spheroids slowly approached each other and interspersed within each other, as one. As this happened, the sparkling electrical activity, a dazzling aura of power, wondrously energized.

The filaments and striations began to parallel one another, as if they were in a mutual three-dimensional embrace: a mutual immersion. Around the two enveloped beings, there seemed to be a brilliant mist of increasing size, essentially a haze that was the same color as their predominant gold. There was a stirring of cobalt blue merging into the backdrop of space surrounding our environment. The filaments and tendrils were swirling, accompanied by a distortion similar to thermal waves on a desert floor. The fabric of the background of space seemed to warp around the convergence of the two beings. The image, the visual effect, was elating, beautiful and magnificent.

There was also a profound emotional impact within myself! The feeling that surrounded the event was that of a powerful, expansive, electrifying and all-encompassing love.

Then, without any observed distortions, they separated into the two independent forms that they had been initially. Nothing seemed to alter or distort after they had conjoined, except for the amplification of my feelings, which remained.

These beings were giving me acceptance, respect and facilitation, that I could only call love. The effect was profound. There was a stirring within my being. My being was changing, opening, advancing. My soul, my whole state, was given an energetic magnification - simply by inspiring me to release the remaining impediments to what I had been holding back and suppressing.

I felt compelled to express my curiosity and desire to participate. "In society, we tend to seek knowledge of how we are progressing toward a goal. This usually causes individuals to measure themselves and possibly gain confidence about what their status may be. My level of…attainment, may I conjoin with you?"

"We do not measure ourselves for the purpose of self-importance, self-assurance, or vanity. We do not attach labels or titles based upon levels attained. We continue, each unto ourselves, in accordance with our abilities and attributes. For your benefit, to aid your understanding about the attainment of abilities or attributes that converge in the personal power of self to continue, we can present a scale of increasing attainment. We've devised an allegorical scale of 'zero through five.' Zero would signify that there is an insufficient and energetic coherent being of self, intent and ability, to project

beyond the body's form and continue. Beyond zero, there is continuance with increasing ability that we call attainment. The gradient of attainment extends to a level 'five.' The energy of self represents the abilities of self, and consequently the level of achievement in our allegorical scale of attainment. Remember: Launching consciousness beyond the body, as you have now, requires an immediate reserve of self-coherent energy to be available. Your own image of your spheroid exhibits your attainment level. You are about mid-way toward your ultimate evolution."

"Oh… 'Only' mid-way? Humbled - I am humbled because as you recited your levels of attainment in continuance, I had hoped my evolution was greater – I thought I might have attained a four! What a presumption I've had about myself – because using your scale I've only evolved at most to a three! Before this discussion, I was actually not fully aware of residual inefficiencies within myself. Surely, inefficient use of my abilities has diminished my advancement! What is getting in my way?"

"Reflect upon your former existence in life. Recall how you acted, and could be obsessed with your role of how you defined and labeled yourself. How do you feel about your reactions to those activities now?"

"Arrogance. Primarily I lived with an arrogance of presumption: clients would always demand my time and service. I thought that I had been seriously committed to the path of my consciousness and awareness expansion for at least three decades. Arrogance is a form of self-importance, fed by my dependency of my clients needing me. You are giving me a reality check. I now understand that I still have much work to do. The characteristics of my field sphere have been showing me that vividly, in comparison to your characteristics."

"You have noticed that alterations in your sphere have been building. This is because you have not been arrogant during your journey or in meeting with us. You have been cautious and observant, working with the challenges we have given you at each moment. You have used reason to meet our challenges, and you have been true to yourself."

"True, there is now more gold and at least some red filaments interlaced with a new gold overlay that I have learned, somehow, represented my attributes and abilities. I am learning to accept my status and how to work to prevent stasis. Whenever I become stuck in indecision, I recall that 'nature abhors stasis,' and that motivates me to make my decision and move forward. I have concluded that learning the knowledge of the universe starts first by learning the knowledge of self. I am convinced this is true because without a firm understanding of myself, the way I think and react to stimuli in any way that might waste my energy, I would not be able to envision anything with neutral objectivity."

"You have approached an integration of facts that you derived through your rational examinations of yourself. There is greater knowledge within your grasp that will bring abilities to help you integrate the energetic state of your being.

"Self-love and trust is the foundation of self-esteem. The ability to love and trust is set by the magnitude of the ability to have self-love and to trust self. Those with high self-esteem have no need to flaunt themselves, have nothing to prove, nothing to display to impress others. Those would be examples of self-importance or ego. Dependency on the accolades you received from your clients shows limits to your knowledge of self, frailties in your self-esteem. With high self-esteem there are no dependencies or inclinations to have power over, or with, others. Those with high self-esteem can simply be in the current moment, each moment, in the immediate present we call 'now.'

"We know that you already have experienced that the immediate present, the now, moves with you through time and space seamlessly, and your state of being that brought you here to be with us displays that as reality to you. Every individual comes into being with a set of attributes. A crime against self is to not identify and develop those attributes. Attributes have a purpose – to fulfill one's evolution. Self-denial, angers, fears, self-importance and emotional dependencies are stepping-stones to self-degradation. Those, in turn, may be preconditions for withdrawals that could lead to serious

depressions or even suicide; and, suicide is the ultimate expression of
self-degradation – the cessation of being."

Internally, I started recapitulating some of my history that seemed
germane to this wonderful excursion. I found a powerful mentor
to stimulate my being. Working with that mentor, I was able to
wholly expose myself, clearly see his aura, and project my consciousness beyond my body. Together we were able to extend
my abilities to see all auras, and significantly increase my use of
even subtle perception. Through my acceptance of visions, precognitions, and lucid interactive dreams, I had also been able to
increase my abilities. I had been slowly learning to accept myself.
I had managed to overcome the admonishment of the exorcist
to hide. That admonishment only resulted in my withdrawal, hiding in self-denial. My response had taken a very high toll on the
energy of my being. I had abilities as a child, and then muted
them because of dictums I had received and believed in life.

   "Your messages are powerful confirmations of concepts that
I had been attempting to develop into maturity. I have learned
that my connection with you is my connection to the consortium, my mentors, and that all interconnects energetically. I
also learned that what defined me in my early life was not only
what happened to me: it was how I emotionally reacted to those
events, and how I imprinted those emotions, then used my impressions as beliefs to redefine me, and to influence my decisions
and actions later on."

   "The energetic field of self, in the various degrees that you've
learned, is reduced and confined within the body during withdrawal.
Confined fields will dissipate within the body that will negatively
affect physiology. The physical body will suffer in proportion to the
confinement of internalized negative emotions and depression and
the metaphysical being – the energy of self will suffer. You have
learned this by experience and pain. Self-directed actions such as
depressions, self-annihilation, and factors of self-neglect that affect
physical health will reduce the energy of self-being. Neglecting the
combined health of mind and body will highly limit one's ability to

evolve, since this is self-neglect. Negative opinions of self, negative emotions become negative influences to internal organs, including suppression of the immune system that is part of the natural order to survive."

"Yes, I have learned these things. I had lived much of my life internalizing my feelings. When my body suffered in consequence of my withdrawals then, by extension, my energetic mental capability suffered as well. I know that self-directed negativity influences the performance of bio-functions. Since many of those functions supply fuel to the mind, and since the mind requires coherent energy to expand and project as consciousness beyond the body, it becomes an integrated system if one's primary focus is to evolve the mind. The mind evolves sentience itself. I know that the body is only a support-appliance for the mind, not the other way around. From all I have learned, the integrated system of body supplying fuel to the mind that in turn evolves consciousness has one primary goal: self-evolution!"

"We know that you have worked within yourself gathering information, integrating it to the best of your ability by experience into your being, setting your attainment of eternal evolution as your ultimate criterion. Your effort has made a profound and expansive difference that has brought your being to us. You realize that you have not yet achieved your ultimate evolutionary goal."

"I understand with every molecule of my being that I am already known by and wholly exposed to you. Humbled, as a term, seems inadequate to express what I am experiencing. Yes, I have disappointment when I learned of my attainment level on your allegorical scale but that was not the primary impact on me. Humbled, quite simply, is my lingering feeling. I realize the feeling of humility is actually evidence of my progress! In prior times, that humbled feeling might have quickly become defensive, then depressed! That would be horribly inefficient in this circumstance of vulnerability because withdrawal would immediately diminish my energetic form.

"What must I do to amplify my commitment, my effort, and attain greater awareness – the knowledge of myself? Is my current level of attainment at this moment my ultimate state? Has my body irrevocably perished? Is this the end of my journey? Is this the final phase now being presented for me to accept as my state of being into infinity?"

"The answers to your questions all depend on a decision you must make, as you will soon learn."

"Decision?" I asked…

CHAPTER SEVENTEEN

DECISION

A *decision I would have to make…* implied immense possibilities. My thoughts tried to grasp the possibilities of what the decision might be, and failed because the list seemed endless. That failure resulted in spasms of anxiety! My field of being was trembling in uncertainty. Once again I was being subjected to a test, and I felt an ocean of furiously roaring waves within my field of being, knowing that there would be immense consequences my decision would have.

Before, in the encounter with the cleric, I had deduced that the cleric would challenge me to make a decision that involved an all-or-nothing experience. Behind the background of my roiling thoughts and emotions, I allowed myself a semi-facetious feeling: *Here we go again.*

I had to know: "What decision?"

"Be patient," they replied. *"Impatience wastes your power. We will present you with an option through which you will define your journey to your ultimate state. The concepts we will provide cannot be individually selected when you make your decision. You must understand these concepts simultaneously and collectively for you to integrate them successfully into your being. You will recognize your*

challenge as you consider the entire group of these concepts in order to make your decision.

"To increase your level of attainment, you will be required to elevate your self-esteem to lose any remnants of self-importance over others. You will be required to exorcise your residual forms of defenses, protections, and anger. Anger, one of the most destructive emotions, dissipates and squanders energy since it accomplishes nothing, and it impedes gaining the higher attributes of attainment. These human failings limit your attainment and therefore the expansiveness of your field sphere as you can recognize, confirm and experience by observing your own. Accept that the energy of self, when confined, defended, and withdrawn, is then internalized to no efficient use. Part of this relates to the connection you have to others.

"The abilities and perceptions you possess and are obtaining must be put into interactive use with others. Not developing your abilities to the fullest is a violation against yourself. Hiding and concealing yourself, which has been your historical failure mode, squanders your energy, dissipating it within your body. Failures such as these waste the energetic being, and if you do not surmount these, you will not increase your attributes. Even your relationship with your spouse can be used as a prototype for your development."

"My wife?" I said as a combination of exclamation and question. I couldn't quickly grasp what Rosy would have to do with my personal development.

"Those who are close to you, notably your wife and children, can be powerful allies for you during your quest. There are historical behavior patterns between you, your wife, and children that include almost everything in the human emotional experience. Some are patterns of guilt, others of anger, and others of power struggles or defensive compulsions. Some are patterned behaviors of dependency or co-dependency and others, importantly, are those of conditional or unconditional love. Learning how to lose the negative influences in your relationships with those who historically know you will be a very effective process for your evolution.

"Those in your close relationships will have their references about you. These references are primarily instilled about how you have behaved around them in the past. Since the historical experiences they've had with you define the way they know you, then altering your patterns, advancing your attainment into a higher form, can challenge those references. Those challenges will be both from your perspectives of the others as well as their perspectives of you.

"By engaging and working with these others, you will be challenged to examine your approaches to emotions. The others, in their reactions to changes, would be stimulated to examine their approaches to you. This will demand that you, and all connected to you, examine the responses and interactions.

"Understand that those with high self-esteem are able to experience love that is not dependent on condition. You have learned of your ability to selectively focus this form of love as you have proven to us throughout a very long period. Many un-evolved individuals only experience conditional love based on the performance of those in the relationship. That degrades the concept of love to something akin to a mundane economic barter system. Your ability to be able to feel and project love toward another, upon your choice or decision, with no need of it returned, is an expression of your freedom to feel as you choose to feel. This is not altruistic, since your investment will result in your higher attainment with an increasing sense of your personal freedom – to love and trust yourself – as your volitional choice."

I reflected on what I'd learned earlier in my life about altruism. I'd seen how the precept of altruism sets up control of lives and actions by serving others at expense to self, sometimes enforced by guilt. Alternatively, it often is a guise to conceal self-importance, hiding an ulterior motive of superiority. I'd learned that those who cry out for altruism, as if self-sacrifice were good, usually have agendas that are not in support of the individual. Early in my life, I fervently tried to accept that self-sacrifice was a mandate to achieve eternal reward. Society often preaches that altruism is the epitome of self-sacrifice. My conflict permeated me. Guilt consumed me in conflict because intuitively I could not understand how sacrificing my natural state without compensation could be good for me. I now recognize that my acts of giving are for my enjoyment, and others benefit from my act of selfishness. I do not delude myself with pretentious claims of serving others!

They immediately perceived my thoughts and advised: *"When you connect to others, you may facilitate their evolution, and you will benefit by facilitation in return – facilitation through the knowledge you will gain by interacting with others and by learning not to form dependencies on these connections. None of this is altruistic.*

"For those who are committed to evolve, the expansion of their attributes can cause them to become candidates to join us in our consortium. When they evolve to this state, all of us mutually benefit. Test yourself by stripping away your labels and roles of self-importance."

"OUR consortium? Labels of self-importance!" – These words echoed in my being as I strove to gather the meaning, timid to accept the implications, so I responded:

"It seems so simple to understand that labels, when applied to the self, seem to be innocuous societal references. With your inspiration, I realize that the 'I am's' of - wealthy, poor, victim, tyrant, important, unimportant, husband, father, wife, mother, manager, lawyer, vice-president, engineer, doctor, consultant, and many others, are all just labels or roles we assume. Labels describe function (such as job position) and responsibilities in life that bind to function (mother, father). Labels are useful to the order of society, but damaging, limiting, and confining to individuals who rely on these labels and roles to define themselves.

"I have been dependent on labels to prop up my self-esteem throughout my career, hiding behind them, using labels to define myself! Labels all eventually fail because they do not truly define or optimize the individuality of self. People who confine themselves through labels might never reach out beyond those role boundaries to explore other, more expansive possibilities of being. By limiting self-definition, labels can compartmentalize lives and be protective barriers that partition away other individuals. They can be utilized as a guise to conceal or deflect attributes, even to disguise who or what an individual really may be, or could attain!"

"Yes. Labels and the roles that come with them are like costumes. In the course of their lives, individuals may put on many costumes like actors in a play in an attempt to define themselves. They can go through life acting out these dramas, as if the character roles were definitions of their self-being."

"Yes! I understand this! At different times in my life, I decided to be a manager or an engineer and defined myself by what I thought those roles might be! The narrower the definition, the safer it seemed, yet the more limiting it became toward awareness of one's whole self. My mentors said that even my personal name is just a label. Personal names might convey nuances of how society sees a person. A male named Scott might imply a very different personality trait from one named Marvin, at least in terms of societal judgments, and the nuances can change the very definition of that individual. Names can imply character or personality as interpreted in society.

"I clearly understand this concept. I no longer depend on labels or roles to help define my identity. I am comfortable with saying that I am only myself and can think about no other way to legitimately define myself. I feel that the human need to judge, to categorize, and to set defining references of self-being, all obfuscate a basic truth: we may ultimately only be ourselves. Humans withhold who they are and hide behind costumes and labels so they will not be vulnerable."

"Societal categories can be used to define an individual's functions in life for social convenience, but all must move beyond these limited definitions to find the authentic self. Now you realize why we do not use names or labels. We had to lose these concepts that narrow self-definition in order to evolve ourselves.

"Your mentors identified themselves only to help you understand where they came from in human history. You will save yourself much

expense by not wasting time on various character roles and other attempts at guises, at any point, for any assumed purpose. You are transparent to us."

"The efficacy of my self-being is increased by these realizations – not to hide again. I have always been obvious, exposed, and openly vulnerable to you. Sure, I could slither into my little hiding places and feel sheltered, but given your perceptional ability, hiding would only waste –essentially squander – my energy."

I introspectively realized the possibility that this would be my one, possibly last, great, opportunity to comprehend in the deepest and fullest sense the essential process to ultimately evolve yet my impatience came to the surface.

"I understand and agree with all you have said, and you are affirming the concepts that I have discerned though my work with others, and my volitional commitment to seek the truth. I accept your instruction and guidance, and that acceptance foreshadows a decision that I will have to make."

"Be patient. Contemplate. Introspect. You have not yet been presented with the decision you must make."

The overused expression, that failure could not be an option, seemed to hang like a weight on my consciousness. Insofar as I knew, I had no body, no backup, and just possibly, no recovery if I made the wrong or inefficient decision. The residuals of my impatience and anxiety remained as a reverberation, although subdued within me. The continuing thought lingered that I would soon have to *make a decision* that would have the greatest conceivable consequences.

Then, it all thrust up from within the depth of my being. Everything was going to hang on some decision: a decision I must make, whatever and whenever they would present options to me. I could quite simply define my purpose: *I want to continue to evolve!*

What simple tool could I use to guide me to make the correct decision? It had to be simple. Suddenly, the inspiration came to me: *efficiency!* The intent of extending my self-energy is to gain the largest reward at the least expense to my being. I must bias my response, to any challenge, toward increasing my efficiency in my progression! Recognizing that simple word, *efficiency*, identifying that combined concept - efficiency to continue to evolve, yielded not just a sense of relief but of increasing confidence.

Now settled into a condition of improved assurance approaching quietude, I discerned that the moment had arrived. Something of incredible significance was persuading me, even beckoning me. It felt as if the whole of this experience beyond the tunnel of light had been forming into a crescendo of beauty, magnificence, and purpose, all orchestrated and advancing to this specific moment. Softly, with confidence and without anxiety or impatience, I again issued the question. "What decision?"

No response: just a pause of silence – silence that penetrated my sensations. Was I being given a moment of time to reflect on what might occur, or even anticipate it? This interval would unquestionably test my tendency toward impatience again, knowing impatience is not an efficient emotion since it wastes energy. Yes, this had to be a test of my ability to be at peace, and to *consistently maintain that peace at each moment under any circumstances they might throw at me.* I intuitively knew that I was ready for this moment – to encounter the challenge that would lead to the decision. I knew this, and without doubt, so did my mentors – the entirety of the consortium.

The field spheres of these consortium mentors had been gracefully moving about at random up to this point, but now the seven field spheres were slowly repositioning themselves. Though subtle at first, a pattern started to form in their positions, setting up the shape of a "v." The apex of the vee pointed toward me, somewhat below my position. The open end of the "v" angled diagonally away from me, ascending to a position somewhat above me. Another moment of intense vision, awe inspiring, approaching overwhelming, was occurring.

The background of space, a "fabric" that had been quiescent black or indigo blue with royal or cobalt blue filaments, was now set into motion. Beyond the open end of the vee, it looked like space stirred into a vortex. The predominant feature was the opening, huge in diameter. Around the circumference, the vortex continued to swirl with striations of grays and blues and variously interspersed dark reds that eventually became predominant. The shape took on the form of a mathematical torus, or doughnut, as I watched it develop before me. *The moment had arrived, and the message was simultaneously soft and powerfully clear:*

"You may now enter this aperture into your eternity with the attributes and abilities that you currently possess, and be welcomed. Alternatively, you may return to your human form and commit the balance of your life on Earth to advance your attainment. You have already been inspired and instructed to understand what this means."

"I feel stunned by the profundity. You are giving me the opportunity to proceed into the infinite starting with the attainment that I possess now, or return to my body to continue my evolution… my eternity.

"Can't I continue to evolve after I pass through the portal? Your evolution must continue: nature does abhor stasis."

"Yes, evolution continues. The consideration is where your starting point is, and how well you work and learn by facilitating others. You have already mentored many, and they have advanced their sense of themselves, as you have advanced as we mentor you. This leaves you with unfinished work on Earth, yet the decision must be yours, for yourself, alone."

Automatically, my thoughts turned inward: "Michael …… your eternity… think! Efficiency, you can use efficiency as your guide. No! That is not enough. What was the tipping point that brought you here? I remember! One concept at the beginning of this journey changed everything: Nature abhors stasis! Entering eternity with my level of attainment now – without having attained my potential – is premature! Would that represent eternal stasis – abhorrent to the order of nature? It is true that I may facilitate others still on Earth, and they could evolve to connect with the consortium. Yet, my condition now has become so peaceful, I have no pain or anguish just freedom to be myself."

I stalled, churning around the possibilities while I processed the decision. To relate to you that this was an impressively powerful decision would be a vast understatement. I considered the possibilities that this option presented to me, and I hope that you will too by applying it to yourselves. To continue into all of eternity in this wondrous state of being was actually alluring and tempting. The peace and tranquility of my current state was comforting, and thoughts of returning to my Earth-bound life rippled me with conflicts. Despite the comfort in my level of attainment, I knew that for me it represented *stasis*. Reason had to prevail. The consortium seemed to perceive my dilemma.

A statement that rolled into me like an ocean wave interrupted my silence. *"You have your destiny in our consortium."*

"Our consortium?" …. . I trembled, and if I then had a body, I would have cried ……

"You must make an informed decision, one based on experience. We will allow you to experience what your ultimate evolution can attain. Nothing of this can be unknown or arbitrary for you. That would be asking you to decide based on faith, not on reason supported by experience."

What occurred then was profound, wonderful, powerful, and magnificent! Having said that, I must admit that I have no words to adequately express this for you - none at all. It all happened so fast that it seemed to be following a predetermined sequence. With a flash of the now familiar brilliant electrified amber gold, almost instantly a projection of intensity inundated the field sphere of my being. The projection had come from the consortium. They had conjoined to project their field intensity into me. When the flash subdued, my sphere of being was changed.

Transformed: they transformed me. From the previous hues of blues with filaments and striations of gold and red, I was now a brilliantly saturated electrified gold, essentially identical to the mentors. There were filaments of very intense red, almost crimson, that started to align toward a focal point with copper filaments. Awestruck, I instantly realized what had happened. My sense of myself intensified. The power of the universe was connecting into and flowing through me. I was experiencing oneness – of knowledge, freedom and being – with the consortium and the entire universe itself. I conjoined with them, maintaining and enhancing my individuality.

I have never experienced such an amplification, elevation or elation of myself. It was almost beyond comprehension, and it *would* have been if it had not been a real experience. I knew then that I really had no responsible choice other than to *earn* this potential state of being for myself in order to maintain it and grow through it. Efficiency was clearly to be the imperative criterion for my decisions, and accepting my effort to achieve increased evolution was the only efficient choice. It would have been self-deprecating, in an absolute sense, to not accept that responsibility. There would been no point to all of this effort and personal integration for anything of less consequence than to achieve my fullest potential. If I did not fulfill this goal, I would betray myself, and all that I am, and all that I have striven to attain.

Even though the state of peace and transcendence had been wonderful, the new, elevated state retained those attributes and added a sense of purpose and personal power. Now I knew what all of the sensations, impressions, and overwhelming experiences were about. Taken all together, this was now a summation, an acceptance of what I realized was my personal destiny.

I had learned who had brought me, propelled me, into this journey far, far, beyond the tunnel of light which was the protective cocoon of stasis that once held me, and I surmised would never hold me again. I brought myself to recognize a foregone conclusion. I would return to organic life and complete my challenges. I would accept and experience my responsibilities and challenges as they became exposed, and gain abilities as a result. The attainment of pure, inorganic, and free being was within my grasp, but I had to earn this for myself.

Instantly, as if on automatic pilot when I made my decision, the red filaments in my brilliant amber-gold sphere had all collected toward a focal point. This point in my sphere directed away from the torus as the tunnel into infinity. The gathering of my filaments represented the focal point of my assembled intent. I had already been altered and my goal – by using my reason and the force of my commitment – was to retain it, build upon it, forever.

In an intensely incredible flash, once again I projected into and through a stream of particles, the "particle wind" as I have come to describe it. Yet, this travel seemed to somehow be faster, more energetic, more directed.

I had met the challenge, made and actualized my decision.

This time, unlike the other segments of this journey, I knew my destination and my purpose for traveling to that destination.

Observation

Decisions are made in the reality of the current moment, yet they can portend infinite consequences.

Each person, at any moment, is comprised of a finite amount of "energy." Squandering that energy in fears, angers, and depression, or deflecting the energy away from self to the service of dependencies, all mitigate the efficiency of self. On launch of self into the infinite, prodigious energy – the coherence of consciousness – is required to make the ultimate transition.

Do you squander your energy?

CHAPTER EIGHTEEN

THE RETURN

My eyes opened to the pleasant sight of a woman standing behind the top of my head, upside-down from my view. She was looking down toward my face, parallel to hers. As my eyes opened, she looked at me and said, *"Sir? Sir?"* then proclaimed in a loud voice: *"I've got him! He's back!"*

From a more distant place, out of my vision, another female voice replied, *"I've got a pulse. Now there's blood pressure!"*

Slowly, I began studying my new environment and situation. My first impulsive reaction was that my journey *in the particle wind* had simply brought me to another place where new encounters would continue be found.

This time, though, it was different. I had tactile sensations. A repetitive beeping of signals from electronic monitors, coming through a swirl of human activity, seemed to be announcing something. It took a bit of time to finally realize: I was in the ER. The woman whose face was the first image I'd seen was a medical practitioner working with a team to save my life, and the monitors were announcing my presence. I had returned to my body.

I didn't attempt to move. I actually felt quite serene and very much at peace. I realized that I returned to meet and surmount the challenges I would face, with the goal to attain an enhanced level of being and awareness as my ultimate state of my evolution.

My attention, drawn toward the face of the woman, revealed alternating expressions of intensity as she looked at the monitors, and concern, when she looked into my eyes. I felt that I had met a long-time friend.

My next sensation was also pleasant and reassuring: She had my face cradled between her hands. Her touch was warm, gentle and sensuously soft, and her touch felt nurturing. Probably she was just feeling the re-emergent pulse coursing through the arteries in my neck. Even with that mundane realization, I took this as a *welcome back* gesture as her expression glowed with a smile.

On reflex, I decided to use the observational process that had served me well during my journey. Elated and fascinated, I watched the clamor of the emergency room staff working intensely to stabilize my vital signs, and then studied my situation and environment in more detail. At that point, I realized that an oxygen mask covered my mouth and nose, and tethers connected me to instruments and fluids. Visually and mentally, I examined the life-support tethers connected to my body. The tethers were three I.V. lines stuck into my veins, going to different hanging sacks, connected to different sites on my body. Additional tethers were probes and other sensor wires, connected to my arms, fingers, and torso.

Though mentally active evaluating my environment and situation, I remained physically rather motionless, uncertain as to how much I could move without stressing the various medical tethers.

I was peaceful with the knowledge that I would physically recover and begin a profound new phase of my life. Partially, on my initial realization of what my state of being was at that moment, I found it fascinating that *my return* to inhabit my body did not produce any particular elation or emotion of any kind.

Back in my body, I was experiencing physical and tactile sensations, including pain, again. These sensations, however, did not distract from my enhanced feelings provided by the knowledge I had gained while I existed as a being far beyond my human organic form. My experiences during my travel were all crystal clear – indelible and incontrovertible: there was nothing vague, nothing opaque. I had no doubt about what I had experienced. I permitted myself a flash of excitement: my journey changed my state of being, my sense of reality, and enhanced me, forever! I knew that I would remain connected to my mentors, to those of the consortium of consciousness of the universe.

Even here in the ER, the whole of my journey seemed partition-less, seamless. I was having one experience after another in a continuous flow. I began to mentally move my focus within my body: Check, everything seems intact. Then, I did a quick inventory: wiggling my toes; moving my fingers; checking my temperature that seemed very cool if not cold; feeling the air movements as others motioned about me; and, sensing the rhythm of life that was flowing through my body. I realized that I was lying on what appeared to be an examination table. My fingers could sense the cold stainless steel at the edges below some pad, by my sides.

My body seemed to be just a part of my new environment, though I now realized it was only a support structure. Certainly, I understood that it was not my sentience per se, not "me" per se. It was as if I had just inhabited some sort of appliance or apparatus. Compared to my journey, my body felt confining. It limited my movement!

Something seemed to abruptly happen: a cacophony from alarms and displays of the monitors stirred the staff into action! The clatter of sounds accompanied the continuing flurry of activity about me in the ER. In response to the alarms, there was much commotion and discussion among the medical personnel. I simply lay there on the examination table and listened as carefully as I could to learn what was occurring. There were conversations about *analytical counts* displayed by monitors and analyzers, and something about the blood supply they had on hand to support me.

Under the clatter of commotion, I also heard comments about a helicopter: when the helicopter would arrive. There were continuing exchanges about my medical data in general, and a question if I had arrived at the hospital all-alone. That question signaled to me that my wife, Rosy, had probably not been in the ER, since the staff didn't appear to know if I had come to the hospital by myself.

Then one specific word from the overheard conversations jumped out at me! Helicopter? Oh! Wow! *Helicopter!* I had an instantaneous flashback to the precognitive experience in Salt Lake City. I recalled seeing the helicopter atop the roof of the hospital and had mused to myself, "Is there a connection between the helicopter and the hospital that would involve me? Probably not that specific helicopter," I now thought, "but a medical helicopter nonetheless. Salt Lake City would probably be too far away."

This partially explained why much of this adventure did not seem to be a total surprise. I was acutely aware of my recurring impressions that my historical events were pieces of a mosaic, describing my life and had assembled to *prepare* me for these experiences.

The woman, whose pleasant face was upside down to my view, reappeared. This time she was in motion, passing above my face as she partially removed my oxygen mask and asked: "Are you alone here?" My reflex and internalized thought: *"Alone? No! The consortium…"*

Then I locked on to another reality: "Rosy! Where is Rosy? I've been traveling with my wife Rosy, and she brought me here. She has to be nearby, somewhere in this hospital. Rosy is strong. You can be blunt and truthful with her regarding my medical condition." She smiled, as she gently repositioned my oxygen mask, then moved away from my sight. Rosy appeared after a time, also upside down from my view. Rosy smiled down as she gazed at me briefly, but before she had an opportunity to speak, monitors alarmed and someone pulled her quickly away!

The abrupt motion seemed to me to be unnatural. The bustle in the ER and the screech from monitors signaled something, again, was happening. At that exact moment, I experienced a very sharp abdominal pain, followed by a warm sensation: the torrent of more blood loss. The pad or sheets beneath me turned from warm to wet, from dry to sticky, and then to very cold. That event brought everyone in the ER back into a flurry of activity.

I remained motionless with no control over the events, and not knowing what exactly was happening to me or what medical crisis my body was experiencing. Somehow, I did know that I would survive this event and that knowledge allowed me to calmly wait, without anxiety or fear. It didn't seem plausible that the consortium had invited me to return to my body, for only a few minutes of drama in an ER.

Eventually the activity settled down once again after adjustments to the I.V. lines. It was very clear that this medical team was very pleased that they had recovered my body from death. It was also evident that they were very competent, professional, kind, and even nurturing. In a way, I felt pleased that I had rewarded their effort by choosing to return.

After an indeterminate amount of time, a new female voice announced, *"We've got him stabilized."* It was at that point, as the image of the upside-down woman was again moving quickly across my limited view, that I asked her (she was in normal dress – not in medical clothing), *"Who are you?"* The oxygen mask muffled my communication. She responded, "I'm a physician. I am the chief physician on staff here."

Another woman, wearing a white lab coat, appeared by my side with a pleasant smile. She must have been the other female voice I had heard from across the room. She indicated that she too was a doctor. She said that the others called her in as backup for my care. She instructed a nurse to remove my oxygen mask and then gave her some additional instructions regarding my care.

I elevated my head just enough to view down the length of my body. I could clearly see the plethora of probes and tubes

connecting my torso, arms, hands, and fingers to various monitors and hanging bags of fluids. There was also a putrid smell: my
blood mixed with intestinal waste.

Then, I noticed something! They had cut off my tee shirt! It
was a collectors' tee shirt from a unique car club! On impulse,
in an attempt to lighten the mood with humor, I was going to
mutter something about their insensitivity about destroying the
shirt, but decided against it. They might not have appreciated
my sense of humor at that moment.

I overheard the doctors advising Rosy about what they
thought had happened to cause the sudden and severe loss of
my blood, though there seemed to be some uncertainty in their
tone. More tests would be necessary to determine the cause,
though for now my physiological stability seemed to be their
only focus. They were explaining to Rosy, away from my sight
line, that it was essential that they transfer me, urgently, to a major medical facility that could deal with trauma.

It seems that the ER in Yellowstone was part of a relatively
small medical facility, and that they had exhausted their supply
of my blood type. They were not certain if my hemorrhage had
actually been halted or only slowed. If hemorrhaging started up
again, they were concerned that they would not be able to inter-
vene with enough blood.

They also had a very limited surgical staff at the Yellowstone
facility. We were advised that a helicopter had been ordered in
to transport me to Idaho Falls, a major regional facility about 100
miles away. They were asking Rosy to sign various medical forms
having to do with the helicopter. Then it suddenly dawned on
me: *"the helicopter!"*

I had never been on a helicopter ride! Surely, the name *chop-
per* might connote the ride quality! I'd assumed that they would
ride roughly, so I complained that I didn't like helicopters unless
they were the size of Boeing 747s. I asked, even urged, if they
would allow Rosy drive me to the other facility.

I'm not certain if they laughed or were annoyed at that
request, but I did see what looked like smirks in their expressions!

I got a stern and quick lecture on the three to four hours it would take to transfer me on surface roads. The chief physician said that the risk was not acceptable, and our Suburban was not set up as an ambulance. One more torrent of blood loss, and I probably would not survive. Leaving no room for further discussion, emphasized by firm voice intonation, they said that I was going to be transported in the helicopter, period! Then it dawned on me that after all I had been experiencing in travel at some incredibly high speed through space, a helicopter ride would be a minor event by comparison.

Being the analytical person that I can be, I realized that something very serious had happened to my body and that I must have bled to death. Recalling the incident at Jenny Lake suggested that. The medical staff volunteered no further details regarding my condition. Somehow, though, I needed to have *medical* confirmation from a physician that my body had gone into clinical death, so I asked the upside down woman when she again passed across my field of view, "I'm curious. What was my pulse and blood pressure when you got me on this table?" She responded clinically: *"There was none - zero. We couldn't find either. We believe that you lost far more than half of your blood supply."*

Her brief report confirmed all of the impressions that I experienced upon my collapse and during my journey. My body had been dying, but I had learned that the essence of my being was not my body. I had not needed my body in my wondrous journey. My consciousness of being, in its entirety, had indeed, launched far beyond my body. My physical well-being was only now becoming important to me.

Now I needed my body well and whole to continue my growth for attainment and progress along my path of evolution. In some subtle way, I almost resented the dependency on this frail and limiting human form. My mentors had given an incredible opportunity to further my evolution. I realized that in death, I had glimpsed my destiny. What a superb privilege!

The hit-and-miss process of periods of quiet followed by flurries of activity continued in the ER. Eventually as my body increasingly stabilized, the activity became more quiet than active as time went on.

From some unseen location, some unclear communication seemed to come crackling from a radio. A female voice in the ER announced, *"Helicopter ETA, 10 minutes!"* I glanced at a wall clock. It was now 7 pm. Three hours had transpired from the time of our entry into the hospital.

Commotion started again! *Now what,* I thought. There was a rush of movement as several of the staff hurried to close the outside-facing windows toward the rear of the hospital. I could hear each of the transom-type windows slam shut in a series of *clunks.* This was, I learned, to prevent dust and debris kicked up by the helicopter from invading the building. Outside, through the windows, I could vaguely see someone watering down the landing site with a hose – dust reduction!

The helicopter landed with the roar and clatter that such a machine creates. Despite the closed windows, the ER seemed to resonate with the sounds of the engine and the commutation of the rotors. I could hear *clicks and clatter* of pebbles or other debris deflecting off the windowpanes. After the noise settled, a flight-suited pilot and emergency flight nurse came into the ER to take over their charge: me.

The staff of the ER and the helicopter team worked together to move my body onto a gurney, untangling tethers, moving I.V. sacks, connecting portable monitors and balancing them on my belly, generally organizing anything required to get my support into motion. Blankets and straps were set around me to comfortably retain me into the gurney, though the monitors seemed precariously balanced. Having my body handled in this way was a fascinating experience because I was completely under the control of others.

Under the normal circumstances of life, yielding control of your body to others to this extent might seem unnatural, even foreign. Yet, during my odyssey into the particle wind, I traveled to meet my mentors and to learn from them, and *I had yielded control to the experience!* Trusting the medical professionals with their equipment and machines seemed like mild events by comparison. I find it interesting to perceive that both this medical experience and that of the journey had one point in common: both offered continuance.

Now here I was in motion again, strapped into a gurney, gently swinging and swaying to the rhythms of their strides as we moved out of the hospital. The transport to, and into, the helicopter seemed tenuous due to the tangle of tethers, IV lines, and support equipment that included battery-powered monitors, all connected to me. There was more clatter as they pushed my gurney into the helicopter, moving bumpily-bump as it slid into the machine. Then a couple of loud *"clunks!"* both felt and heard, when the gurney locked into position.

The emergency flight nurse climbed in next to me. I could hear another firm "ka-*thunk!*" as the outside door of the helicopter slammed closed and latched behind us. There was a transparent partition between the pilot and us. There was very little space available inside the helicopter, especially with the array of medical equipment that had been loaded in with me.

The flight nurse and I were now committed together into the partnership of a patient and an attentive caregiver. We in turn were surrendering our trust and control of our lives to a machine and its competent pilot.

This was powerfully emotional for me. I felt profoundly positive with a sense of appreciation and respect for these obviously well qualified professionals. I could hear voices through the partition, confirming that we could take off.

Slowly, with the precision that powerful engines can bring, the engine and rotors spooled up. The machine rose with the careful authority that seemed alert as it responded to the command of the pilot. We gently swayed as the machine rolled graciously in yaw and pitch, as it and we, became airborne. My adventure into yet another form of flight had begun.

Somehow, this flight seemed to carry greater risk! During my travel into the particle wind, my state of being was under my direct care, my own sense of my self-being, and my own drive to continue existing! Subjugated here and now to the performance of a complicated and unthinking machine with innumerable parts - was a different story! I had never before thought of a machine as a bearer of life. I do now.

The helicopter ride was surprisingly peaceful. The flight nurse was professionally active, working to keep the tethers of my life support in a minimal tangle, and continually checking the monitors. Measurements by the flight nurse on the monitors were constant. Once in the helicopter, before lift-off, she equipped me with a pilot's helmet with built-in headset and microphone. The helmet partially muffled the noise of the helicopter machinery and rotors. It also provided the valuable function of communication, permitting me to easily communicate with the emergency flight nurse despite the din of noise and the full-face oxygen mask. (Only my eyes escaped the mask).

The *rotor-side manner* of my flight nurse was impressive. She gently touched me on my neck near my collarbone to get my attention, informing me when we were about to take off, alerting me to each change in our altitude, direction, and for our landing. Her descriptions included what noises I might be hearing from the machine, and she did a great job to reassure me that everything was functionally normal in operation.

Apart from the muffled sounds of the machinery, and the words of my flight nurse, all I could hear was the sound of my own breath through the oxygen mask. I have to say that I could not have had more professional or better care than I was receiving from my flight nurse. Thank you, Margaret.

If I had any complaint at this point, it was that I was touring the area for the first time – in a helicopter, no less! I could not see a thing other than the fuselage and the face of my flight nurse (who was also partially masked by her own helmet).

The Yellowstone staff informed Rosy that she could not accompany me in the helicopter. There was insufficient space. She would have to drive through Yellowstone into Montana, then Idaho. Her drive would require about four hours. She would be out of contact during this time; unable to learn of my condition or even if I had survived during the flight. Cell phones were not yet common, nor did they work well in such remote areas at that time.

I wanted Rosy with me. I could only imagine what might have been running through her mind as she drove to rejoin me through those long and tense hours, alone in the dusk that blended into night, all the while not knowing if I had lived.

On landing, a contingent of medical staff met us. The motions and feelings exiting the helicopter were about the same experience as the entry into it. Everyone was in a hurry. On entering the building, my eyes caught the reflections of our procession across numerous ceiling light fixtures down the corridors. They wheeled me into the new ER; wherein six new upside down and lateral faces took immediate charge of me: *immediately* was the operative term.

They connected more tethers and probes, handing things back and forth to each other in synchronized precision. Some of the probes were invasive, through my nose, down my throat, and even further down toward my stomach. They called this device-of-torture an *NG* tube. My advice: this is something to avoid unless incontrovertibly necessary! My protestations of discomfort did not dissuade these medical practitioners. They were trying to learn why I had bled to death, to find the source and stop the bleeding. The measurements and probing continued for a seemingly long time.

While the medical professionals were still testing, measuring, and probing me in the new ER, the emergency flight nurse approached. It was the first time I had seen her without her flight helmet. She had a very large grin that lit up her face above her blue flight suit and soft flowing brunette hair. She was carrying a tee shirt that she displayed holding the front outstretched, and then rotated it around to show the back. This shirt carried an imprint with an accurate profile sketch of our helicopter on the front. Below that image were the words: *I Flew Air Idaho Rescue.* She turned the shirt around and on the back in BIG letters, it proclaimed: *For the Ride of a Lifetime.*

Very true, I nodded, and through my smile, I signaled that I couldn't agree more. It *was* a ride, *the ride of my lifetime* - with the helicopter only a minor segment of it. With her wide infectious grin, she proudly presented this new tee shirt to me! I thought to myself, with a sense of justice, that I really deserved that new shirt! After all, the ER staff in Yellowstone had cut off my treasured collectors' shirt from the car club! It was now 10:30 pm.

Tests continued. The medical staff disconnected some probes and connected new ones. These new probes interfaced to a telemetry transmitter that linked to monitoring equipment in the Intensive Care Unit. This clever telemetry allowed for monitoring of my body while they wheeled me around the facility. This is impressively efficient technology.

Another analogy occurred to me. I had been brought into a unique adventure, and I had profoundly experienced awareness as a spiritual being. This happened simultaneously as my body was experiencing sequential shutdown of clinical death, but there, in my non-physical state of being, I learned that I was a candidate to be in the consortium. I allowed myself to speculate that I might be a novitiate in the consortium already – they *had said our consortium!*

In order for this experience to have been set up, they had to identify me across tiers between their beings and mine, and periodically monitored for most, if not all, of my life. I had learned that the group monitoring me comprised those who had brought me to them as an inorganic and spiritual form and had presented themselves to me as my mentors. My recollections prompted questions that I should have asked the consortium more specifically: What exactly signaled my identification? What are the parameters – the characteristics or attributes that they initially look for in an individual? Can anyone in humanity gain the knowledge of himself or herself to attain an evolved state of being? Now rejoined with my body, the answers to those questions were delayed - not for very long, however.

Rosy finally arrived, and her radiant smile disguised her fatigue. After all the hours of crisis and trauma, we could finally have some quiet time together. There was so much for us to discuss to align ourselves with our recent, individual, experiences.

She downplayed the stress and emotions during her long and exhausting drive. I can only imagine the anxiety and angst she must have felt not knowing my condition and not wanting to take the time to stop and call the hospital. I shared with her my sense of conviction that this experience would resolve itself in a positive way.

Then, gleefully with a child's enthusiasm, I shared my joy: I proudly called her attention to my new tee shirt! She smiled.

Finally, we arrived at my room. The staff allowed Rosy to stay with me through all the procedures. There seemed to be a test about every hour through the entire night. The staff still had not learned why I had bled to death. They decided to map my entire vascular system with a nuclear scan. Rosy followed the progress of all my tests in real time, even the nuclear-gamma-scan imaging of my vascular system performed in the wee hours of the morning.

Rosy would not leave my side, and I had learned long ago not to argue with this woman when she was determined. Arguments with her would be a waste of energy.

The vascular nuclear-gamma-scan resembled many of the medical imaging procedures, with the exception of the irradiated blood. A technician extracted a vial of my blood, and then immersed the vial in a field to cause it to be temporarily radioactive, then re-injected the irradiated blood back into my body for detection by the imaging system. The images produced provided a detailed view, a map, of the blood vessels to inspect them for any leaks. The test did not produce any noticeable or unique sensations, though I felt very warm during the experience. It was during the quiet time in the imaging process of the nuclear-gamma-scan that the answers to the questions posed before (what identified me as a specific individual and what characteristics are required of individuals for the facilitation of mentors) were revealed to me.

A glow of brilliant and very comfortable, light, reminiscent of the initial cocoon that extended into a *tunnel of light* just before my breakthrough into the voyage *in the wind,* immersed me. I could still see the medical apparatus, interspersed or filtered through the haze of this light cocoon. This reminded me of how my dying body appeared to me in the ER, just before my impulsion into the wind. Unlike that experience in Yellowstone, though, I was *not alone* in this field of light.

Telepathic communication began, identical to the communication I'd experienced with my mentors. The consortium had challenged me with the decision: to either continue into the infinite with the attributes I then possessed; or, return to human life to attain my full potential, and I surmised must have remained connected with me. Their statement, *"You have your destiny in our consortium,"* seemed to be true, since now I knew we remained connected. I felt a high intensity in the communication, a loving field of nurture and embrace borne of our mutual interconnection.

"You increasingly drew our attention because of your responses to the perceptions we stimulated in you and that are natural to your abilities. In your natural state as a child, you did not run from those perceptions, and you did your best to use them.

"The characteristics or attributes are already known to you, and they are known to us. They reflect the commitment you eventually made to yourself to advance your evolution with rational and directed thought as you matured. You probed deeply into yourself to unravel the puzzle of self-development that for many others might seem prohibitively complex. As you have recognized, that complexity is not prohibitive at all: Each individual's evolution is a personal responsibility. You eventually discerned that no one is under

the guidance, judgment, or control of divinities, since those do not exist. When you came to that conclusion, you began to realize that continuation into a spiritual form is actually a natural process: the physical to the metaphysical, as you yourself would say in the vocabulary you've learned.

"That natural process starts with the human body and the energy it provides as an organic bio-electric source. With evolution, it then moves as a continuum into high sentient awareness, then subsequently projected beyond the body that is not dependent on the organic form, other than to initially stimulate and fuel, and launch, the consciousness. The focal point is a realization of the existence and magnitude of one's consciousness, the expansion of awareness to embrace the energetic and non-physical form of all sentient being. With the use of personal willpower, using reason and volition, anyone can evolve to a level to project their sentience into eternity. Recognizing that this process is real, you have taken actions to advance your state of being. The attainments you earned, that we amplified in you when you were with us during our meetings in the infinity of the universe now permeate your being."

Then, the field of light faded away. I realized from this early example in my newly re-entered body that I would always be, continually, interconnected to my mentors when inspiration was called for - *always*. The powerful reality of the words, *"Our consortium…."* was finally sinking in.

Later, back in the private ICU hospital room, Rosy asked the nurse what the policy was on visiting hours. The charge nurse replied that the hospital had a general policy, but on the ICU monitoring floor that policy does not apply. The charge nurse then directed Rosy to a pullout bed in my room. She could stay with me without limitation. Rosy stayed, and my room became our room. We settled in for the night, though it was now the small wee hours of the morning.

This ICU room was not particularly luxurious. I must give them credit, though, for an excellent facility and staff. The ICU room provided quiet for a change, and a place with time to rest.

Rosy refused to leave the hospital for a more comfortable hotel room, no matter how much I urged her: stubborn woman. It was now 3:00 AM, Monday 13 June.

Our period of quiet lasted all of about an hour. More activity and more tests followed. Staff performed some tests on an hourly basis in the room; others required that they wheel me to various labs. The final test was a full colonoscopy. The clattering disturbances of the night finally slowed down as I continued in my process of stabilization, and as daylight appeared.

So on it went through Monday, but that night was *relatively* peaceful, as my body had stabilized. Tuesday was actually very peaceful. No difficult tests were required, with only regular measurements of my vital signs taken. The medical part of this adventure had now become routine, actually boring, and I was looking forward to going home

Staff advised us that they anticipated my release for the next day, Wednesday, provided certain test results verified the stability of my condition and that I continued to steadily improve.

The tests indicated that the bleeding had stopped, but I would require additional testing and monitoring when we returned home. The colonoscopy had shown a probable location where the hemorrhage had occurred: a ruptured diverticulum, which, thankfully, did not rupture through the colon wall into the abdominal cavity. The images gathered during the colonoscopy also indicated a need for surgery to remove a polyp, though that had nothing to do with the hemorrhage. We could postpone the surgery until we settled at home. The senior staff decided that although they could have easily performed the surgery there, I needed to rebuild my blood supply before undergoing surgery, and they didn't want to risk any bleeding that might have signaled another crisis.

Something impressive occurred to me: from the point of entering the hospital at Yellowstone to the point of collapse with zero pulse and zero BP, less than three minutes went by. That tiny time window, which allowed for my organic survival, occurred after a 350-mile drive from Salt Lake City, and about two hours after the Jenny Lake experience. I find great significance in that narrowest of margins. There really are no coincidences in life, it would seem.

We left the hospital, though I was feeling somewhat weak, and Rosy held me close as we entered our Suburban. Rosy took the wheel to drive us home, since my body's reflexes were a bit frail – wobbly in fact. After a few hours drive, near St. George in southern Utah, Rosy abruptly turned off the highway into town, almost as if she were following some unheard command. She found a delightful and cozy motel room for our night's stay. Our room had an unusually large Jacuzzi, and we found that to be just the right therapy at the right moment in time.

We enjoyed a great dinner, relaxed ourselves in the Jacuzzi, and celebrated all of life itself with a glass of wine and our mutual love. Upon my decision alone, I'd accepted the challenge to reenter the realm of organic life. I had chosen and committed myself to a renewed path of attainment. The events and experiences of my journey amplified my value of life, my state of being, and my purpose, forever. I had gained essential information, connected with mentors, and returned to expand my personal quest with renewed vigor.

My journey beyond the tunnel of light also brought a profound appreciation for my life, my being, and for each of the mosaic of events, each a tiled piece that assembled into a new and magnificent vista as my sense of myself.

As time goes by, Rosy and I enjoy visiting the nights of summertime, at a desert resort. There, as I gaze into the midnight sky, I feel enhanced by the visual clarity that the high desert brings to the heavens on a cloudless night. My sensations delight in the warmth of the gentle breeze washing over me. I reminisce about my feelings on the rim of Canyon Muerto, my perceptions in the searing forces of the hot wind, and the magnificence of my Journey as I flew through, and supported by, the particle wind. I re-experience the events in my Journey and the awesome power of understanding, transcendence, sense of acceptance and knowledge that I gained. With my consciousness embraced with peace, the glory of fulfillment and unconditional love shared with my mentors and protégés, I sense an appreciation that is so wondrously emotional; I tear in joy and gratitude even as I write this.

The warmth of the breeze connects with a glow in my being, and it naturally intensifies as it has so many times before: it is now part of my life. I love the feeling, the feeling of empowerment, embellished by knowing: I have earned this state through my commitment, decisions, and volitional actions.

Expanding my energetic sphere toward the universe and the consortium, I delight in my sense of purpose, knowing that I made the right decision to return to my body, now so many years ago. The reward I give myself is the liberation of my spirit, my purpose to experience the glory of eternity with incredible awareness as I conjoin with the consciousness of the universe.

I marvel at the expanse and indescribable energy of the universe, and yet know there is wondrous simplicity in the way we evolve. The circle of life on Earth is but a microcosm of the circle of all being. Assembled as we are from the stardust of the universe, we may return as conscious fields transcending our organic form as we ride upon the fabric of all being.

The knowledge of self, as an individual, is the foundation from which all other knowledge derives, and that, quite simply, is my personal quest. Each person who is inspired and motivated to commit to themselves and attain their own path toward their ultimate evolution can potentially add to the fields of consciousness of the universe. In doing so, they may touch and motivate others by their example and implied inspiration to evolve, build-ing a geometrical progression of enhancement.

My purpose in being is to facilitate my evolution, and in so doing, to open myself to others, who as individuals, would choose to commit themselves similarly.

ATHEISTS CAN GET TO "HEAVEN"

PERSPECTIVES FROM THE JOURNEY *Beyond* THE TUNNEL OF LIGHT

PERSPECTIVES

OVERVIEW

T he experiences gained during my *journey beyond the tunnel of light* yield a magnificent conclusion: that one's eternal essence of life being does not depend on deities, religion, or faith. Nor *must* consciousness end upon the death of the body, as die-hard atheists would assert. I've discovered that individuals can attain their ultimate state of being, their destiny, as they evolve through the use of reason and self-actualization: the deliberate, volitional, course of action to determine one's fate using free will without subservience or compulsion to blind, unconscious, beliefs. Reason, freedom and volition are the fundamental tools of personal discovery.

Using introspection and reason, you can learn what causes you to waste your energy, and what factors elevate your sense of being, gaining knowledge of yourself in the process. Often, I've found, personal discoveries will happen simply by asking questions about why and how you are inclined to react to different circumstances in your everyday life. Using your volition, you can probe into your mind, use reason, untangle what holds you back, and change your destiny. Your advancement into the eternal is actually a natural continuum: that the metaphysical state of being extends from the physical, and does not in any way, involve mythologies of the supernatural.

I assure you that my memories of the events of my *journey* are as clear, real, and as defined as if the events were occurring at this very moment. The mosaic composite of these experiences, when gathered as a whole, form a breadth of understanding leading to universal knowledge, founded upon direct personal experiences.

Some among you may be doubters; others among you might be emotionally uplifted because, after all, *mine is a story of hope!* The hope is borne on what I've learned and discerned: that any individual's ultimate personal evolution is a matter of personal responsibility. Personal evolution advances with commitment: to be responsible and in control for your own attainment, using the power of reason.

My own connections to those inspirations I've called *the consortium* are not faith-based. My connections, derived from my individual quest to learn about my own authentic nature, sequentially exposed increasing and enhanced awareness. Awareness increased, in the broadest sense, enables greater consciousness, and that expands knowledge. My history and my inspired interactions with the consortium led me to fully experience and realize that the use of *reason* – not worship or leadership or the totalitarian and limiting nature of blind beliefs – can result in evolution which ultimately means *crossing the boundary, transcending* from the physical to the metaphysical. In other words, I am convinced that anyone can attain their ultimate state of evolution for themselves, should they make the choice to do so and consistently focus their effort toward that purpose.

Any rational person can easily offer alternate explanations for what I have reported to you as my experiences. If that is your intent, you may be predisposed to dismiss my experiences as fables that I have either fabricated or distorted. Should that be your inclination, I can only suggest that you might first evaluate your motivations in making those assertions. I've learned by observation in my efforts as a mentor to many individuals spanning across more than four decades, that people have tendencies to protect, even ferociously defend, their psychological comfort zones telling themselves various tales to justify why they do so. From what I have discerned, individuals will cling, often desperately, to what they feel is familiar, even if "the familiar" holds them in conflict with their true nature and binds them to stasis.

Because my experiences contrast sharply with institutional precepts, the beliefs held by many in society, I feel very similar to the characters in Carl Sagan's novel *Contact*. In that novel, Sagan has certain characters journey to other planes of awareness, and perhaps even other galaxies, through a device or machine designed by extraterrestrials. Each character returned to Planet Earth after profound but very different experiences, specifically designed to fit each character's needs. By analogy, your experiences during your journey will doubtless be very different from mine in detail, yet the mission of each journey can be the same: an incremental progression of expanding personal awareness that when combined, forms one's evolutionary path of attainment.

My effort is very different from fiction because it relates factual, personal history and experiences as they occurred, arranged in a progressive sequence. Space-transport machines were not required, mind-altering drugs were certainly not used, and no vehicle energized other than the sphere of my own being, carried through the streaming energetic impulsion of a particle wind.

Anyone has the ability to advance in life and thrive for all eternity, empowered by his or her will, intent, and by using volitional minds to actualize reason. To actualize self and enable freedom of the open mind, it takes courage and alacrity to depart from the negations harbored within the self, no matter how familiar they might be. You must first be responsible to yourself to start your personal journey of attainment. Your responsibility, when directed away from the blind unthinking belief systems of an unconscious automaton or to a supposed deity or even a societal cause (however those might be institutionalized) advances you to your preservation, determination, and expansion leading to the fulfillment of your true essence, your authenticity. These are your rights: the right to exist, to thrive and prosper with freedom of mind, and you can claim them for yourself.

PERSPECTIVES

RESPONSIBILITY

Fundamental questions

There are fundamental questions facing each of us: Where to look for our true nature, our authenticity; and, when found, how to extricate it from entangled brambles that often make it difficult to grasp. Either your true nature is what others influenced you to believe, or it is deeply within you awaiting your discovery to actualize. If you accept responsibility for your own development, you may soon discover that obscurity overlays your true essence. What could have obscured and even possibly obstructed your grasp of your true being? Candidates are: various family and tribal (societal group) beliefs that compelled you to deflect your awareness and purpose away from your true nature; personal traumas, where events and experiences exceeded your ability to cope; or, harsh judgments thrust upon you that caused you to feel you could never measure up to the mandated standards of personal performance and be accepted by others. Conceptually, the process is quite simple: free yourself from embedded impediments in order for your evolution to move forward and progress.

The basic decision in life, then, is between moving forward and standing still, between sequential attainment and the stagnation of stasis. Should you decide to examine yourself to find what holds you back, it might be helpful to recognize: *it is not what actually happened to you that matters; rather, it is how the memories of what happened became embedded in your mind, and continue to influence your emotional responses and decisions.*

Behavior loops and the brain

Researchers studying the brain have noted that repetitive behaviors actually set up neural loops in the brain, tantamount to being addictions. These loops then operate as non-volitional, automatically running *programs* that control behavior and emotions. The loops of one instilled program can connect to other loops, causing a matrix of patterns to become impressed that collectively respond in complex ways, stimulated by circumstances we're exposed to during our lives. Habitual behaviors and emotional response patterns are diametrically opposed to rational, volitional and purposefully thought-through processes. Automaton programs *can* be broken with commitment and intent - but first recognition, identification and awareness of the patterns must occur, and then analyzed to determine their origin.

How behavior loops form

If anything may be clearly extracted from what I am reporting to you, it is that anyone's life is composed of a matrix of experiences, superimposed onto the basic structure of your familial legacy: the genetic patterns that constructed you. The embedded matrices that influence thoughts and emotions are impressed within people often in ways so subtle their conscious awareness doesn't recognize what happened. Subtle impressions, when embedded, can set up unconscious reactions. Sometimes we just overhear or see something during childhood that grabs our attention and when imprinted with a lack of understanding about what happened, can influence our actions and emotions throughout our lives.

Nevertheless, we can carefully inspect and evaluate the thoughts and emotional reactions that cause conflict, turmoil, or that just fail to be harmonious within us, to find the causations. By probing into our minds, we increasingly become self-determining and self-actualizing, making decisions and choices using reason and volition, rather than reacting emotionally through reflexive responses. The alternative is to live life as an automaton, operating according to programs running unconsciously in the background of your mind.

The open questions for anyone include: Am I basing my choices using rational thought and volition, or upon blind unthinking compulsions; do I really have freedom of my mind, and know how to use it to consider all options; or, am I bound by limiting precepts of a belief system that deny me possibilities to expand? In other words, do you *think all things through* or just emotionally react?

Neural loops are self-protecting

Those who have identified themselves solely with their entrenched beliefs, locked into controls that limit their vision of what might be possible, will tend to see, feel, experience, and hear only what they *want* to believe and accept. When their exposure to events and information supports their preconceptions, they will see that as affirming, so it must be "okay" even when it is detrimental to the person. Should new encounters produce conflicts with patterned beliefs, they might reflexively denigrate what is new as wrong, irrelevant, daunting, foolhardy, or even evil, rather than evaluating the efficacy of their beliefs! Some individuals will spare no time, energy, effort, or money to fabricate an acceptable storyline – even as distortions of reality – into a fable in which they *feel compelled to believe,* no matter what the cost might be to their self-esteem, health, or emotions. History is replete with examples of societal delusions, instilled and perpetrated upon the masses, resulting in wars, bloodshed, loss of freedoms, and massive suffering that have thundered across the planet for millennia, ravishing populations and destroying lives.

Tribally approved actions are not necessarily rational ones

I've observed that humanity has an amazing tendency to seek comfort through tribal (group) consensus, even if it means death and destruction to others. My observations and experience suggest that the tendency starts early in life as children seek acceptance from others, often at the expense of surrendering their authentic, natural selves. Individuals can learn early in their lives to subvert themselves, losing their true nature by spinning webs to weave superficial costumes and presenting themselves to others in ways to gain the acceptance of *their tribe* or those in authority. By doing so, they place higher value on the drama roles they serve, or are taught and accept that they must play, far beyond the value the assign to themselves.

Many tribal forms are available to influence us, adding to the complexity of how we can be enticed to neglect our inherent nature. As we move through life, tribal exposure becomes increasingly evident as a sequential progression. In youth, the first tribes are the family, followed by various school groups, even groups within groups for specific activities. Careers and jobs bring more tribal opportunities to our lives, and any individual might participate in multiple tribes all established for various purposes. Some people may become so dependent they do not feel whole unless they have acceptance of tribe membership.

Tribal consensus may involve many guises, all under the allusion to bring comfort or benefit to each member of the tribe. There is an *expense* for tribal consensus, which members must pay: someone must *lead* the tribe, and to that person or group, members could yield control over all or part of their lives. Tribes, in this context, can have many functions, ranging from the purely social to: educational, political, activist causes, career/business promotions, or may be simply religious. In many of these forms, exemplified by religions and social "causes", the tendency is to convince others to believe and behave as the tribe believes in order to gain acceptance by the community of the tribe. To me, the yearning for acceptance by a tribe, or even by another individual, is the antithesis of personal evolution because it often results in valuing the consensus more than the self-values-self, and that means the diminishment or even destruction of self-esteem.

The primal human tendency to seek comfort through tribal (group) consensus applies to many "institutional expectations" foisted upon society as well, presented in formulaic ways of marginalized credibility. Do you want to be happy in your life and career? You must be accepted: not just by any credible university; but by a "highly vaunted" university, society responds. This reflex response places the name-value recognition of the university before the veracity of education. What is the process to gain acceptance by these (tribes) institutions? Outstanding test scores are the first key to acceptance, they say. Do test scores really signify that you possess comprehensive knowledge and ability, or that you have just developed good memory skills and have learned how to excel in tests? Is this approach from "learning institutions" really resulting in true knowledge, an assurance of success, or is it simply an artificial process: a formula that institutionalizes dictums and are able to function partially because many "believe" in the formula which then feeds on itself through the "institutionalized expectations" of employers. Perhaps the assembly lines of institutions do not effectively construct "minds of knowledge." When viewed as tribes, institutions tend to work in the interest of promoting the institutional tribe, forcing students to comply with its demands and not adapting the tribe to the needs of individual minds.

In religious institutions, which to me are simply large tribes, if members believe a figure is *a savior*, then there is someone else, other than you, to hold responsible to save you. Are those who believe that a messiah will save them, simply looking for a stand-in to absolve themselves of their personal responsibilities? Shepherds have flocks of sheep. Shepherds assert that they are protecting and guiding their flock, but are they nurturing them for fleecing? Could those who follow simply be seeking another to blame for their failures or someone to save them despite any actions they might make?

We might laugh at the stand-up comic who asserts *the devils made me do it*, yet humans might live out their lives in submission to what they've allowed their *tribe* to manipulate them to do, just to be in compliance with tribal dictates and to gain group acceptance. *What happened to self-acceptance as an individual?* Is there really a difference between the *devils made me do it* versus *the tribe made me do it* when pleading self-defense against offenses inflicted on others?

Beliefs will often instill fear and guilt, even when you have done nothing wrong. For example, the absurdly ludicrous accusation that you are guilty of *original sin* against a deity – simply because you were born a human being – immediately affects self-esteem! How can your birthright be sinful, making you responsible for crimes against an imagined deity – before you even existed? These same psychological mechanisms will promote fear, manipulating you to believe that when your body dies you will either cease to exist or will move into the unknown, probably defined as heaven or hell. Beliefs through these postulations may pretend to offer you an eternity where you have little control of your destiny (other than what your programmed-in fear suggests that you must do), yet you may be seeking compliance to an illusionary goal.

While the reality of your body's eventual death is by itself superficially obvious, why accept that your consciousness must end or that you cannot continue to evolve? Why limit your potential through fear, foisted by the controls of others, from thriving to what only seems to be unknown, when it can be an extension of your life force driven by your ability to achieve without limit?

It's obvious that you do possess a life force, because you exist. Your body is composed of bioelectric activity, and the most important area of that activity is your mind – your consciousness. Through that, you have the facilities of reason, and can even have *intuitive feelings, perceptions,* about things that eventually come true! Personal evolution is definable by the way you choose to gather, orchestrate, develop, and utilize your bioelectric force!

The invention of Hell

Human institutions tend not to necessarily promote, or even support, personal evolution without help from the institution. Once they have imbued their followers with fear of death and the unknown, religions then play on the manufactured fears they have instilled. They come charging in to provide the answers *for you,* coming to your rescue! Rescued? From what do you need rescuing? Do you believe you need salvation, and if so, from what? Do you need saving from the eternal flames of Hell, or saved from ending in extinction? What if Hell is an imaginary human invention designed to cause your compliance to forces attempting to control you, hidden inside the preposterous assertion that those same forces will save you?

The *same processes that humans use to thrust out and expose any fear from people probably fabricated the evil of Satan.* In recent times, these notions seem largely leveraged off the sadistic imagery contrived by Dante Alighieri early in the *fourteenth century* in his allegorical work, *La Divina Commedia* (The Divine Comedy). In this work, he offered an imaginary tour through the Inferno (Hell), Purgatory (limbo), and Paradise (heaven). The nefarious feature of the Hell as contrived by churchianity is that there is no way of escape for all of eternity! This contrivance is a powerful device: to induce the hope for "salvation" – if one will obey the doctrines of those who invented the punishment.

Although almost certainly influenced by the teachings of churchianity in his time, Dante's allegorical work of sadistic ingenuity devised many images used to promote fear in those followers convinced to believe, and consequently controlled at the expense of their individuality.

At least *the hells* of earlier (pre-Christian) religions offered some means of escape, notably the Hindu. For these believers, a sentence might be limited to a specific number of years, as defined by the teachings of the religion. The mental anguish carries the imaginary specification that one day in human life equals 6,400 years in their version of hell. (We can imagine a sentence to hell for a major crime, such as slaying a religious leader, equaling hundreds of billions of human-years.) Nevertheless, no "sentence to Hell" was eternal in earlier times.

In contrast, my direct and very personal experiences indicate convincingly to me that effective *salvation* really means that I take full responsibility for myself, *saving me from myself!* This means that I needed to dissolve my own *programming* that compelled me to subjugate myself to the controls of others who claimed to be able to *save me* – if only I would obey them. I discovered that much of what they demanded in obedience, such as the pernicious prohibitions against even *thoughts* about sex, are against the primal nature of the human species and consequently *impossible to obey.* The contrived dictums effectively keep the believer in a sense of sin, vulnerable to controls through guilt and responsive to corresponding need for churchianity, which, perhaps, is the secret point of such prohibitions.

Against reliance on faith

I have learned that *faith* is quite passive. Should you simply have *faith* that you can float along your *river of life* and go with that flow, you might be surprised when the river places you in peril, unwittingly crashing you down a malevolent cascade of rapids in turmoil and anguish, beyond your control. Alternatively, when I will myself into action, my volitional intent is active and self-actualizing, and certainly not passive. Driven by my intent and choice, I am able to develop and actualize my life as I define myself. If you limit your self-definition to include the controls of others, or at the mercy of others, I can suggest that you could experience a self-fulfilling prophecy of limited attainment. That prophecy implies that you will be bound to those *limitations devised by others* and embedded in humanity to keep individuals suppressed and controllable.

By virtue of my experiences, I have learned that we, in humanity, are not powerless little chemical-organic creatures that exist at the mercy of a supernatural deity. Is it the years of habitually following beliefs blindly, or just laziness, that causes people to willingly surrender control of their destiny, their sense of themselves, to tribes and to mythological beliefs? Does it seem easier to wistfully believe that someone else will guide your eternal soul if you follow the rules they impose on you rather than taking up direct decisions for yourself? I have learned that eternal life is indeed possible and wondrous, enabled through our own power as we begin to actualize ourselves as evolving beings. To gain knowledge of the power within the self, you must first *intend* to gain that knowledge. After intent, something must actually happen, and that means breaking loose of the preconceptions that bind you and taking action.

Here is one practical tool for evaluating preconceptions. People have an affinity for devising words to disguise their realities, even from themselves. Given that observation, you might be inspired to check out your own words: *When actions and words are not the same in yourself or others, what would change if you trusted only actions?* In other words, what do you say versus what do you do? When words and actions do not match, trust in actions to reveal the truth.

My suggestion is that you can break free of instilled tribal beliefs that you carry. To break free, it is essential *not to abandon your personal responsibilities* to a system of *passive faith* that only reinforces fables. You might consider that faith is like an outer wall circumscribing and protecting self-limiting beliefs, designed to keep you confined under the guise that faith can miraculously offer you salvation. The imperative to "have faith" means that you are better off if you learn to live with, rather than question, the internal contradictions that a tribe (even a social cause) or religion has embedded in you. However, "having faith" also means that you would be abandoning your sense of self, absolving yourself of the need to take direct action on behalf of your self-interest of evolution.

I'm quite confident that each person, as an individual, can actually realize and embrace the unlimited potential that is both human and, through personal development, metaphysically eternal.

The question of fear

Examine the question: *Does fear hold you back from becoming your own advocate?* Fear of the unknown is a very powerful device, and the fear of non-being upon death of your body may elevate fear of the unknown to a paramount sense of vulnerability. I have discerned that religions and all blind belief systems leverage society primarily on fear. To assuage the fear, they make use of the natural primal desire to survive, and expand that to continue into the eternal. This plays into an intrinsic desire to be more than just a temporary little chemical-organic blip on the time line extending into eternity, or a blip of biological interaction. To an extent this explains why there are so many religions are offering salvation, telling you that you were important enough to be created by a super-being, while degrading you by simply demanding command and control for you not to offend the super-being. It also explains why there are so many "social and activist causes" playing on your fears as they beckon you to "believe in them", even if there is only scant validity to their superficial premise. When you "believe", they and social consensus may praise you as incentive for you to comport yourself according to the beliefs. When you think and act as they wish, they will instill a satisfaction that you are "doing good" for the cause as a form of acceptance and sometimes, self-importance. With subliminal control comes power to those wielding its sword. Those in control may compulsively use all resources including death and bloodshed – to protect their power base.

The control issue

Individuals, or even groups, can disassociate from themselves, effectively deeding over ownership of their sense of who they are and their actions to others, and these span the range from religious and political leaders, activist causes, to cults, personal tyrants, and even to gang bosses.

We can recognize the malleability of the human mind by observing the distortions accepted by the battered woman who is often beguiled, then manipulated by a tyrant to gain control. The battered woman disassociates herself from reality, spinning herself the tale that she deserves the beatings. Remaining with the batterer eventually becomes a brain-washed response, and seems less fearful than leaving his control and abuse since she has deeded over control of herself – her self-esteem - to the batterer. Kidnap victims can form dependencies on the kidnappers, a transference of love to the perpetrator and away from the self. The delusional idea is that love, given to the abuser, will protect the victim from injury at the hands of the abuser. This is a form of dependent love: a "love" that seems real, yet reflexively devised by the victim solely by survival instincts, no matter how specious the premise.

When victims believe and trust in their love of the tyrants to whom they have relinquished control of their lives, the tyrants become more important than they are to themselves, and the bondage of dependency takes control of their self-being. The tyrant can become dependent upon having a victim, as the victim can become dependent on the tyrant, setting up a co-dependency.

I observe that relationships, tribes and institutions based on controlling concepts are not limited to religions: *any cause presumed to do good* can be utilized by manipulators, spanning the spectrum to include political, environmental, and other social issues. Typically, they all use fear as their incentive to gain control. Do you fear that the environment is collapsing? *"Fear not! We'll fix it! Donate your time and money to the cause!"* they say, even when only specious data and speculative suppositions support the "threat." The more bewildered society is with the undercurrent and entanglement of fear, the more vulnerable to manipulation it becomes. What percentage of *social causes* use volunteers-in-service simply to increase the wealth (and control power) of those directing the effort? How many politicians are in office *based on the blind beliefs of their followers* rather than demonstrated performance that they are qualified for the job and deserve trust?

Those who are vulnerable to being controlled are those who do not possess sufficient objectivity to use reason and detach themselves from dependencies. They are unwilling (or have been permeated with control for so long that they are unable) to be free as individuals, positioned spaciously apart from the tribal consensus. When they fail, are they victims of others or nature, or are they victims of their own inability to use reason and evolve themselves? Once again, is it just easier to believe in an illusion than to make the effort and do the research to learn the truth?

Are those who live near active volcanoes or on flood plains actually victims of nature when disaster occurs, or are they victims of their own arrogance, with its partner ignorance, that causes them to place their lives in harm's way? When the peril erupts, and their lives or families are taken or shattered, do they accept responsibility for their self-imposed crisis, or do they blame their imaginary god or their leaders for the calamity? Do they pay homage to their god so that they will not be stricken again in the future - even as they continue to position themselves to re-encounter the same peril? In the process, do they whimsically accept what has happened to them by saying, "God must have other plans for us," or "This is God's will"? Do they answer their cries of pain by extolling that "God works in mysterious ways"?

Deity is not the answer

The only mystery here is why so many refuse to take responsibility for their actions and continue to place themselves in harm's way, physically and psychologically. Perhaps they have so invested in the concepts of a harsh and judgmental god who issues punishments as painful retribution for sin or guilt that they actually believe *they deserve* the suffering they experience. Inspecting these phenomena with other dependencies that cry out for individual self-esteem in humanity, they appear much like the battered-wife syndrome, except that an imagined deity is the batterer and humanity somehow must deserve the beatings.

PERSPECTIVES

CHILDREN OF THE UNIVERSE

Although pieces of this writing relate my personal discovery that there is no god (meaning a supreme omnipotent being that is responsible for all creation, life and death) along with my rationale for that conclusion, it might be obvious by now that this writing is not solely about religion, per se, nor is it about belief in a deity. Those are only mechanisms, devised by humans that tend to prey on humanity. Rather, this is about *the rational and intentional choices* that any person may make in their lives. Through your choices, driven by your volition, you can evolve and enhance your state of being. Choices, once committed and brought into actualization, restructure the brain's peptide neural links, and that results in a reconstruction of your inner self and psyche. An incredible *journey* can occur for each person - and it happens incrementally in sequence, an orchestrated crescendo where one decision, one choice becomes an instrument that connects to another then another, as a symphony of being evolves.

Universal beginnings

You are, as are all things organic or inorganic, sentient or not, constructed of sub-atomic particles derived within the universe that are energetic. Energy, as described by the first law of thermodynamics, is convertible from one form to another but energy cannot be created or destroyed. This fundamental truth about the conservation of energy must apply to our beings and consciousness as well, since these are forms of energy!

In physics, a hypothesis could describe sentient energy as an electromagnetic field structure, interacting as a quantum electro-dynamic process to form consciousness. That said, we know that the glue that holds all matter and structure together, including the cellular structures of your body, is comprised of electric fields that when set into motion, transmute to electromagnetic energy. Since energy cannot be created or destroyed, the energetic ingredients of our beings are eternal.

In the sense of the (sub-atomic) particles that compose us, and the related fields that bind us into coherent beings, we have always been here and always will be - at least in energetic form. The statement from Genesis, "Remember man that you are dust and unto dust you shall return" is quite apropos when we consider that our energy and structure is composed of the particulate dust of the universe, which really is the stardust of all being.

Since we are derivatives of the universe, it follows that *we are children of the universe*, constructed from dynamic processes within the universe itself. That means that all human beings have been constructed and born of the same elements as any being is, has been, and ever will be. As children of the same parental source, the universe, we are brothers and sisters to each and all no matter what our status is on the tree of evolution.

For sentience itself to evolve, an electromagnetic, quantum-dynamically interactive, self-adaptive process is required. An intriguing concept to consider might be that those quantum electro-dynamic sequences would not necessarily have to start up in biological organic chemistry as found in humanity. Any mutually adaptive process (probably seeded initially at the quantum sub-atomic level) that could establish the equivalent of neural network links would suffice to evolve consciousness, leaving open for contemplation the matter of probability.

With these thoughts in mind, it is reasonable to conclude that everything, including all thought, are interconnected in one vast and majestic reality: the universe through atomic and sub-atomic particles, fields and waves. Even the regions of the universe, once thought of as only vacuum, are composed of a fabric filled with energetic particles and waves. The universe, as our source of our being, is with us, flows through us, and connects us together, as we are part of this interactive and dynamic process.

Evolving beyond the material state-of-being

As derivatives of the universe, you may suspect that sentient consciousness, the self-being (what would otherwise be termed *the soul*), is in hypothesis a process of natural evolution, a natural extension of the organisms of the biological mind. For example, we know in physics that once an electromagnetic wave launches into space, it continues into infinity – it is forever.

If sentience could be defined as a quantum electro-dynamic, adaptive, and interactive electromagnetic field structure, one could continue into a state of being that was not dependent upon any organic form – once launched beyond the confinement of the body. The concept of sentience, of consciousness, was defined in the early 17th Century by René Descartes as a rationalist premise: "I think, therefore I am."

If that rationalist premise were to be founded on, as arising from, a structure of quantum electro-dynamic interactivity, then it could hypothetically become metaphysical (at a stage of development currently beyond conventional physics) and accordingly, *spiritual.*

Because we are sentient, conscious beings, our self-intended actualization can direct changes to our minds and our bodies. Those actions effectively cause us to become our own "creators" as we define and "assemble" ourselves.

The health problems I was experiencing in Chapter Eight, *The Crater of Self-Deprecation,* tend to confirm that observation since my negativity overloaded my body's ability to compensate. Positive connections when willed into self will yield, in contrast, affirming results.

Additionally for emphasis, during my challenge with *the cleric,* not taking a position about the presence or reality of a deity would have essentially been deceitful, given the understanding that I had attained. Deceit in the face of those to whom one is already wholly known and transparent, is sheer folly. The very same challenge when presented to another who is committed to the concept of a deity could probably have a similar result, though there could be variations that are significant in detail.

For your contemplation, the test challenge statement, "Come with me, I will take you to God" could, for one who monotheistically believes in a deity, have had almost the same outcome as my own – *almost.* Since I recognized that challenge to be partially a test of my commitment to myself, and partially a test of my self-inspection affirming that I was doing my best, the question would have been a good test even for one who believes in a deity. Such a "believing" person might have thought, *"Ask yourself: Why would an all powerful, omnipresent God position a representative to take me to him? As omnipresence, I would already be with God. Why should I submit to being led by one I did not know, on a presumption that could be a delusion, that I might be taken to God?"* So a response of equal integrity would have been: *"No! God is with me always! You cannot take me to what is already within me! You must be a charlatan!"*

With that decision not to be led, it is implied that personal objectivity would be in place so that *you would not blindly follow one you did not know, and could find truth for yourself.*

To me, there is no question that there is a life force within and among us, developed from within ourselves connecting with, and flowing through, all living things. The derivation of that life force is from processes in the universe that began some billions of years ago. Consequently, I can *confidently* attest to you that my "god" is the universe itself, the source of all structures and fields of matter, organic and inorganic, all energetic fields of being. My god is not a monotheistic super-being but rather the process of forces, fields, and energy that encompasses all of nature. Since I am *child of the universe*, as you are, in popular terms the universe is my parental base: my father. Accordingly, I can emphatically say that my god is omnipresent and within me, and interconnected to all. I find peace and joy, and a sense of personal freedom, through this knowledge. I am free of guilt and the need to seek salvation at the hands of another. My spirituality is the whole of my awareness and comprehension of universal truth.

I can also suggest to you that those who enter a deep form of loving meditation called fervent prayer, believing they are extending themselves as energetic forms to their deity, are actually extending themselves in connection to the fields and sentience of the universe.

The open questions for any monotheistic believer: Are you following your individual path in full and efficient harmony with yourself, or do you impulsively accept that burdens are demands of your deity for you to carry a cross? If so, ask yourself why an omnificent being would demand that service of you, and for what purpose - if he were truly omnipotent. Are you open in spirit, free in being, to make course corrections to your process of evolution, or are you bound to dependencies? Ask yourself: As you follow your path, are you truly gaining knowledge of yourself, or are you acting as an automaton following the dictums handed down by others that compel you to blindly and obediently follow beliefs that cannot be challenged?

PERSPECTIVES

THE CREATION OF DEITIES, EMISSARIES, AND BELIEF SYSTEMS

With respect to belief systems involving a deity, or religions and other institutions, it may be useful (if not
deliberately provocative to inspire thought within
you) to explore how social structures tend to create deities.

The hidden purposes of groups and causes

Are belief systems limited to deities, religions, and other factors of mysticism? No, they are not. Talk to any person who *re-
fuses to listen to rational discussion* about any subject and who
resorts to emotional defenses. That person has replaced logic
and reason with emotion, perhaps based in fear, captured only
by beliefs, absent the use of reason to understand the consequences. The subject could be a social ideal or almost any social
or political cause. *Anything a zealot can use to invoke a state of
fear will suffice to impress vulnerable minds*. Even reasonable and
understood things subject to technical analysis, such as measurable environmental issues, can become blindly reflexive in emotion, making them "beliefs" essentially tantamount to a religion.
The issue to inspect is if the conclusions inspiring the fear, the

social promotion of a threat, are based on hard, factual, provable data, or on speculative projection (called complex simulations) about "what might" happen over a time span of decades.

When you encounter an individual or a group that operates only on the consensus of speculation or emotion, you can easily find an active but blind belief system made into a treasured cause. The zealot will seek out, and gather, volunteers to support the cause for the supposedly greater good and instill zealotry as an attitude that can develop into fanatical obsession, whether the cause is in reality good or not. The zealot's often-unconscious motive is to gain power, wealth and veneration from exerting control over others, justified by threat and fear.

People have often demonstrated a willingness to gain acceptance by conforming to the consensus of their social group. In these socially approved roles, they are rarely inclined to take independent control of their lives, whether material or spiritual. This can be true even if a madman is leading their group and taking control and power over others. Why is this true? Because those who belong to the group and who follow its leader, are often unconsciously motivated by their desire to be accepted and empowered by their identity with the group. (The sense of empowerment can be heard when followers proudly, boastfully, proclaim their importance through their association with a socially accepted group cause.)

Acceptance and social empowerment, per se, has nothing to do directly with what the "cause" of the group happens to be. The group's official objective is actually irrelevant to its true purpose, which is dual: gaining control, power and even veneration for the leader; and, a feeling of acceptance and the allusion of empowerment for everyone else. Moreover, the greater the fear the leader can implant, the greater will be the harvesting of power.

Tyrants such as Adolph Hitler only take or have power at the expense of others. Take away the victims, and the tyrant would have no power. Since tyrants cannot be self-sufficient in their being or their energy, they cannot evolve and neither can their followers since they have given their power to the group's leader or to group consensus. Only those who extricate themselves from these loops of energy-restricting dependencies can attain their ultimate evolution.

The alternative to such dependencies, encouraged by my own life experience and that of many others, is to use rational choice to develop your own reality. This is accomplished by thinking as an individual and by not being afraid to question – even if your questions are in contrast to the consensus of the group that you may be tempted to join, or in which you are already a member. Using your reason to discern the truth will open you to a strength of self that will provide you with an incredibly valuable asset: unconditional love and trust in yourself that will by extension apply to others, when you choose (through your volition and not emotional reflex) to love and trust others.

Deity as a Way of Accounting for Natural Phenomena

For millennia, probably since the evolutionary dawn of human consciousness, human beings have sought to understand events and forces of nature that they were witnessing or experiencing. Humans have yearned to learn what the significance of these events or manifestations might be – to and for themselves. After all, what one doesn't understand will often seem frightening.

Initially, whatever humans observed they accepted as *being real*. For example, early humans could only see across their surroundings to the limit of what appeared to be a flat horizon, so it was easy for them to conclude that the *Earth must be flat!* What would happen to the person who said, "Maybe the earth is not flat?" Would tribal (societal) consensus deride the individual for having a unique thought?

When viewing the night sky, the stars appear to rotate around the Earth. It seemed obvious; therefore, that the Earth must be at the center of everything else (in other words, the universe!), since everything seemed to move around it! That idea possibly caused the reassuring thought that if the Earth were at the center of the universe, humans must be too! What a wonderfully gratifying feeling: humans were at the center of everything!

Observations of unexplained, phenomena became "understood" as *various sorts of mysteries and magic.* What makes rain? Since humans could not make rain, some mysterious force must make it!

Early humanity understood that they, themselves, could construct certain things (shelters, tools, canals for irrigation), and they even learned how to develop agriculture. They could not, however, construct or influence the fundamentally vital processes of nature. So the forces of nature were personalized, which tended to assuage their fears as well. Since the five senses are often insufficient for learning the cause of anything observed or experienced, the attributed explanation was to an unknown force. This brought the *magic theme* into an alternate concept of reality, through which *they believed* they could identify causation. If humans didn't cause it, maybe *magic* caused it! The magic of rain, for example, became the responsibility of a *rain god.* What if there was insufficient rainfall to sustain a group? They would assume that they must have offended their rain god. Then the question arose of how to appease this god (often with dances to entertain him, or with sacrifices to please him).

As another example, the warmth and light of the sun are very powerful, so there must be a *sun god.* Thus the process of groping for answers continued, personalizing not-understood forces and assigning causation to deities, eventually touching all the manifestations of nature. In this way, the explanations for a seemingly limitless number of natural forces (e.g., health, oceans, agriculture, volcanoes, earthquakes) simply allocated power to magical deities. Humans gave each deity both a personification and a responsibility. This offered people some form of human-like identification with these forces. In effect, *humankind created gods* to serve its basic need to reduce fear through consolation, providing solace through "explanations."

Even common language and its definitions can get in the way of human understanding. What exactly is a god anyway? Is a god something that causes manifestations of nature? Certainly, a

Christian would have a monotheistic definition, invoking a powerful, singular being that is mighty and omnipotent. To a polytheistic pagan or a pantheist, however, the question begs a new question: *"Which god?"* Buddhists might relate that *god is nature itself*, involving the essential life-supporting elements of water, earth, and fire.

The Emperor of Japan during World War II, accepted as a living god, demanded service from his subordinates as gods tend to do, and they acquiesced control of their lives to their deity. Japanese folklore, mythology, and tradition prevailed over the use of reason, and the beliefs led the populace to horrendous defeat. The famous Kamikaze pilots, a group that splattered themselves in suicide missions, took their title from the presumed divinity of their emperor: kami (divine) + kaze (wind). In effect, they knew of no other way to live or judge reality except through the powerfully imprinted social consensus of blind beliefs set firmly into place during their early youth.

On occasion, gods were simply historical humans deified at some later point, often because of the magic they practiced (or were rumored to practice). Leaders and societies also anointed Prophets and Saints with god-like powers, worshiped and followed them by millions of believers.

An Example from Ancient Egypt

Going back in time to approximately 2,600 BC in Egypt, we find a great genius in architecture, medicine, and astrology in the person of Imhotep, who at the time of his life, they called *a court magician*. Later on, a group worshiped Imhotep as a deity. In Imhotep we have an example of a human process: What we would now say is a physician or technologist, was called a magician in his time; then he was elevated to a deified status, and worshiped, about two thousand years later, in 525 BC. Society has a history of assigning magic as a label for what it does not understand, and even worshiping those thought to be proficient in controlling (or influencing) natural forces.

Siddhartha Gautama, a Seeker

Moving forward about two thousand years from the time of Imhotep, and overlapping the time of his deification, Siddhartha Gautama was born in 563 BC as a prince of a small kingdom (in Kapilavastu), and a member of the Sakya warrior caste. He was inspired at about the age of 29 years to question the sheltered luxury of his upbringing when he renounced attachments to worldly things and embarked on a personal quest to find "enlightenment." Eventually he settled on a middle path somewhere between a life of indulgence and self-denial. His quest "enlightened" him to find ways of overcoming suffering, primarily by advancing knowledge over ignorance. The cause of suffering, he said, is ignorance about the nature of reality, with the consequence that human craving, attachment, and grasping for things are the result of ignorance. Wandering extensively from place to place to preach the philosophy of what he discovered and his methods of discovery, Siddhartha Gautama became The Buddha, or "Enlightened One."

Refusing to designate his successor, his advice to his followers was that it was their responsibility, as individuals, to work out their attainment of enlightenment for themselves. The Buddha left no written record of his philosophy. His followers verbally passed the philosophy down across the span of centuries until the version that emerged became written down about the 1st century, BC.

I mention The Buddha, and a small fragment of his history, not because he was deified but because he extolled a philosophy - that his followers converted to a religion. It seems evident to me that the concept he related, that the method of attainment he found and developed for his personal enlightenment, tends to match what I've learned: that achievement of personal evolution occurs through self-responsibility powered by volitional discipline to introspect and seek knowledge. The fact that his followers banded together to form a tribe, that approaches a religion, speaks to a primal human need to have psychological comfort through companionship.

The Origins of Christianity

The human need for direction and consensus of tribal embrace converged in many of the same processes to develop the institution of Christianity. Saul of Tarsus, initially a bitter enemy of the new movement, later became its leading missionary. Known later as *Saint Paul,* and who never actually met Jesus in physical form, he "marketed" the small (originally limited to Judaism) sect to the Greek and Roman world beyond. As its self-appointed missionary, Paul converted the small sect of Christianity into what would become a worldwide institution. His letters, though they only expressed his opinions, became central dogma in the new religion.

The chain reaction started by Saul of Tarsus caused followers to group into many small sects, each with different ideas about the faith and different stories about Jesus. Some sects were in radical disagreement on key points, indicating that there were serious differences of opinion about Jesus, his role, and his state of being. The historical record indicates that these small, discordant, sects had no central point of reference for their faith, though in some cases the philosophy tended to agree with Buddha's. The original texts of various sects were written in Koine Greek by *unknown authors* between 45 AD and 140 AD. Compilations of edited, selected, writings from various sects happened around 180 AD to become the early bible stories – written by men and presented as the word of God. The officially sanctioned accounts were only four of the more than thirty that were available about 150 years after Jesus' death.

More editing and revision occurred around 325 AD at the direction of Constantine, through his Council of Nicaea. Constantine was seeking to harmonize control over his empire and had to factor in the growing number of Christians among his populace. To harmonize his empire, he also had to consider the beliefs of the Roman military, which mostly followed the sect of Mithras, an ancient Persian sun god considered as a guardian against evil. The organized version of Christianity that emerged actually resembles the structure in the sect of Mithras, even to the point that December 25th, Mithras' birthday, church luminaries assigned to Jesus as well.

The Beginnings of Islam

The historical story about the formation of Islam is similarly awkward, though it extracted (and re-stated) many segments of the Torah, the Old Testament, and the New Testament. The Prophet Muhammad died about 632 AD, approximately six centuries after Jesus. An individual named Ibn Idhaq, whose original work has been lost to history, first documented Muhammad's life 120 years after his death, around 750 AD. Then, around 830 AD, more than 195 years after Prophet's death, Ibn Idhaq's information was recounted by Ibn Hisham in a new compilation that included stories told across the generations for over 190 years. From what I have learned, it is generally accepted that the written fragments from his disciples, augmented with verbally passed-down stories, were eventually collected to become many hundreds of verses, each recorded over time separately by his followers. The structure of the compilation is not set into theme, date or significance, but in descending order of the length of the verses.

Common Approach of Other Religions

There have been many books written in the history of the world's major monotheistic religions. These include the dictations of Joseph Smith (who appears to have been illiterate), first to his wife Emma and then to his neighbor Martin Harris that resulted in the Book of Mormon. Smith claimed that the texts he "read" for dictation were inscribed on tablets of gold, delivered by an angel, and that God would strike dead anyone who saw the tablets, other than Smith. That explains why he was "obligated" to conceal himself, and the tablets, behind a cloth partition as he dictated, to prevent his wife or his neighbor from incurring God's wrath. It only follows that the gold tablets vanished to heaven, never seen by anyone on Earth again.

All of the books initiating a religion have one thing in common: These are the stories of human experience, conceived, written and edited by humans, and presented to mankind to be of divine origin when a deity was said to be involved.

How is this Book Different?

Based on my direct personal experiences, I am quite certain that Jesus *never claimed* to be the *Son of God* or a deity himself. I am equally certain that Jesus had, or has, no interest in saving anyone, or to be a leader. When he gazed into the sky and meditated about his role with his father, he was referring to his and to our parentage from the universe itself, the source of energy and sentience for all of us, implying the recognition of nature that Buddha learned for himself.

Working with the concept that "the consortium", the consciousness of the universe that includes Jesus and many others, have attained their ultimate phase of continuing evolution, questions arise: *What is their role with humanity, and why?*

Having asked that, it might be useful for you to imagine what you think *your role* would be if you achieved their level of attainment, and then examine the possibilities implied through your introspection. Would you seek to take control and direct the lives of humans? Why would you (since they could never come up to your attained level while under your control, and as an ultimately evolved being, you'd have no need of being worshiped since that is a dependency of ego)? Would you be inclined to facilitate others to evolve? If so, at what expense to yourself?

In the important interest of conserving your own energy, using it carefully when needed, would you require that any candidate worth your consideration and effort as a mentor would have already demonstrated - by their actions - their own commitment to their evolution? Would you lie quietly back and just observe them, until they proved their commitment through their actions? Finally, since you would have evolved through your own volition and self-interest, what would be your reward by inspiring others?

To begin my response to those questions, I'm reminded of the character of a proto-angel, Clarence, in the movie (1946) starring Jimmy Stewart, "It's a Wonderful Life!" The character played by Stewart, George Bailey, was on the brink of suicide by jumping off a bridge. Clarence, showing up on the scene just in time, gets Bailey's attention, convinces Bailey to stop the suicide attempt, and then mentors Bailey into higher awareness to understand the significance and value of Bailey's life. When Bailey asked Clarence why he was doing this, he replied that he was "earning his wings" as an angel.

Allegorically, Clarence would be seen as a partially-evolved being, already in spiritual form, evolved to just the right energetic level to "match" with the needs of Bailey, at exactly the time of need for fulfillment for both individuals. It can be construed that Clarence was positioned somewhere in a chain of mentors for Bailey, that would eventually extend to those who are ultimately evolved.

During my journey, I extract for your review the quote (Chapter 17 – "Decision") from my mentors: *"When you connect to others, you may facilitate their evolution, and you will benefit by facilitation in return – facilitation through the knowledge you will gain by interacting with others and by learning not to form dependencies on these connections. For those who are committed to evolve, the expansion of their attributes can cause them to become candidates to join us in our consortium. When they evolve to this state, all of us mutually benefit."*

They followed this by *"You have your destiny in our consortium."* - The implication being that by working as a mentor, I will facilitate myself.

Hence, there is a chain of mentors ranging from those who are ultimately evolved to those who are lesser evolved, matched at various levels in their evolutionary state, to the conditions of candidates seeking increased attainment of their personal evolution – that they must earn individually. An energy efficient system works through the chain because energy is not wasted upon those who choose not to evolve; and, provided to those who demonstrate their resolve.

This explains why this book exists: I am demonstrating by my actions that I will not revert to my historical mode of failure by hiding; I am earning my "wings."

The reward for others, who have progressed to high attainment, is that candidates without losing anything of their individuality, who increasingly elevate themselves toward their ultimate attainment, become full members of the consortium that, by definition, increases the energetic consciousness of the universe. In the meantime, during the progression of their paths, they enjoy a life of purpose with freedom of mind, spirit and being, to inquire and explore the potentials that inspire them.

Personal Experience

My reports to you are those of my personal experiences and do not entail a belief system that demands compliance. My experiences suggest that one can choose personal responsibility, the use of reason, the development of one's abilities, and ultimately an extension of the self through natural and evolutionary processes. There is a sequential development of self-esteem that leads to trust in self; that takes nothing from others; and that requires no servitude to an illusionary higher being, or to emissaries that claim to represent the wishes of such a being.

It seems reasonable to propose that human frailties are the fundamental reason why religions and other institutions exist: to offer comfort and solace to humanity with belief systems that rely on faith alone. People will believe in something that comforts them, even if it doesn't provide any real answers. For example, consider the phrase, *God moves in mysterious ways.* Each individual in a group might accept and recognize the phrase, even take comfort from it, yet the phrase explains absolutely nothing.

As I found in my early life, if I questioned a belief, the programmed response would be to turn the questioner into the accused. *"You don't have faith!"* simply converts a question into a challenge! The effect is that the questioner is being told that he or she is now inadequate, has failed to have the quality of faith demanded of them, simply because they asked a question.

Those elevated in stature by blind beliefs of their followers, that claim their uniqueness as emissaries of the divine, gives them access to incredible imaginary knowledge, and sometimes power. They bolster their positions by saying that their knowledge is far too complex for *ordinary* humans to understand. Sometimes they claim that ordinary people would be struck dead, if they were to see or hear the source of this special knowledge! What intimidating and ludicrous propositions these are, all to protect their manipulations! To solve the dilemma they cause, the emissaries bring their profound "knowledge" down to terms people can understand. When challenged, they cannot tolerate questions, since any interrogation undermines their authority.

Blind faith directs people not to question and simply to follow. Faith might be absolving you from your responsibilities and your sins, as those who compel faith from you also *contrive those sins* you must be absolved of, even if the "sin" is just a natural feeling of sexuality. In natural human expression, it is not possible to comply with these commands without conflict that is easily converted to guilt. If compliance fails for you, all of your troubles become your personal failure. Maybe your guilt will lead you into a pernicious crater of self-loathing, as it did with me. Because your faith is not strong or sufficient, you could be defined *as inadequate,* hammering down your self-esteem. The feelings of inadequacy can cause you to follow others *you believe* (but do not know) to be more adequate than you are, just as the batterer controls the beaten woman.

Some religions have even created a salve for these feelings of failure and inadequacy in the doctrine of reincarnation, which allows a person to say "Okay, I don't have to worry so much about my failures today because I can make it up and fix it in my next life!" *But- what happens to you if the next life is only a fantasy?* Do people improve their self-image and take comfort when they believe that they are old souls with the experience of past lives? If that is true, how many lives are required to *get it right*? Perhaps those who have, or believe they have, intense memories of past lives are simply responding to resonances carried forward within them through their DNA. Since DNA represents a microcode that assembles our bodies and our natural abilities, could it carry forward memories?

Even the origin of life itself is "accounted for" by belief systems. How does life, particularly human life, form? After all, life is a very complex process. It is so complex that it must be mysterious, and to solve anything mysterious, humans devise gods to provide explanation. Perhaps human life came from something like a soul descending into and occupying a body, they would have you believe. However, if that were true, where do human souls come from? Is there really a vast reservoir of undeveloped souls floating out in the universe just awaiting the opportunity to inhabit a limiting and frail body – so they can develop to please god?

There are more humans alive today on Planet Earth than ever before. Does that imply an excess of souls were stored somewhere – without bodies – just waiting for humans to produce enough offspring to absorb those souls? What would happen to those souls if an asteroid extinguished humanity? Would those souls have any cognizance of what they were before they inhabited a body that they needed to develop from an undeveloped soul-state? What self-identity does a newborn infant really possess, since obviously they are not highly developed? If children had no one to teach them that they were divinely created, or that they had to obey rules to please a deity, would they intuitively know that their origin is nature?

Which seems more probable to you - that some vast storage pool of souls has nothing better to do than to patiently await for a body to inhabit, or that a mythical deity creates souls "on the spot" when he notices conception is occurring somewhere, or, that human sentience develops by *natural* processes within the body itself, and, that consciousness may then expand into the universe through natural processes of evolution? I have come to the firm conclusion that evolution applies not just to species but to individuals as well.

Those who control through belief systems have used the planets, stars, galaxies, and the universe itself to support the notion of a vast and powerful deity. Even the natural processes of biology have been brought under this aegis by creation-believers to support their dependency on a deity, through the pseudo-science of *intelligent design*. However, we note many instances in nature where the design is clearly flawed and therefore *not* highly intelligent.

The Beginnings of the Shaman-Priest

As tribes continued to assign various responsibilities for their quality of life to their deities, a more organized approach to appeasing and directing this power was required. It became logical to assign someone within the tribe to be certain that the tribe appeased the demands of the deities. Of course, humans also invented those demands, just as they had created the deities to control the tribes in the first place!

Accordingly, the function of an individual or group that appeared able to interpret and respond to the *desires of the gods* continued to mushroom, along with ever-increasing control over tribal actions. These "special individuals" now served as intermediaries between humans and the gods. Consequently, we soon had shamans with imagined control over natural events, medicine men, Pharisees, priests, and more – a whole class of people serving as society's interface with gods that did not even exist (though we can respect that some of these included homeopaths skilled in healing and herbal medicine, and even functioned as proto-psychologists).

Powerful gods, logically, required powerful attention, and by implication that required powerful human representatives to the gods! (Apparently, no one openly asked the question why powerful gods needed service from puny little humans.) This attention could take the form of ritual, veneration, or worship, and the power assigned made some of these emissaries not just powerful in terms of control, but wealthy in the worldly sense as well.

The Beginnings of Sacrifice

According to these intermediaries, the gods might also demand sacrificial gifts from the tribe. Beginning perhaps as tokens such as flowers, these "gifts to the gods" soon expanded to gifts of food (for the ever-growing priestly class) and then to offerings of blood, forcibly taken in pain, which were for some reason specially favored by the gods. In some cultures, these blood offerings included self-mutilation and human lives *as sacrificial offerings*. Various ceremonies were increasingly devised that included: dances; incantations; prayers, and, expansively massive pilgrimages to sacred places. By giving the gods increasing power, their intermediaries received increasing power, to the extent of expansive control of the tribal culture.

The Beginnings of "Religious" Warfare

How long would it be before the will of the gods wanted to bolster and justify tribal warfare? Not long, and the battle cry *Kill in the name of our god,* has been going on ever since. Given the pernicious and even nefarious history of organized religion, it would be very difficult to convincingly assert that belief systems actually cause humans to behave better than they would if those beliefs did not exist.

Historically, we recognize that authorities of the church *believed* that they were "doing good" during the hundreds of years of the Inquisition and the witch-hunts that came with the Protestant Reformation. The German SS in World War II *believed* it was "doing good" by exterminating Jews. The Islamic fanatics *believe* they are "doing good" by attacking the West – and slaughtering those who do not believe in their faith or their god (even though their god and faith were extracted out of The Torah, the Old Testament, and the New Testament). These are all simply manifestations of humans seeking domination or control over others, yet doing so in the name of a higher power.

Monotheistic religions divide the world into good and evil, believers and nonbelievers. This comes down to deciding whether an individual or group is adhering to a certain belief system, or not. Everyone else is "out of control," somewhere between "lost" and "evil." Ask yourself: Is this really a case of good and evil? Alternatively, are these simply the judgments of people seeking control over others?

The universe does not divide itself into good and evil. Likewise, the consortium of consciousness permeating the universe does not see things in terms of good and evil, nor would it have any reason to care what humans might do since humans are responsible for their own actions, whether they realize it or not.

Then what are the interests in the universe and the consortium of consciousness? I suggest to you that there are two principles at work: one is balance, and the other is life and attainment through a path of evolutionary growth.

View first the concepts of balance. Consider that all of the forces in the universe are continually in motion, constantly restoring energetic balance and equilibrium. Balance applies to human interactions as well, and these tend to follow Newton's law that *action equals reaction*.

If fanatics based in blind emotional beliefs blow up the USA's World Trade Center, citing Allah as their moral authority - it is easy to see that a motion started. Every motion requires a counter-motion to seek balance. The counter motion is that the USA then blows up the fanatics by taking the war into the territory of the aggressor. (History teaches us that when wars are *not taken* into the territory of the initial aggressor, the original *victim of the aggression will be defeated*.)

The achievement of balance in this example is by force and opposing force. To both sides there is momentum that can require continual re-balancing: The West and non-believers are evil to fanatics; fanatics are evil to the West and the believers of other faiths, in essentially equal measures of emotion. Tracing this thread back to the Crusades, 1095 to 1270 AD, Western Christianity wanted control of the "holy land" and set out to achieve it with papal sanction. The balance for this action happened by the military and political genius of Saladin who overwhelmed Jerusalem in 1187. The region has not rested from this cycle of action and counteraction since then, and the strife, power struggle, and terror have become a way of life.

In contrast, there is a way of life where all may choose their own path and decide their own destiny. Nature clearly favors life, growth, advancement and continued differentiation, all through movement and completely natural processes of evolution. As you learn to make the choices that lead to your greater freedom of mind and increased energy, you'll unlock more energy that will be available for your personal growth and development.

For me, one of the great discoveries of my life is that evolution into a metaphysical state of spiritual consciousness is a *natural* progression, one that requires no deities, belief systems, or faith. There is a condition attached for your attainment: that the extension and enhancement of sentient consciousness into a metaphysical state of being is a natural progression, available only for those who *choose to evolve.* This choice implies a willingness to withdraw one's life energy from any self-negations, as well as embedded control belief systems directed into the servitude to others that are not in one's self-interest, and to redirect this energy with intelligence and reason.

PERSPECTIVES

MAGIC, SCIENCE, AND THE EVOLUTION OF THE INDIVIDUAL

As human intellect moved into more objective investigation and experimentation, what was once magic and under the control of deities gradually changed to become understandable and natural processes.

In our own day, most of human society no longer requires rain or weather gods to explain and describe circulating pressures of water vapor, thermo-clines and jet stream movements in the atmosphere. As the technical tools of observation and measurement increase in diversity and capability, investigation and description moves into more subjects. Science, per se, really discovers nothing. Science only describes – often with mathematics as a vocabulary of description – and seeks to explain through meticulous examination and observation what occurs in nature: how various motions, structures, and forces of nature behave and mutually interact.

From this intellectual expansion of examination and inquiry, the magic of the past is either science already, or it will be in the future.

Is Science Itself a Belief System?

Science is essentially a system of observation, description, review, analysis, and explanation. The primary difference between science and the beliefs of religion or faith is that the statements, hypotheses, and conclusions of science are *falsifiable.* Those who *believe* in religious faith-based systems, or hold *intractable beliefs* in a cause, particularly one promoted by social or media consensus, often reject solely on emotional grounds the premise that their beliefs are subject to hypothetical or testable examinations in order to demonstrate veracity. Those beliefs, especially those held by emotions, are not falsifiable. *If human involvement in any cause, even a social cause, cannot be examined for veracity and altered, cannot be subjected to test, reason, and experiment, it is not science: it is a blind belief system.*

Should a science become dependent upon the mind-set of the scientist with a strong bias as to the outcome of the research, *it is not science*. It is just another form of faith and consequently just another *belief system pretending to be science*! The notion, posited by churchianity, through the obvious oxymoron called "scientific creationism" is such an example of pretense. To be true science, the pursuit of inquiry must *always* possess freedom of mind, the freedom to inspect and follow the evidence without prejudice to the outcome.

Manipulators aiming to suit alternate social agendas other than the pursuit of truth can distort even treasured theories such as "The Big Bang" or "Darwinism", and when that happens - they cease to be science. For example, the continuing investigation to learn about the origins of life cannot be prejudiced by labels such as "Darwinism" or "intelligent design" and still be science since both labels imply bias for the direction of study, and consequently the result. Missing pieces in any explanation do not falsify a hypothesis. Simulations based on a large number of variables, particularly those projected out over a large time span, do not validate a conclusion of a hypothesis and most certainly do not prove anything. When objectively applied, finding missing pieces in a valid evidence chain, or gathering indications from projected long-term simulations, only motivate increased inquiry and inspection of the subject. Cries for action and social consensus, borne on fear, when based on simulations purported on a large number of interdependent variables, become specious pretense disguised as science, and are often the tools of manipulators predisposed to their agenda.

The singular beauty of science, apart from the enormous knowledge it has derived, is the mental and emotional discipline it instills. The "scientific method", a process of logically and systematically exploring and evaluating a study each step of the way, searching for inconsistencies or conflicts in the results, is arguably the greatest single achievement of the human mind. Emotional attachments and religious beliefs are normally left behind at the doorway in the practice of science that requires curiosity, an open mind, and the emotional willingness to discard whatever does not survive rigorous testing. These same criteria should apply to any exploration of the "metaphysical" realm, which considers questions such as the meaning of evolution and investigates different evolutionary potentials and possibilities in a rational way.

Personal Commitment

My own journey is infused with these values from the beginning of my inquiry, largely because of my background in science and my disillusionment with organized religion. Even so, everything I've experienced and learned is subject to verification by other, future, investigators who may be motivated to push explorations beyond known physical manifestations into metaphysical hypothesis, which will be eventually subjected to experiments and tests.

My experiences gathered through my life and journey, suggest a path for our evolution that may qualify as the first to be completely free of religion and its un-testable beliefs. That is, I posit that my experiences indicate a new and rational foundation for future human evolution into nonphysical (beyond the organic body) reality, a foundation free of deities, emissaries, dogmas, and attempts at control through guilt and fear.

Replacing these relics: a personal commitment to your own evolution, based on responsibility, reason, and self-esteem, and on the willingness to extricate yourself from anything that would drain you of your energy. These energy traps include early traumas, irrational beliefs, faith in a god as defined by institutions in humankind, and the limiting expectations of self that extend from the potential confinements of one's various tribes. You are not required to have faith in anything, even the consortium as I describe that to you, in order to have perception, inspiration, and intuitive power that is already in your being waiting to be fully unlocked.

You are, by birthright, a free and independent being, capable of rationally navigating the course of your life. The guidelines that apply to this adventure are entirely experiential and natural, and you may discover them for yourself.

I share what I have learned only to inspire and stimulate you to introspect how you feel about yourself, question if your individuality is being suppressed by who or what you are serving, and learn to leave belief systems behind and embark on the journey of your own evolution.

My own venture began when I became compelled to recognize that my quandaries, consternations, and conflicts were essentially related to my low self-esteem. Some portion of that low self-esteem was related to guilt complexes arising from my inability to contort my natural attributes to fit the dictates of churchianity, or even pressures applied from other social forces "to conform" in ways that distorted my appreciation, my sense of my self-worth.

To conceal my lack of self-esteem, I developed various defenses, sometimes including anger and often withdrawal that repeatedly became serious depression. I felt I had to hide my perceived inadequacies, eventually pushing myself to believe that I was wholly inadequate, and thus justified hiding myself.

Though your own defenses may be different from the ones I developed, the process is the same: induced guilt and fear causes inadequate feelings, and lowers self-esteem. We then try to hide ourselves behind various defenses, leading to even lower self-valuing and eventually to depression, and possibly even suicide. In the meanwhile, low self-esteem can cause dependency upon others to lead you, or upon structures such as the belief systems of churchianity, or even any "tribal group" bound and determined to serve "any cause to do good." If the other person or group also has low self-esteem, then the trap of co-dependency will become evident, yet you might not be aware because you'd be receiving emotional support in the form of acceptance from the group. Thus, the downward spiral continues until your physiological health finally becomes impaired, and you realize that you must turn your sense of yourself and direction of life around, or perhaps die. You realize, often with a sense of shock, that you have been wasting your life and its most valuable resource: your conscious energy of being and awareness!

Your motivation to *restructure* your mental patterns to free yourself from the negative components of your thoughts, feelings, and relationships is your key. The chief (and early) warning signals, besides the bad feelings that accompany any form of negativity, is unnecessary conflict in your life that can result in issues manifested in your body that have specious medical causation.

You are an individual beyond anything else, with essential responsibilities to yourself! *The most fundamental choice you will ever make is to accept responsibility for your own evolution and not deferring that responsibility to outside forces.* Assuming you are beginning or continuing your own self-directed journey, I think you will find the following questions useful.

a) What are my emotional dependencies?
b) Do I lead myself to my own destinations, or am I conditioned to being led?
c) Have I committed to my own responsibility to evolve?

d) Am I more concerned with what others think and feel about me, compared to what I think and feel about myself?

e) Do my beliefs cause me to exist in conflict or guilt?

Had I previously asked myself, or been asked, the question, "Who is the most important person in my universe?" my answer would probably have been someone or something – almost anything - other than myself. That meant I was then living my life for another, which implies that I was placing my sense of being in the control of some external concept, or someone on whom I was emotionally dependent and had forced myself to believe in. That was then: this is now.

The old adage that *God helps those who help themselves* seems very apropos here since it directly implies that being attentive to self is important, and it even promotes the notion of the energy progressing analogies to a chain of mentors, a link every step you take in your journey. People who help themselves are engaging with their own lives, actualizing their potentials, and accepting their individual responsibilities, and in turn, strengthening and building their self-esteem. This, as a broad concept, is what I learned during my voyage and experiences in the infinite expanse, far beyond confinement within the tunnel of light. During the journey, I made the fundamental choice *to be only myself and to be true to myself.* Within that context, I have striven to stay free of labels and to make the best choices I could make for myself.

This doesn't mean that there weren't better choices I could have made and then taken into action. It only means that each choice was the best I could make in the moment of the now and the now is the only state of time any of us have to work with. Making the best choice you can at the time fulfills your responsibility to yourself.

I find it continually useful to inquire of myself if I am doing my best, given the experience and information I have - now. If something does not feel right, if there is any nuance of conflict, I halt my reaction and ask why, as I start to dive deeply inside to learn the answer. Questions I ask myself at any moment of reflex reaction:

What do I really know — right now?

Are my feelings based on expectations, anticipations, or speculations?

What can I learn – right now – by being objective?

Is my feeling truly objective, or disproportionably elating or degrading to myself?

I continue to engage with the consortium of sentience, of consciousness, in the infinity of the universe. These are my mentors, intuition and inspiration, connected in a continuum and functioning with me in a mentor-protégé relationship, yet I experience no dependency on them and no concern that I might offend or be forced to conform myself to their wishes. My evolution can only be my agenda, not theirs. Through inspiration, my mentors have provided concepts and perspectives for me to evaluate and utilize, and which I am now passing on to you for the same purpose of your personal exploration.

PERSPECTIVES

ETHICAL BEHAVIOR & TRIBES

Belief systems often present themselves as the voice for moral authority, particularly when they claim that their authority stems from a deity. Moses and the Ten Commandments is an example of how men using words, ascribed to a deity, can gain control and rule their tribes at times where circumstances demand leadership. Given that humans seeking control over other humans to gain power from them wrote these "scriptures", it is appropriate to examine such systems of ethics and morality, and to learn to whom advantage is given.

It is obvious that humans are born with certain primal instinctual drives, including survival (from which fear is derived), emotional expression, social connectedness (being drawn toward tribes) and the desire to procreate (sexual drives). These drives entangle and interact with each other, generating behavior that is simultaneously territorial and possessive. A primate (including humans) male with a female might automatically feel possessive of her, and this would cause him to be protective. The same male may seek partnership with many females to seed his offspring, spreading his legacy as widely as possible, while the female will seek a male who will protect and provide for her children.

Clearly, humans as "social beings" possess an instinctual need to form common emotional bonds with others to provide solace and gather support for common purposes. This drive causes tribes to form, and people to be "part of" the mutual facilitation that tribes can provide.

At issue is the nature of the tribe and membership within the tribe. If the members of a tribe mutually support each other for specific purposes, without usurping or impairing the individuality of its members, and not demanding that the members value the tribe more themselves, then the tribe has an ethical constitution. If a tribe issues intractable service demands from its members that are inequitable, out of balance compared with the value returned to each member, then the tribe is not ethical. In other words, for a tribe to have an ethical foundation of operation, the constitution will require that the member gain at least as much value as an individual as they put into investing in the tribe, and that the members can reshape the purposes of the tribe without contravention by leaders.

Beyond the comparatively few primal tendencies that are inherent to the species, we have *morality*, consisting of a learned set of rules defining ethical behavior. We require these rules for the harmonious and non-conflicting interaction between people, and for the development of human potential. Derivation of these standards of behavior and conduct come from various sources, primarily social customs and pronouncements attributed to a god. Reason, introduced later on as an arbiter and ethics as a discipline, becomes more rational and more philosophical.

Ethical behavior stems from a balance of value, a rule accepted by your mind with reason, and that in balance is true "morality." If tribal dictums, under the label of "morality", cause you to relinquish your self-interest without "equitable balance value" being returned to you, the dictums are examples of blind beliefs, not of reason, and perhaps precepts of force.

I would submit to you that an ethics based on reason encourages the seeking of value in a way that maintains balance for all involved. That is, truly ethical behavior discourages one person or society from seeking gain at the expense of another without an equitable return: Exchange and balance are the keywords here.

The frailties and dangers become obvious when we probe into who provides the ethical instruction, and for what purpose. If the instruction balances benefits to the tribe in proportion to benefits the individual receives back from the tribe, a balance becomes evident. If, on the other hand, the mandated instruction supports only the tribe, without regard to individual value, the tribe will diminish the individual.

Most tribes (including nations) throughout history have ignored the principle of balanced exchange. Even some philosophers, such as Immanuel Kant, assaulted reason and undermined the individual by saying that an individual has no value other than the value the community (that is, the tribe) assigns! What a travesty!

The *emissaries of the gods that I call churchianity* would have found support for their control positions in Kant's philosophy. Paradoxically, even the atheist political-social systems of Karl Marx and Vladimir Lenin would have found an ally in Kant, since communist society aims to control every aspect of life, completely subordinating individuals to the society.

It is useful to evaluate most ethics in terms of Newton's action versus reaction energy exchanges, which in societal terms means actions versus consequences. An individual can judge the value of an act by considering probabilities of risk from the action versus the potential resulting reward. Some members of society routinely ignore the risk and look only at possible rewards.

The concept of the balanced value is not limited to the realm of individuals and tribes. The same balance even applies to relationships between intimate partners. All exchanges between individuals, be they for one night or a lifetime, are actually contracts. The conditions of the contract agreements are determined by the individuals involved, yet to be moral, to be ethical, the conditions must apply equally.

A person who cheats on their spouse risks contracting disease, they risk loosing marriage, family, and perhaps a significant portion of their net financial worth. A public official, who takes a bribe, violates the trust of his employers (the public) and risks the loss of career for no matter how paltry a sum received. Those who steal and those who inflict damage on others have ignored risk, and may lose their freedom. What is the risk that the family or allies of the victim, including modern law enforcement, will return harm to the perpetrator?

A predator that kidnaps or abuses another is usurping the life energy of the victim. The victim might reflexively attempt to find balance by sympathizing and even forming an emotional bond with the perpetrator (e.g. The Stockholm syndrome), just as the battered woman might believe she deserves the beatings by disassociating from herself from the reality of her situation. The sadistic degradation, even mutilation, of women in some cultures has parallels – the freedom of choice has been taken way, or was never instilled or permitted by their society.

No cultures or tribal sects, when built upon inflexible belief systems, can allow reasoned minds to function, no matter the toll taken within the individuals involved.

When options are not available to balance choices that are objectively considered, it is not the province of the reasoned mind but of blindly made precepts - often implanted by manipulative or tyrannical control.

I would submit that a person choosing evolution will not seek to usurp *anything* – not energy, not possessions, not control, not labor, or even loyalty from another. In tribal barter systems, mutual contracts are set up where something (labor, food, possessions) trades for something considered to have like value. Who determines the mutual balance of value? The individuals seeking the trade establish values.

In most societies today, we trade using the medium of money as a store of value. Essentially, the economy remains a barter system, with money as the common denominator of value because it represents the value received of our labor for exchange (through money) on the open market, or the value of our intellect in innovation and design, or from making shrewd investments. If a seller asks for a price that does *not* provide recognized value, the goods will fail to sell. Theft of anything of value is not ethical because it takes from another and gives no return.

What happens if a person is starving to death? Is the theft of food ethical? Consider the factors of balance and opportunity. If the person who is starving offers his labor in exchange for food, balance is evident. If the person steals the food from another, imbalance is obvious. The person losing the food would have the right to demand a return, perhaps through involuntary labor (or confinement), or a punishment enforced by tribal or societal authorities.

Your reasoned mind is your power to decide if the truth of value exists in balance, and that becomes an ethical condition. By basing your integrity on being true to your reasoned mind, your consciousness itself discerns that this cannot be "faked." Honesty means that dichotomies cannot exist: between thoughts and deeds, words or actions, between the veracity of your life, and your convictions that support it.

Most can accept that slaying an attacker to defend one's own life is ethical. Most can also accept that the unprovoked murder or torture of another is a crime of evil. How would an ethical society define *evil*? I postulate that *evil is the absolute absence of empathy for the life or pain of another person.* By this definition, rape, torture, and unprovoked killing are evil. Totalitarian controls by dictators, institutions, or tribes that usurp a person's individuality to act ethically in personal self-interest, result in incredible psychological distortion and pain, are evil, particularly exacerbated where the tyrant or society is oblivious about the pain it inflicts.

The concept here is quite simple: moral individuals and societies seek ethical and equal balances in all of their exchanges and endeavors, be they energetic, the effort of labor, financial, or even emotional. A predatory person or society cannot evolve at all, for they are preying on others for financial, political, energetic or emotional gain. Your principled freedom is your ethic as a reasoned individual, and that gives you the power of choice to direct your life and character.

To evolve yourself as an individual means using your own energy, the spirit of your consciousness powered by your *free will to think with a disciplined mind,* either directly within yourself or in balanced exchange with others.

PERSPECTIVES

CHOICES AND RESPONSIBILITIES
FOR THE SPECIES

My visit to the large asteroid during my journey might seem curious or even incongruent compared to the powerful connections I had with my mentors. While this encounter might appear to have been a side trip when compared with the other, higher purposes, it seems reasonable to assert that the asteroid signifies an important challenge for the population of the Earth.

We have ample scientific evidence of several extinction-level events on this planet. The evidence is clearly visible in the planet's geological strata over a period of some 250 million years. *Each of the massive extinctions was the result of an asteroid impact.*

The last extinction event wiped out the dinosaurs about 65 million years ago; tens of millions of years before modern humans and most other primates came into being. Since the emergence of the human species has occurred quite recently, arguably over only the past two hundred thousand to perhaps one million years, extinction level events are not on the minds of most people. Nevertheless, the information is there, stored in the Earth's record, for anyone to see, who chooses to see. Since researchers estimate that *98% of the life forms that have ever existed on Earth have become extinct,* and the probability that the next large impact will result in the extinction, or near extinction, of Earth's predominant life forms, societies and governments have choices to consider and decisions to make.

Humankind has developed many impressive tools. These are the tools of technology, devised by human intellect, and they include vehicles for space travel. Spacecraft could travel to and possibly even terra-form other planets for colonies. This would provide a redundant population for the human species, though it would almost certainly develop as a different evolutionary branch of the human tree. Other tools could be devised to deflect threatening objects in space and to protect from (or at least warn of) other random events in the universe, just as satellites now warn us of hurricanes and seismic instruments are used to foresee possible tsunamis.

My visit to the asteroid signified the vulnerability of the human species, rather than something posing a threat specifically for me. After all, we are a comparatively new species on Earth, not fully aware of the threat from space or the consequences of presumption that we as a species are immune from such threats.

There are impediments that humanity places upon itself that get in the way of developing a common purpose, namely a plan to protect us from celestial threats. Squabbles that squander energy and purpose within the human species: tribal warfare, ethnicity and skin color, religious beliefs, or even social status and gender, all diminish our resources to one degree or another.

While the species is erratically flailing itself with issues of control, self-importance, and tribal power pitting one faction against another as it has been for millennia, an object wielding potential extinction awaits in space with the populace largely unaware, generally ignorant of the threat.

Human intellect, language, and the freedom to use *reason* are vital components of our evolution that distinguishes us from all other organic species. Intellect, when it emerges unfettered from tribal confiscation, continues to slowly evolve, and that brings action. Actions born of intellect converge with curiosity to produce the explorations of science with its derivative technologies, and technologies are the tools that can promote and defend the species.

The insane absurdities of travail, fostered and maintained by the forces of blind-beliefs and from reflexive non-volitional responses, must be replaced with volition, commitment and reason for the species as a whole to survive and evolve. For individuals who are engaged in their private quests to evolve, it is clear they must *learn* to have the freedom to use intellect and reason to make personal and objective choices. Through our personal efforts, we can reward ourselves by the ability to continue and prosper into infinity, vastly expanding our conscious awareness and amplifying the magnificence of our beings.

When a sufficient number of individuals evolve during their tenure on Earth, humanity itself will consequently evolve and a uniform purpose for societies can emerge and develop: choices based on responsibilities to defend the species!

My visit to the asteroid warns that extinction of the species is possible. Consequently, I have concluded that the intent of my encounter was to inspire me to present this possibility, as a messenger, simply to increase and perhaps broaden awareness. Taking me to visit the asteroid does not seem even vaguely logical without the purpose of informing others. Perhaps my experience simply reinforces a warning about a potential extinction-level threat even though science has this information through the geological record.

"How much time?" you might be inclined to ask. I have no idea.

I have concluded, however, that there must be sufficient time to react and make choices, or this information would be useless. I am assuming, then, that there is sufficient time to implement a strategy to counter the threat.

PERSPECTIVES

CHALLENGES AND STRATEGY
FOR A PERSONAL JOURNEY

E ach individual's journey of evolution begins with one choice: the choice to commit to oneself as an individual. Without this, you remain vulnerable to outside forces, the pressures imprinted as controls to comply with the needs or demands of others you place above yourself. Those pressures would encourage you to retain dependencies on other individuals, tribes, and belief systems.

In order for the process of "making choices" to work productively, there is a profound requirement that they be based on the use of reason. This process is comprised of simple steps. First, there is the rational consideration of what is and isn't objectively in one's best interests. Second, using reason – as opposed to faith, emotion, or letting your societal environment make your decisions for you – carefully compile all of the options related to furthering your best interests and consider the consequences of these options, both positive and negative. Third, *assess the probability* of the various outcomes, as some outcomes are far more likely to occur than others are. From the final values for these options that you develop through the freedom of your mind, you can then make an informed choice and carry out the decision by taking action.

Through your commitment to expand your use of reason, the task becomes how to learn to free your energy from its bound state, so that you can power your enhanced awareness that leads in turn to personal evolution. Nevertheless, if the process were that simple, everyone would connect into their consciousness, introspect and diminish non-volitional reflexes, make choices to change, and thrive.

I wondered why this doesn't seem to happen easily. Why is it such a struggle for individuals to "seek" and find their authenticity?

Then I remembered: I myself had bottomed out in a crater of self-deprecation (Chapter Eight). I had lost, or never had, the tools of objectivity and of reason. I was living my life to comply with the requirements of others. I was unaware that I was an automaton living through programmed precepts; and, because of churchianity's unyielding instruction in my early formative life, I had *never fully developed the freedom* to think objectively for myself.

My version of a "wow! moment" happened when I realized that absent objectivity, a person does not necessarily possess *the freedom to make appropriate choices* to expand awareness, and increase the knowledge of self. Simply said, by persistent indoctrination about how and what to think, unyielding pressures about what to believe, the lessons teaching objectivity are unavailable and people will not learn how to develop freedom of thought!

Freedom of thought and the use of reason are, after all, threats to the dogmas of churchianity and to various precepts of other societal institutions and even social consensus, and are therefore not encouraged. Why is this true? A view of churchianity's or other institutionally demanded blind-belief systems through the lens of objectivity shows that they simply vanish as irrelevant, other than to control humanity. Objectively, when inspected through the freedom of reason, there is nothing of substance there!

Just how does a person learn to be sufficiently free-of-mind to develop and use reason, if this wasn't facilitated early in life?

The depth of my own crater was so horrific that I needed a chain of mentors to facilitate the rebuilding of my self-worth! Yet, the inspirations (and challenges) my mentors provided were not complicated. The complications came only from my emotional turmoil, my clinging to beliefs that, from the view inside of the crater, made the prospect of positive change *seem* so intimidating.

To overcome my negations, I had to adopt and commit to a philosophy: *I am an individual seeking freedom to use objective thought, and through that, gain my ultimate evolution.* That explicit philosophy, with my commitment to it, applied through practice and patience, altered my psychology. *By breaking my pattern of addictive behavior, I freed my self-awareness to advance my evolution.*

Closed-loop addictive behavior patterns that science has found are correlated with peptide neural links in the brain, display in many forms: some are blatantly obvious, others may be rather subtle, but all present challenges to the candidate seeking the authenticity of their free being and true nature.

Challenges: Automaton Behavior

If a person is wholly embedded in a belief system during youth, the majority of their thought processes will be directed to conforming to the belief system – since that is all they know. Even atheists, who are committed to the belief that all life and consciousness ends at organic death, who allow for no other options, have formed an exclusionary (closed-minded loop) system. Thus confined to a limited set of options based on their learned, embedded instruction and confined experiences, they will tend to repetitively choose what is familiar to them. Moving out of the familiar could be a fearsome proposition because they've had no (or insufficient) experience at attempting anything else. The "fear of change" is actually *a clinging to the familiar*, whatever that might be. Also, the belief system of churchianity or that of other "tribal" institutions, *actively suppresses* any impulse to expand one's set of available options, preferring to confine believers to the narrow set approved by those who wish to exert influence to control.

People tend to implicitly tie self-esteem to conformance with a belief system and its reduced set of options, which is degrading to self-esteem in a number of ways. First, churchianity's picture of a human being is, for example, that he is a lowly, sinful, unworthy insect, subordinated to serve at the mercy of a super-being. Second, rigorous compliance with a set of rules that may exclude any natural, biological feelings and even small deviations from "righteousness" generate feelings of unrelenting guilt. Third and most damaging, high self-esteem can only develop as we function effectively in the *real world*, the *objective world*, which requires valuing one's own development by using objectivity and reason. *Automatons do not and cannot experience genuine self-esteem: they do not know how.*

The intense examples of those who follow their churchianity leaders, even to their deaths as "martyrs" as they slay others in the name of their god, are very obviously locked in the routines of automaton behavior – with pernicious results to humanity. Those trained to believe in racial, ethnic, social or cultural hatred, visiting discrimination or pain upon those they hate, are also examples of people acting as automatons. Others, seeking values for themselves that they were not able to find as they wandered through their lives, might hand over their sense of themselves to a cult, even a cult of societal consensus, surrendering their self-interest. Their belief system requires disassociation from themselves and from others they knew before they conjoined with the tribe, or in some cases, a nefarious tyrant. They become firmly convinced, even brainwashed, that the tribe and the tribal belief is the only way of life possible for them, and as long as they believe it, it is true.

Automaton patterns are observable in other, sometimes inconspicuous, ways. These are found in addictions to chemicals (drugs and alcohol), sex, depression, "mind-noise," angry (fight or flight) reflexes, and even to dangerous "thrill-seeking" (life-threatening) adventures. Addictions include workaholic lifestyles, obsessive-compulsive disorders, the gathering of wealth or possessions to the exclusion of all else, or any other pursuit not balanced with other facets of being. The biblical adage that "a wealthy man cannot enter heaven", misrepresents reality: a person obsessed with *anything* (including wealth) cannot evolve. The irony that the adage is an excuse to punish higher achievers for their accomplishments, and drain their wealth into tribes, largely goes unnoticed because the tribe itself can be an obsession. The energy invested in the obsession or compulsion confiscates the flexibility of the person, consumes it into the obsession, and that makes it unavailable for growth and evolution.

Mind Noise

Of all these behavioral manifestations, I suspect that "mind-noise" may be the easiest to overlook. Mind-noise patterns, as I have observed in my mentoring efforts, often develop as protections against emotional turmoil at an early age. The mind races around with churning thoughts about almost any subject or emotion – blocking out whatever it is that the person does not want, or doesn't know how to deal with. Some, said to be spiritual advisors, suggest "emptying the mind" or "stopping thought," as this supposedly leads to higher awareness. Rather than being devoid of *thoughts*, which can be rational and constructive, I would suggest being devoid of "noise" instead, the continual churning of the mind that accomplishes nothing but undermining awareness to all but the noise itself.

Patterned Reflexes

Blind reflexive patterns are unreasoned, unconscious behaviors. They might start out as subtly as presumptions or anticipations, the expectation of what will occur in the future. The subjects of expectation seem limitless. For example, what might happen in an intimate relationship, where the anticipation of losing the relationship often escalates emotion to intensify inappropriate behaviors that may only hasten an eventual break-up?

Imagine, for example, a person who very early in a potentially intimate relationship, has a reflex to "bed" a partner: not simply because they want to, but because *they believe it is expected* of them! That person is not making a choice based on reason but is performing as an automaton, locked in a belief about what they are required to do for the relationship to continue – and it can be an illusion. In this context, the so-called relationship is not balanced: it is one person engaging with another through automatic reflex. Manipulation, deceit, and co-dependency are often the result, taking a high emotional toll.

Patterned unconscious reflexes also happen in relationships that devolve to circular "love-hate" exchanges in mindless, emotional tennis matches. One serves up emotion, the other responds in a reactive way and the volleys continue until someone runs out of energy.

A strategic approach would be to immediately halt the addictive cycle by not returning the serve. This strategy starts with one thought: "stop."

Strategy: Recognize and Accept Reality in "The Moment of the Now"

We exist only in one small segment of time, the current moment that is "the now." Circular patterns of emotion and the endless repetition of behaviors wholly consume and overrun the moment of "now" with emotions dragged up from the past, negations dredged from the depths of depression, or fanciful expectations about the future, whether too elating or too dark.

These emotional responses from the past are usually automatic and habitual. They surface as unconscious protections. Yet, what did not work well in the past will never work well in the "now." Dregs of depression, for example, cause distortions about what is happening in the current moment. Those dregs obliterate the opportunity to release self-negations, clogging the potential freedom of the mind with the sludge of self-depreca-tion. If one is looking through sludge, all one sees is sludge.

Fanciful expectations of the future, likewise, are illusions of happiness or of failure that narrow our openness to objective reality. As these illusions fade or are eventually broken by con-tact with what is real, one is left with emotional confusion and conflict which causes the process to cycle back to re-invade and re-obscure "the now." The *freedom of mind that is only possible in the moment of now* becomes both disabled and fragmented in the cyclical pattern of unconscious behavior and drowned out in noise.

By halting any cycle, a window of opportunity quickly opens: to increase awareness of oneself and to raise consciousness out of unconscious, reflexive behavior loops. When a person has finally *had enough*, the will to stop the noise of the emo-tions and of the mind will force a pause. The pause allows a person to introspect and ask: *What am I doing? What am I feel-ing? Am I thinking with reason*, and eventually, *what are the causes?*

Seize the moment to connect to your sense of what is going on within you, whatever the answer might be. Hone your aware-ness to a precise focus. Probe your consciousness with this fo-cus and find the single point you are experiencing, what you are *feeling*. The moment of self-recognition might at first be fleeting, but holding the focus for as long as you can means that you are learning to exist in "the moment of now" and to seek answers for yourself.

If your answer returns with a jumble of possibilities then the point of focus is either lost, or not identified. I'd suggest that you try again to capture it – because in the moment of the now, there will be only *one* feeling, not a jumble. Jumbles are artifacts of confusion with conflicts and habitual mind-noise from the past, so if you feel jumbled, your awareness is not yet truly "in the now" but swirling around in turmoil.

When you capture precisely what you are experiencing, *the next step is to accept it*. It does not matter whether it is positive or negative. Whatever it is, it is. Acceptance means that you know exactly how you are feeling, what you are experiencing, and that you do not have conflict with it *because it is real.* Conflicts would suggest you are not accepting the reality of what is happening – now. Acceptance means that you are learning how to know yourself, to elevate your awareness and break the loop patterns that have hidden the beauty of your being.

By accepting, you gain a piece of information. Information by itself is not positive or negative – it is just information, and if you emotionally start to feel it as anything but "neutral," the past and the noise has invaded again. Remind yourself: *be objective!* How can a person learn if they distort reality by the tangles of the past?

Moments of awareness – *of the now* – are snapshots of your probes into the moment, and each is separately accepted. These are not the entire long story of your life's situation – they are moments of reality. My suggestion is that at first – whenever you interrupt the mind noise, probe and accept *the now* – that you make a written journal entry about what you have discovered. This entry can help relieve your mind of the tendency to churn about the information (which can become distorted in memory) and make it available for later use.

These snapshots taken at different points of *the now* of your conscious awareness and acceptance, logged into a journal, eventually become similar to the individual frames of a movie film. Each frame is a slice of the story that, when flipped in sequence, will display the larger story – *your* story. Since you will accept each snapshot as they happen along the way of "now", *both your acceptance and awareness of yourself will increase.*

Strategy: Body Scans in "The Now"

Our bodies can provide valuable signals to use as triggers to say "stop", and then open consciousness. Physically traumatic or sensual events imparted to the body will store memories in the mind. The body will trigger the mind, and the mind will connect to the body to relive the events, bi-directionally: body-to-mind and mind-to-body. Stress in the mind can cause physiological responses in the body, even degrading the immune system, and these effects can be profound, as I reported to you in Chapter Eight. A process I call "body scans" can sensitize your mind-body interaction.

Set yourself into a quiet, comfortable, and peaceful environment and halt the noise of your mind. Use your hands as objects of focus to start the learning experience. Place a hand at a comfortable distance away from your face, and stare at your fingers or the palm of your hand. Use your eyes to focus on your palm or your fingers, and when you feel any sensation there, strive to increase the intensity by increased focus. Do not analyze what you feel: only experience it.

If you are not able to make a mind-body connection to your palm, place it near your face, about an inch away from your cheek. Close your eyes and bring your mental point of focus to your cheek. When you feel temperature sensations in your cheek, or hand, slightly increase the distance between hand and cheek. If the sensations remain, continue to increase the distance. If they diminish, focus more to re-establish the connection or reduce the distance. When the connection is re-established, experiment with increasing the distance again. Eventually, reattempt the earlier exercise of using your eyes with your hand held out in front of your face.

As you learn to sensitize your mind-body connection, use the palm of your hand to experience other regions of your body, the torso being the most obvious; then move into other regions. With increased sensitivity, it is possible to probe the body without using the hand to set up the connection: only the focus of the mind is required. When lying comfortably, it can be useful to imagine a small and brilliant shaft of light illuminating the soles of your feet, or your toes. With your eyes closed, focus your mind to "find" the sensation of the light-warmth at your feet. When you learn to reliably make connections, you can learn to hone your focus to your toes, then feet, then ankles. Work your way up the body slowly and carefully as you experience your body's sensations, feeding back to your mind.

If you experience sensations of physical or emotional discomfort at any point of your scan, "stop" and probe into the sensation
in the moment of the now. If it is significantly uncomfortable,
make a note to probe the area later and learn the causation –
usually an event lodged in the past.

Mind-body sensitivities, once learned, are usable at every
moment of your life to capture the trigger point of "stop" and to
increase awareness in "the now."

Strategy: Recapitulation

As your journal of experienced awareness builds, you may
be inclined to meditate and connect carefully with the past to
learn the causations of what impedes your energy in "the now."
Should you run across any bitterness or conflict that involves
other people, including your parents or others that influenced
you in your early years, remember that you and the others "did
their best" that they could with their understanding, their abilities, at the time. Resist the tendency to revise history: whatever
it was, it was, and "no" they could not have done better because
if they could have, they would have. Acknowledging that fact is
acceptance, and your awareness will be freer as a result.

When Bob Morella realized my horrific condition, he guided
me into a state of meditation that developed into an incredible
moment of awareness, and that started to change my life and
state of being, forever. To extricate me from my crater of deprecation, of hiding, he used the tool of guided visualization. I was
able to project myself into a scene of beauty.

Bob didn't do this for me. I did it through the tool of his inspiration. Through that inspiration, I experienced for the first time
in years my own beauty, and I tear with joy as I write this. Bob
was a vital link for me, the first link in a chain of mentors that
advanced my awareness magnificently.

Starting with one event triggered by Bob Morella, I eventually
learned how to be free of my obsolete belief system. I learned to
use my mind with a true freedom of intellect, reason, and choice

by carefully recapitulating all of the negating experiences of my life. I realized and accepted that "I did my best" at any point I could with the awareness I had at the time; accepting the events and my responses of my life in the now; and evolving to trust and love unconditionally.

Later, as my body entered the throes of death, I took advantage of an amazing and profound opportunity to join others whom I call the consortium and my mentors. As the precondition for this opportunity to open, I had shaved off many layers of emotional tangles and boundaries, which freed my awareness to advance to the next level and to cross the boundary into post-physical being and awareness, and a joy so profound that it cannot be conveyed in words.

The Flow of Attainment: Ramps and Plateaus

As you engage in your introspections and make progress to enhanced awareness and greater attainment of your being, your flow of progress will be evident in a sequence I call "ramps and plateaus." The flow of self-enhancement starts when you are in an emotional plateau, whatever that might mean for you.

With your commitment and effort, inquiry and acceptance in each moment of "the now", you will find personal discoveries that lead to increased knowledge of yourself and that brings incentives to take the next steps. As your personal story unfolds, you will enter a transition – from the plateau to a ramp - leading to increased attainment, and within that transition, there are often trials. The trials come from reluctance to let go of the familiar, to resolve the barriers that held you back, and these will test you on the most-sensitive topic that cries out to be harmonized within you. Passing the trial means that you've sufficiently dealt with the topic of concern, and brought it to resolution, so it no longer deflects or consumes your energy. Then, a magnificent ramp, a ramp of discovery and knowledge, will become evident.

Ramps, which can endure for weeks to years, are followed by plateaus, and in between the ramp and plateau there is transition. Because the ramp had become a way of life, the change to the plateau means adapting yourself to accept your elevated state of being and often new responsibilities that the plateau provides. The period of the plateau is where you learn to put into practice, understand, explore and integrate all you have learned during your ramp into your state of being in every day life. Plateaus can bring impatience, a longing for the next ramp and sometimes an arrogant assumption that you've done your job, which suggests you've moved into the comfort of stasis. If you climb to the top of a ledge on your mountain of attainment, be careful not to slip and fall - which means maintaining your impeccability to yourself and your commitment.

It follows that after the plateau, the natural flow of life and attainment will present you with a transition, and then to the next ramp in a wondrous sequence of evolution to your ultimate state of being.

An Invitation to Yourself

You are invited to gaze inside yourself, to enter into a self-exploration and introspection that could challenge you and allow you to unravel some of your greatest mysteries: why and how you feel or behave in any moment of the now. All journeys, all explorations, start from a point of reference. That reference is who and what you are in the moment of the now. The starting point is your self-image and your self-esteem – now.

See yourself in the reflective image of the mirror, the introspective reflection in your mind. Inquire of yourself, *"what do I see"* and your journey will begin as soon as you commit to your evolution.

The 19th Century scientist, poet, novelist, and dramatist, Johann Wolfgang von Goethe, offered this call to action: *"Enough words have been exchanged; Now at last let me see some deeds! While you turn compliments, something useful should transpire. What use is it to speak of inspiration? To the hesitant it never appears......So get on with it!"*

Goethe's call to action can become your action and commitment, a plan to release the magic of your spirit that is already within you, held within yourself. It is your challenge and perhaps your ultimate responsibility to yourself to unlock it from the tangles that ensnarl the full ability of your mind and being.

Nowhere will one find a bolder or more purposeful journey than that of the introspection and attainment of the self. When you volitionally engage in your journey, then examine and enhance the reference of who you are by bringing information into experience, and from experience into knowledge through rational thought, your journey can progress toward your ultimate evolution.

AFTERWORD

INSPIRATIONS

A bout four years after the experiences of my *journey be-yond the tunnel of light* occurred, I was bedridden again with an intestinal infection that was life threatening. Heavy dosages of antibiotics were slowly quelling the infection so that rupture and hemorrhage, I hoped, would not occur. One afternoon, while fully immersed within the state of deep mediation and in intense pain, a vision of an image appeared above me.

That image was that of the familiar torus, a circular tunnel which appeared again precisely in the same construct that I saw during my journey and previously related to you. A solitary being, an image that I recognized as one of my mentors from the unique life-altering events that started through premonitions on the Defiance Plateau, and actualized in a small hospital in Yellowstone National Park, appeared within the torus.

The instantaneous communication issued to myself, was profound in its simplicity: *"You have made progress in elevating your awareness, attributes, and you are conjoined with us. You may enter this passage to attain your infinite state in spiritual form, leaving your human organic form forever. Have you attained your ultimate state of being? Now - are you ready to enter your ultimate destiny?"*

With only a fraction of a second's hesitation as I carefully took inventory of my attributes and abilities, my immediate response compiled and telepathically transmitted was a resounding *"No!"* Instantaneously, the torus vanished, leaving me with the responsibility to heal my body and advance my state of attainment.

Being true to the commitment that I made to myself before my return to my body, I had fervently strived in the intervening years to attain my ultimate state of being. When in my inorganic state of sentience, I had been treated to experience what my full destiny in evolution would be and accepted that I have more work to do.

The sound of my "No!" seemed to be deafening as though it reverberated throughout the universe with high energy. I had been presented with another test, I passed another milestone, and a renewed purpose was initiated.

A decade has passed from the time of that significant test. I have extended my efforts to complete my development, engaging with many others who have been identified as candidates to evolve and connect to me, and hence to the consortium of consciousness. Many of these individuals, by demonstrating their progress on their paths of attainment, provided inspiration for me to write this book.

If this all seems too incredible or inconceivable for you, ask yourself: *Are you a component of consciousness in the universe?*

You are on the Planet Earth. The planet, in turn, and its solar system are in a galaxy that is one of countless galaxies in the universe. Since you are sentient, self-aware as consciousness, you must be a component of consciousness in the universe already. *The open question is how you use that status, connect to others, and evolve yourself.*

In addition, I feel it important to recall that I had an *intense flash of inspiration* that started the preparation of this effort for you.

You might be interested to learn that just a few weeks after the vision I related to you in the Preface occurred, signaling me to start this book, I heard the dry words from a physician that I will never forget: *"We have the results of the biopsy, and there is no easy way to say this: you have cancer."*

To say the least, moving from an inspired vision to a critical diagnosis within three weeks provided intensified impetus for me to complete my tasks: my personal wake-up call! Thanks to the professionalism of alert and attentive physicians, the diagnosis and treatment happened very early in the progression of the malady; before symptoms from the cancer itself could be experienced. We rapidly followed the diagnosis with effective treatment to obliterate the disease taking hold within my body.

I clearly understand that presenting the reports of my experiences to all who may be interested to challenge their assumptions is another test for me. I hasten to add that many of the concepts that I relate to you have been circulating around humanity for millennia in fragmented ways. Realizing that history became my justification to again hide, and not write this book until I accepted that I would fail myself by not taking action.

Despite all of that recorded human history and its implied potential for personal inspiration, I compelled myself to openly relate what I have discovered, and I have done this for myself. For me these are reports of experiences, conclusions and progressions of what I consider knowledge that I have gained. You might consider my reports simply as ideas for you to contemplate, and perhaps, utilize for introspection, and that will bring value to you.

Oh yes! I forgot to mention! I managed to replace my treasured car collectors' tee shirt that the medical staff destroyed and discarded in the Yellowstone ER!

APPENDIX

MAY "THE FORCE" BE WITH US!

The realms of "magic and metaphysics" are less mysterious than one might think – and there is, indeed, an energetic force that exists within us.

For example, references to physics experiments suggest "field or force connections" between sub-atomic particles that are expressed as paired electron movements, show that even when separated from each other, forces applied to one electron will alter the spin direction of its partner that has not experienced a force - but reacts to the change in its partner. The effect noted relates to the concepts of mind-body awareness and connections. Deepak Chopra touched on these implications in his book "Ageless Body, Timeless Mind" where he describes reports that show when a few heart muscle cells are clipped from a living heart, and separated by significant distance from the originating heart, the removed cells will still track the heartbeat intervals of the heart itself. (One hypothesis is that these dynamics might occur through interconnection by the Higgs field, the subject of inquiry at CERN and other high-energy physics laboratories.)

Connotations of what some would think of as "magic" are actually, slowly, surfacing as metaphysics in the sense of quantum electrodynamics and field motions where "metaphysics" are the extension of science that are not yet fully described by exploration and experiment. The fields, with their flow of motions exist in the realm of energetic forms already understood, or that await discovery.

It is interesting to note that in various texts, journals, or even discussions about perceptively paranormal activity, such as empathic connections, "the energetic flow between people", and even ESP, there are many connotations that involve the use of the word "energy." More accurately consider that connections within the self and with others are structures of "fields" and not energy per se. While it is true that fields placed into motion will exhibit an energetic effect, it is the "connection" and perception that we experience. There are several concepts that can be applied, all hinting that what we could call the "metaphysical" is really an extension of "the physical." In fact, many things that seemed as "magic" in prior centuries are only "science and technology" today.

The implications seem clear: one does not "surrender to the connection"; one drops the noise of the mind to allow the projected consciousness of self to become aware, and in consequence connect to and perceive others similarly evolved at various levels.

From my training and experience, when the brain and it's sentient consciousness develop into adulthood with the physical attributes of the body, including the natural electric field structures within the body, the thought-intent-will processes of the mind can, with volitional intent, "direct" the field structures of the mind – the consciousness - to specifically interact with the body's bio-electric, organic, processes. Using field intensities developed within those organic processes, through intense personal focused commitment and effort, the presence of the consciousness can be expanded "in the now" to higher awareness. The projection of "Chi", the life force, would occur in that manner.

One of the standard characteristics of known electromagnetic wave physics is how electromagnetic waves, once launched into space, remain intact - into infinity. During the 1960s through the 1980s, scientific experiments were performed to determine the interaction between human brains and electromagnetic fields and waves. We learned from the experiments that the mind could respond with a "closer-my-god-to-thee" sense of euphoria when immersed in quiescent, intense, negatively-polarized (with respect to the Earth's polarity) electric fields. Another result was that when those fields are variously modulated at low brain-wave frequencies, one could produce nausea, blackouts or disorientation. The hypothesis reached by researchers was that if electric and electrodynamic fields interact with the mind, the mind must be electrodynamic in its processes.

Individuals tend to exhibit different sensitivities to electric fields and the effects they play in the consciousness. Anyone can experiment with their perceptions and the effects they experience with immersion into extraneous electric fields. For example, if you stand near a waterfall (the higher and more free-falling the better, in terms of quiescent electric field intensity – such as Bridal Veil Falls in Yosemite National Park) position yourself just at the boundary of the water spray where you will not get soaking wet. Close your eyes and meditate, facing the waterfall. Try to connect yourself to nature, to "feel" something happening in the environment and in the water motion. If you feel elevated, positive, then open your eyes and turn around with your back now toward the waterfall – then feel again. When you have connected to all you think you can gain, walk away from the waterfall at least 200 feet, meditate and feel the new environment. Emotions can be altered by the influences of electric field intensity.

On a smaller scale, you might have noticed that, if you have a plastic shower curtain in your shower bath, and turn on the water to the showerhead at full pressure for maximum water force, the shower curtain will tend to be dragged into the water spray. This is a form of energetic interaction that could be thought of as a prototype for telekinesis – the reason why the plastic curtain is being "pulled" into the spray is because of the electric fields produced by the impact of the water molecules against the atmospheric molecules. The field intensity at the base of Bridal Veil Falls will be approximately 3 to 5 times higher than at your shower, yet the effect is the same. If you "feel good" after a shower, it is possibly and partially because of interactions between the electric fields have and your consciousness: *your mind.* If you feel uneasy during a wind when low cumulus clouds are moving above you, particularly if the clouds are dark as if they could shower rain on you – you could well be sensitive to modulations of the fields upon your consciousness since the intensity of the electric field will vary with the motions of the clouds.

A professor emeritus from a major university in the 1990s decided to experiment with the concept of telekinesis. Like other experiments, he really didn't know exactly what to look for, so his approach was to use something "known" and learn if humans could project "their fields" into what was "known and measurable" to learn if there would be a dynamic interaction. Because he was looking for kinetic effects, he used easily set up devices to use as a basis for effects, such as a small stream of free-falling water. From my view, if humans could "project energy" into the experiment, particularly if they were projecting an electric field structure, then it would have an impact on the water stream. It's only logical to some extent: if a water stream produces electric fields (as we know in science is true) and if those can deflect a shower curtain energetically, then the reverse might also be true – fields could deflect the water. The results of the study suggested that indeed, humans "can" project energy and deflect (for example) a small water stream, and "some" individuals had much more focused power to do this than others had.

In the 1960s, there was a program to develop a method of communication with nuclear powered submarines while they were deeply underwater during their six-month long missions. The research was to find an efficient way to transmit and receive information that might be available in nature. It is known that if a resonant structure is set up at a particular frequency, one could apply a comparatively small amount of energy at a harmonic that coincides with the resonance, and realize "efficient" propagation of that energy throughout the resonant structure. An example of this effect is that if you strike a bell, you will hear a ring that has a long dwell time compared to the short strike that illuminated the sounds of the bell.

Researchers discovered in our environment exactly such a structure: Planet Earth. It turns out that there is a cavity-based spherical (concentric) resonance formed in the gap between two overlaying spheres: the ionosphere, and the surface of the planet with its oceans. Radio amateurs can get their radio transmissions to "skip" over the horizon by "bouncing" their signals off the ionosphere, expanding their "reach" to other radio-hams around the planet. Studying the natural resonant frequency and harmonic structures within the electromagnetic spherical-concentric cavity formed between the planet's surface and the ionosphere, researchers found that it naturally matches lower brain waves, with a spectra measured in low-Hertz frequencies.

Like the natural resonance of a bell ringing, it is possible to recognize that if there is a spherical resonance in the media between the surface of the planet and the ionosphere, the resonance could "be struck" and excited to carry a field. If the "strike" were to be a transmitter operating at the same frequency as the media resonates, a high efficiency of transferring the field would be achieved. Because the media would be concentric around the planet, the transmitted field would surround the planet rather uniformly. The system based on this concept to communicate with submarines while deeply underwater has been in use for decades.

This brings us to a hypothesis: With the concentrically over-laid spherical media naturally set in the environment of the Earth, viola! - we have a natural - physical - transportation layer for tele-pathic/empathic connections for any individuals who learn how to "tune" their consciousness to the resonant structures of media that is inherent to the planet. If you study any of the anecdotal reports about empathic connections, it's typical that it doesn't seem to matter how far apart the individuals are, or where they are located on the planet. This makes perfect sense if the "connections" are based in the projection and reception of electric field structures and intensities.

Every molecule, every cell of all matter, organic or inorganic, is glued together by one thing: electric fields. The electromagnetic field structures in the universe are strong forces. The elementary particles are protons, neutrons, and electrons, though there are more than 200 subatomic particles identified that make up all matter of the universe. When considering the electric field structures that hold you, or any other structure, together there are factors of distance between the molecules and the electric field intensity that develops across that distance. The distance between the cells of the body is about 300 nanometers, and across those boundaries exists an electric field potential of about 10 million Volts/meter. If you were to measure the field intensity from a 50,000 Watt AM radio-transmitting antenna at a distance of about 1/4th mile, you'd have a field intensity of about 10 to 20 Volts/meter.

Why so much field intensity across the molecular structures of the body? It's a trick of distance. One-forth mile is vast compared to 300 nanometers, and field intensity has proportion to distance. You might be interested to realize that the human body, when at rest, represents a power of about 100 Watts. Of that amount, the brain utilizes about 25 watts - about the same as the communication transmitters we used on the Apollo missions to the moon. Certainly if any portion of that power can be projected beyond the body in a quantum electrodynamic state, it is adequate to continue and "make connections" to those who are "aware" and in the present of the moment.

The subset of the quantum mechanics process that deals with the motions of subatomic particles such as electrons, when expanded constitutes and adaptive and dynamic hypothesis: that sentience itself is electrodynamic as its physical state. Werner Heisenberg, generally regarded as the founder of quantum mechanics, hypothesized that the act of measuring pairs of variables describing motion-velocity and position, or energy and time, will influence the behavior of that under measurement. Simply said, the act of observation alters the behavior of what is being observed.

Is it possible that when you enter an environment with other people, and you bring your consciousness to be highly aware "in the moment of the now" with a quiet mind, you are influencing others by your presence and connection? Have you ever noticed that people might stop and stare at another person entering a room, even though that person has said or done nothing to call attention to him/herself?

A group of curious researchers at an august research laboratory complex (that for about 100 years issued a new patent in technology at the rate of about one per day) had an idea. They were trying to learn if electrodynamic fields from people could be measured even though they had no idea what it really was they were trying to measure. The central question was: *What can alter a field structure?* Well, perturbations from conductive planes or other fields can alter structures - of course. So they went into a completely contained "vault" shielded from electromagnetic fields and waves, and set up a known value of a very long wavelength electromagnetic field that was measurable. The concept was that IF humans could project their fields of unknown characteristic into the "known" field, the implied interaction could be observed by the alteration of the known field caused by human projection. The researchers even hooked up with the local psychic society to connect them to members of their society to use for measurement evaluation. They found that indeed, humans can project their field and yes, it will interact and modify a known field. Thanks to the volunteers of the psychic society, they found some individuals whose intensity had "more influence" upon the known field than the "normal" person did, who were usually lab techs.

If consciousness can be projected, it would be able to explore and "remote view" (something that in the time before surveillance satellites would be valuable to the "intelligence" community). The experimental program, run by "special groups", was real. The program resulted in limited success, but clearly some people were able to "remote view". If you're curious about this, Paul H. Smith wrote a book entitled "Reading The Enemy's Mind" describing his participation in the latter phases of the program just before it was shut down. The results were impressive but inconsistent compared to the reliability of today's surveillance technology.

From all I have trained for, practiced and experienced in normal life and during my *journey beyond the tunnel of light*, I am convinced in hypothesis that human consciousness is comprised as a form of electrodynamic fields, developed and enhanced in "the physical", and honed to a fine level that can be projected into the metaphysical. In that context, one does not "surrender" to mythical forces. Individuals may learn their responsibilities for themselves, to learn the intrinsic nature of their authentic selves using the attributes of the physical to indeed, become metaphysical and connect with others in the presence of "the moment of now."

May the force be with you?

Yes. The force is already within you, channeled and directed by you, and ready for you to bring it through your commitment into the attainment of high, transcendent, awareness.

ACKNOWLEDGEMENTS

T he relationship between mentors and protégés is a dynamic, fascinating and expanding process. Viewed as a journey, a mutual trust develops to form a bond, and the nature of the relationship evolves, empowered by trust. A partnership is structured, and over time, that advances to become a true friendship where each mutually shares in contribution to the other.

On this page, I am privileged to acknowledge my friends that have developed in that manner: Russell Lait, Amy Louise Maher, as well as Eddie and Lisa Pavlu, for enduring the first-reads of the manuscript draft, and finding places where missing pieces needed to be added, or areas that required expansion. To Eddie, I express my deep appreciation for his amazing astro-photography that I assembled as the cover-art for this book.

About eight years before this publication I was privileged to become mentor to Sarah Masteller, who found the resolve to commit to her personal journey, overcame her daunting life-situation and has learned to thrive in her own being. Engaging with Sarah played a definitive role in preparing me to connect with and become mentor to Amy Louise Maher years later, whose own commitment to herself caused her to extricate herself from a deep crater, to redefine her life, as she became empowered into the vast realm of personal attainment.

Zoran and Sveta Babic similarly realized that the basis of self-attainment begins with the commitment and quest for the knowledge of self, and using the tools of exploration they've found in themselves, are motivated to explore their roles in mentoring others.

Anne Dennis reviewed the second manuscript draft cycle, and found parallels to use in her own introspections. Other long-term protégés, including Charles and Sue Grasso, also found analogies in my descriptions to apply in their lives. Their commitment to their personal journeys has enhanced their awareness.

Through it all, from initial inspiration to the final draft and publication, I offer my deepest appreciation and profound acknowledgment to my life-partner, Rosemarie, for her unrelenting guidance, editorial assistance, and support as I relived the events, and opened myself to write this book.

Thank you.
W. Michael King

May 2008

Made in the USA